52 CHURCHES:

A YEARLONG JOURNEY ENCOUNTERING GOD, HIS CHURCH, AND OUR COMMON FAITH

Peter DeHaan, Ph.D.

52 Churches: A Yearlong Journey Encountering God, His Church, and Our Common Faith © 2018 by Peter DeHaan.

ISBN: 978-1-948082-07-5 (paperback)
ISBN: 978-1-948082-06-8 (ebook)

Published by Spiritually Speaking Publishing

Credits:

Developmental editor: Cathy Rueter
Copy editor/proofreader: Robyn Mulder
Cover design: Cassia Friello
Author photo: Chele Reagh / PippinReaghDesign

I dedicate this book to Candy, my partner for this adventure and in life.

Table of Contents

Other Books by Peter DeHaan

Women of the Bible: The Victorious, the Victims, the Virtuous, and the Vicious

95 Tweets: Celebrating Martin Luther in the 21st Century

How Big is Your Tent? A Call for Christian Unity, Tolerance, and Love

Look for Peter's upcoming books:

- *Dear Theophilus: A 40 Day Devotional Exploring the Life of Jesus through the Gospel of Luke*

- *Dear Theophilus, Acts: A 40 Day Devotional from the Book of Acts for Today's Christian*

- *Friends and Foes of Jesus: Explore How New Testament Characters React to God's Good News*

- *Woodpecker Wars: Discovering the Spirituality of Everyday Life*

- with more to follow

Be the first to hear about Peter's new books and receive monthly updates at www.PeterDeHaan.com/updates.

The Beginning

"Where do you go to church?"

Oh, how I dread that question.

It isn't that I don't go to church or am too embarrassed to answer. Instead, my frustration comes from the scowls I receive as I fumble through my reply. No matter what I say, I cause confusion.

This question about church attendance comes from clients at the local food pantry, where I volunteer. The pantry is a community effort started by local businesses, service organizations, and churches. Now staffed mostly by church members, church attendance is a common topic of our patrons.

I serve as the point person for the clients. I explain our process, guide them through the paperwork, and match them with a volunteer to help them shop. As we move through these steps, we often chat. This is when the awful question about where I go to church comes up.

The problem is that I don't attend any of the churches that support the pantry. Instead, my wife, Candy, and I drive some fifteen miles to a church in another community. Though I long to worship God in the community where we live, he has sent me to one further away and less convenient.

Sometimes I explain all this, but the clients' eyes glaze over, either in boredom or bewilderment. Other times I only share the name of our church, but no one recognizes it. Since it's not a typical church name, they wonder if I'm kidding. Occasionally, I change the subject, but they don't like that either.

Eventually, I realize they ask because they're looking for a church. Sure, some people are being polite, others feel obligated to ask—since nearly all our volunteers go to church, and a few desire to label me based on my church affiliation. But most of them just want to find a spiritual community to plug into.

The pantry's mandate is to serve residents of our local school district, which has ten churches within its borders. I don't know a thing about some of them. I know a little bit about each of the five churches involved with the pantry, but I don't know enough to answer folks' questions or direct them to the best match for their needs and background. What if I visited all ten? Then I could better help clients who were looking for a church.

Yet, it isn't that simple. What about churches just outside the school district? Should I consider nearby congregations too? In addition to the ten within our school district, five more are a few miles to the southwest, twenty-one to the west, and scores more to the east.

* * *

All my life, I've gone to church. This has been a regular practice, pursued with dogged determination. Yet, in considering the churches I've attended—first with my parents, next by myself, and then with my family—our church of choice was seldom the nearest option.

Why don't we go to church where we live? This is a deep desire of my heart: to live, worship, and serve in the same community. In addition to being practical in terms of time, effort, and cost, worshiping locally would also provide more opportunity to connect with and form a *faith* community in our *geographic* community, not somebody else's.

Another perplexing question is wondering why each of our church-attending neighbors goes to a different one. I long to worship God *with* my neighbors. Are the forms of our faith so different that we can't go to church together? The answer should be "no," but the evidence proves otherwise.

My hunch is that each possible church opportunity offers a fresh perspective of pursuing God or perhaps a different understanding of what it means to worship him. If I can learn from each one, my comprehension of the God I love will grow and my understanding of worshiping him will be enhanced.

These reasons propel me forward, to undertake my unconventional faith journey of visiting different churches.

* * *

This isn't the first time I wondered about the practices of other churches. My grandmother went to a Baptist church. It was so different from the mainline one I attended, that as a young child I thought she was a borderline heathen or perhaps part of a cult.

I was even more concerned about the girl next door, my only consistent friend for the first ten years of my life. She went with her family to a Roman Catholic parish and attended a parochial school. Based on misinformation from people who didn't understand Catholicism — or perhaps didn't care to — I was convinced she was on her way to hell. She likely thought the same thing about me. I assumed I was on the side of right, and she, on the side of wrong. The idea that we could both be right was beyond my comprehension. I even wondered how I might convert her to my church practices, not knowing we both looked to the same God, just in different ways.

When my family moved, my exposure to Catholics increased. In middle school art class, where the teacher had no clue what went on in her room, some classmates started arguing about Purgatory when we were supposed to be making art. A group of us ditched our projects to debate the issue. We aligned our teams on opposite sides of a rectangular table. We stared at each other until I framed why we sat there glaring at each other. "Is there Purgatory?"

"Yes," answered the other side of the table.

"No," came the retort from my side.

No one said anything more. We each had our opinions, but we lacked support. The debate ended without any discussion and without a winner. We slunk away from the table. It bothered me that I couldn't defend my unexamined position and that I learned nothing about Purgatory. How could Christians—who all claim to follow Jesus—hold such polarized opinions over the same faith?

* * *

I was a voracious reader, and my grandmother kept me supplied with a steady flow of books, all from a Baptist perspective. This influenced me significantly during my formative years, causing me to wrestle greatly in attempting to reconcile a traditional Christian mindset with evangelical teaching. Later, I discovered the Holy Spirit—the third part of the Trinity that mainline and conservative Christians downplay, sometimes even dismiss. I immersed myself in a pursuit of the charismatic.

We're all on the same team, I lamented. *Why can't we get along?*

This so vexed me that, years later, when it came time to select my dissertation topic I had no hesitation. I chose Christian unity. My imperative need to learn why we were different and to advocate Christian harmony became even more urgent as I studied Jesus's prayer in John 17, which he uttered just prior to his capture and execution. With an agonizing death only hours away, Jesus took time to pray. His final request was that all his future followers would get along. He knew the impact of his sacrifice would be lessened if those who later professed to follow him lived in conflict with each other.

Now, with my dissertation complete, I have a theoretical understanding of the need for unity. Despite that, I lack the practical knowledge of how the different streams of Protestants express their faith and worship God. And I'm completely ignorant about the rest of Christianity.

* * *

As I wonder what to do with my idea of visiting area churches to better inform myself and help the food pantry clients, God prompts me to pursue a grander vision. At his leading, I plan an unconventional faith journey, one of adventure and discovery: to learn what he would show me by visiting a different Christian church every Sunday for a year. I eventually call my sojourn "52 Churches."

Oh, how this vision resonates with me. All my life I've yearned for more, spiritually. More from church, more from its community, and more from our common faith. I've searched for answers, answers to impertinent questions I can sometimes barely articulate. Yet something deep inside compels me to ask them, even though I confound others every time I do. A primal urge forces me to reach for this spiritual "more," one I know to exist, as surely as I know my own name. I dare to extend my arms toward God and have the audacity to expect him to reciprocate, perhaps even touching the tip of my outstretched fingers.

We're content to drink Kool-Aid, when God offers us wine.[1] Yes, there is more. So much more. I'm desperate to discover it—and visiting fifty-two churches offers the potential to uncover more—or at least get me closer. This is something I must do. For me, this is no longer an option but a requirement. My faith demands it. My spiritual sanity requires it.

This adventure earns the support of my wife and willing accomplice; my pastor, who encourages me to move forward; and my fellow elders, who after initial apprehension, support me, even anticipating what I will learn and share. This isn't a church-shopping romp, looking for a perfect faith community. Instead, I seek to broaden my understanding of God, church, and faith by experiencing different spiritual practices.

To do this, Candy and I will take a one-year sabbatical from our home church, intent on returning, armed with a greater understanding of how to better connect with the God we love, worship, and serve. Yet I realize God might have other plans. He could tell us to join one of the churches we visit. He might instruct us to extend our quest or end it early. He could fundamentally change our understanding of church and our role in it. Or perhaps things might work out as we plan, with

---

1 This is an interesting metaphor, since I don't drink alcohol—except for the occasional communion service that serves it.

us simply returning to our home church, one year later, better equipped to worship and serve.

Along the way, I suspect each church will show us a different approach to encountering God. I'm determined to learn what I can each week to increase my comprehension of him and enhance my worship. I want to expand my understanding of our common faith, and I expect to boost my appreciation for the diversity of the local branches of Jesus's church.

Whatever the outcome, I know God will teach us much, and I intend to come back well-armed with helpful information for the clients at the food pantry.

As I tell close friends about my plan—actually, it's God's plan—many resonate with it. This isn't just a journey for me but for us all, albeit vicariously for most. This isn't one man's narcissistic pursuit. It is an adventure for all who sense a need for more.

- **To those disenfranchised with church**: This is a journey of hope and rediscovery. Don't give up on church. God has a place in it for you. Yes, church can be messy at times, and the easy reaction is to give up. Maybe church left you disappointed, or her members hurt you beyond comprehension, but there are many people, at many churches, ready to offer love and extend acceptance. Don't let a bad incident, or two, cause you to miss a lifetime of spiritual connection with others. I pray this book will call you back to Christian community.

- **To spiritual seekers**: You have a place in God's family. I'll share fifty-two ways to expand your perspective. Diligently seek God as you explore churches, and you will find him. But don't shop for a church as a consumer.

Instead, travel as a pilgrim on a faith journey, seeking fellow sojourners to walk beside you. I pray the end of this story will mark the beginning of yours.

- **To the inquisitive**: The church of Jesus is bigger, broader, and vaster than most of us have ever considered. Here, I share fifty-two reasons why, fifty-two variations of one theme. I pray you will begin to ask brave questions about church practices, explore fresh ways to worship God, and accept those who hold different understandings.

- **To church leaders**: I offer a narrative to help you reach out more effectively, embrace more fully, and love more completely. You're sure to catch glimpses of your church reflected on these pages, with anecdotes that will cause you to smile — and to groan — with each impression offering insight to those willing to accept it. May this book serve as your primer to celebrate what you do well and improve what you could do better. I pray this will mark a new beginning for your local branch of Jesus's church.

- **To advocates of Christian unity**[2]: We're part of the church Jesus began. It's time everyone embraces this reality. I pray this account will encourage you to pursue greater unity in Jesus, to help churches in your area work together for God's glory, so that everyone will know the Father, just as Jesus prayed.[3]

* * *

2 The technical word for this is ecumenical: "Of or relating to the world-wide Christian church," (http://www.thefreedictionary.com/Ecumenical).

3 From Jesus's prayer for unity in John 17:20–26.

Candy compiles a list of churches within ten miles of our home. She initially identifies fifty-seven, but we keep discovering more. Our file eventually balloons to ninety churches located within a ten-mile drive.

Not on the list is our own church, an outlier congregation that is part of a small mainline denomination, even though many assume we're nondenominational—because that's how we act. God told me to help start this church. He called me to go there. Despite aching to attend church closer to home, he hasn't released me to do so.

To realize the most from our sojourn, we form a plan. We'll visit those churches nearest our home first, picking them in order of driving distance. Toward the end of our journey, we'll choose other churches from the remaining list, visiting those most different from our norm. Making the list is the easy part.

Next, we set some guidelines. Each week, we'll check their website, hoping to learn about them before our visit so we can more fully embrace our time there. Still, knowing that websites are sometimes out-of-date, we'll email or call to verify service times.[4] If there are multiple meetings, we'll go to the later one, since second services, which usually have a higher attendance, possess more energy, and lack time constraints.

We'll dress casually, as we normally do, for church. For me this means a T-shirt, shorts, and tennis shoes in the summer and a casual shirt, jeans, and boots in the winter. This is practical because my wardrobe best allows it. It will also help because casual attire is what a non-churched visitor would likely wear. Though I don't want to come off as an unchurched

---

4 This is the corporate "we." I never once did this. My wife faithfully handled this every week for the entire year.

9

outsider, I'll learn more if they don't view me as a conformed insider.

We agree to go along with any visitor rituals, but we'll do nothing to imply we might come back or consider joining their community. If they want to give us literature or welcome gifts, we'll graciously accept them. When asked why we're visiting, we'll be honest, saying we're seeking to expand our understanding of worshiping God by visiting area churches — but we aren't looking to join one.

Also, we'll avoid showing up at the last minute, instead aiming to arrive ten minutes early. This will allow for possible pre-church interaction. Afterward, we'll look for opportunities to talk with people and will stay for any after-church activities — except Sunday school[5]. Through it all, we'll do our best to be open and approachable, interacting with others any way we can.

Perhaps most important, we'll participate in their service to the degree we feel comfortable, while being careful not to push their boundaries. For more exuberant expressions of worship this means we'll have the freedom, but not the obligation, to follow their lead. For more reserved gatherings, we won't do anything to alarm them with our behavior. I'll write about our visits, but I won't keep the dispassionate distance of a reporter. I'll engage in the service and with their community.

* * *

---

5 The original purpose of Sunday school was to teach poor children how to read. By the time public schools took over this task, Sunday school had become an institution and continued (**Pagan Christianity?**, p 212–213). At most churches Sunday school is now little more than an obligatory expectation, where frustrated faculty seek to fill time that antsy children strive to avoid. Too many Sunday school programs bore their students and effectively teach kids that faith is boring.

Throughout our adventure, I will continue to participate in a twice-a-month, midweek gathering at our home church. It is a nurturing faith community where we encourage and challenge each other. This will serve as my spiritual base during our sojourn and help keep me connected. I'll also listen to our church's sermon podcasts and attend elder meetings.

As friends pray for our journey, one asks that we make a positive impact on each church we visit. This surprises me. I strive to make a difference wherever I go, but I never considered it for *52 Churches*. I assumed we would receive, but I never considered how we might give. With an expanded perspective, our adventure becomes doubly exciting.

Talk is safe. Action is risky. It's easy to consider a bold move in the indefinite future. But I need to pick a date, or this will never be anything more than an intriguing idea that never happens.

It's the season of Lent, and our church is marching toward Easter. What if we start our journey after that? I share the timing with my wife. I expect resistance—or perhaps, I hope for some—providing an excuse for delay. But she nods her agreement. My pastor and fellow elders also affirm the timing. Some are envious.

Candy and I celebrate Jesus's resurrection with our home church. Then we slip away to begin our sojourn the following Sunday.

I expect this to be an amazing adventure, and I invite you to journey with us.

Part 1:

Getting Started

It's Sunday morning, and we've yet to visit our first church. Even though it's only been a week, I already miss my friends at our church. I already miss what I know and expect, even though I know to expect the unexpected. At least the unexpected happens in a familiar place and with friends.

As an introvert who excels at social awkwardness, I relish familiar surroundings. Going somewhere new produces a deep fear I yearn to avoid. I have driven into a parking lot at a new place, panicked, and driven away. Instead of fighting fear, I prefer to flee it. I understand panic attacks. It takes prayer and God's help to subdue them.

I get up around 6 a.m., as usual, but Church #1 doesn't start for five hours. That's far too much time for me to wait. I wonder, and I worry. Doubt creeps in. My fear grows. If only the service started earlier. Then there wouldn't be as much time for the enemy to whisper his lies: "This is a stupid idea." "You will fail." "No one will read your book."

I must resist the devil, so he will flee from me[6] — or at least I can distract myself by working on this chapter. My insides churn with equal parts excitement and fear — or perhaps it's just the sausage pizza from last night.

---

6 A personal paraphrase of James 4:7.

It doesn't help that my bed provided more restlessness than rest. I add "tired" to my growing list of reasons not to go. I now understand why the non-regular church attender can so easily stay home despite their best intentions. The living room recliner and television remote are much more inviting and much less threatening.

Yet I press on. This isn't due to my character but to avoid embarrassment. Too many people know about this project for me to abort my mission on day one.

The first of fifty-two churches is a small one in an old building. I know nothing about them, even though they're a scant one mile from home. For years, we've driven past their tiny church, yet I've never met anyone who went there. How strange. We've lived in this community for nearly a quarter of a century, and my connection to it goes back even further. I know people from the other local churches, why not here? *Does anyone actually go to this one?* Learning about them online isn't an option. They don't have a website or even a Facebook page.

Candy and I discuss when we should leave but don't agree. We don't want to breeze in at the last minute, removing any opportunity for pre-service interaction. Yet, arriving too early opens us to awkwardness if there's no one to talk to, leaving us with nothing to do but squirm.

We pray before heading out. I ask God to bless our time at church and teach us what he wants us to learn. I request his favor, so we can have a positive impact on this church and the people there. We say "amen," and then we leave.

Candy shows no apprehension, and I doubt she's aware of mine. She keeps our conversation light. In the two-minute drive, there's no time for my angst to grow. Before I know it, we're there. My palms grow sweaty and my heart pounds. Nausea overtakes me. *What have I gotten us into?*

Takeaway for Everyone: Make it as easy for visitors as possible. Providing helpful information online is critical: what to expect, how to dress, a theological overview, and any distinctive characteristics.

Church #1:

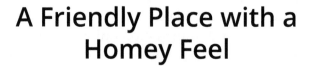

A Friendly Place with a Homey Feel

We arrive ten minutes early and are the eighth car in the lot. It's an older one-story building of simple wood-frame construction. An unwieldy wheelchair ramp tacked onto the front desperately needs painting. We bypass the ramp, but it remains our focal point as we approach, forming our first impression — and it's not good.

I can't believe what we're about to do. I'm in a near panic. My impulse is to run. *Put one foot in front of the other. Remember to breathe. Act calm.*

I exhale slowly and open the front door. Ever the gentleman, I gesture for Candy to go first. She scowls as she walks by. It's the smallest of entries and dark. Three people, hovering just inside, act surprised to see visitors. We take a couple steps forward and are in the sanctuary. With no room to mingle, we sit down, second row from the back.

As we wait for church to begin, the pastor's wife introduces herself, but a hard-to-understand man has already cornered us, recounting the diseases and deaths of his parents a few decades ago. We can't escape his plodding monologue. This guy has mental issues.[7] Some people acknowledge our presence

---

7 This, of course, is an unqualified diagnosis.

with a quick smile or inconspicuous handshake, but no one rescues us from his unfiltered spew of personal information. The pastor also squeezes in a brief introduction.

The sanctuary is a rectangular room with paneled walls. On our right hangs the Ten Commandments, the opposite wall displays their Church covenant. Mounted front and center is a traditional cross, adorned with a crown of thorns and a purple cloth. On each side stands a flag, one for the United States and the other for Christianity. A Sunday school placard in the back reveals last week's attendance was twenty.

The building has a distinct odor, but we disagree what it is. Rotating ceiling fans keep the air, and the smell, moving. I soon forget about it, but Candy isn't so fortunate, with the aroma lingering in her nostrils the entire morning.

A pianist plays a small upright. She's skilled at her craft. Having background music is nice. In addition to the piano, there's an electric organ. I also spot an electric guitar and amp, which seem out of place, but they're not used today.

I count seventeen people, including us. Most of them are well into their senior citizen years. All the older men wear suits and ties, with their wives in dresses. A few people, in their thirties, sport casual attire, but none as informal as me — even after I passed on wearing a T-shirt and opted for a polo shirt I found hiding in the back of my closet.

There are no school-age children, teens, or young families, but there are two toddlers with their grandmothers. Numerous times, the grandmas remove the crying tots from the sanctuary. At one child's third outburst, grandma leaves and never returns.

One member opens the service, leading us in a song. Neither Candy nor I know it. I find it hard to even mouth the words, let alone sing. The song leader then asks if there are any birthdays. The pianist stands for us to honor her, leaving no one to play Happy Birthday. After a bit of scrambling, the pastor does something out of sight to generate music as we sing.

There's also a second verse, something about a second birthday. Candy later tells me the words: "Happy Birthday to you, just one will not do. Born again means salvation. How many have you?" The song leader says his second birthday is coming soon. It will be thirty-eight—or is it thirty-nine—years.

Apparently for our benefit, the pastor shares that there are normally forty to forty-five in attendance, with this Sunday's number being unusual. Some absences are due to illness and he reels off a list of names, but, for the rest, he's unsure why they're gone. The pastor was sick last week, and the song leader quips that today's illnesses are his fault.

The pastor conducts some church business, roughly following Robert's Rules of Order. He wants to go to a conference, which will cause him to miss a Sunday. The song leader moves that they approve his request and use "pulpit supply" to find a replacement. Someone seconds the motion. After no discussion, he holds a voice vote. Motion approved.

The minister looks at us. With a pleased smirk he says, "If there are any first-time visitors here, please raise your hands."

Isn't it obvious? I groan—hopefully to myself—as I force a pained smile. Reluctantly, I raise my hand. *Can things get any more awkward?* Their focus on us lasts too long.

Although foreign to me, the service matches Candy's childhood church memories. Though there's nothing remarkable about it, she's comfortable with their format: a few old-time hymns with piano accompaniment, sharing prayer requests, an offering, a message, and a low-key altar call.

The people make the difference. They're comfortable with each other, accepting one another. There's no pretense, just nice folks. It's like family, albeit quirkier. Despite the creepy guy who first cornered us and the ridiculous request for visitors to raise their hands, I feel contentment, a peace perhaps best attributed to God's presence.

The two-hour service is mostly preaching. The message rambles a bit, peppered with frequent mentions of Jesus, faith, and heaven. Our future in heaven is also the topic for many of the hymns. I wonder if these themes are common in their services.

The pastor says there are seven thousand promises in the Bible. We need to accept them by faith, know them, claim them, and believe them. With much alarm, he also alerts us to the "rapid worldwide growth" of Chrislam.[8]

Afterward, everyone lingers to chat. Our stomachs tell us it's past time to eat, but we tarry. Many thank us for visiting and invite us to come again, but they aren't pushy. I'm not going to mislead them, so I simply smile and nod to let them know I heard.

The pianist invites us back that night for their monthly hymn sing and meal. There will be plenty to eat, so there's no need for us to bring anything. For a moment I consider it, even though church music bores me, and I hate to sing.

We leave feeling appreciated and accepted. This is a friend-

---

8 Wikipedia later informs me that Chrislam is a comingling of Christianity and Islam, but I don't get a sense of "rapid worldwide growth," as the pastor claimed.

ly church with a homey feel. If it was necessary, I suppose I could join this congregation, but I'm so glad I don't have to. I worked hard to have a positive attitude today and still struggled. If our visits at the next fifty-one churches are all like this, we'll surely never make it to the end of our journey.

Fortunately, I anticipate something much different next week.

Takeaway for Leaders: While providing a safe place for people with mental illness and boundary issues, churches need to keep these folks from accosting or scaring away visitors. Also, churches should examine every aspect of their service through the eyes of a visitor and then make appropriate adjustments.

Church #2:

❖

Growing Deeper, Not Wider

Today's church is three years old. I met the minister before they opened. He's a postmodern guy with a modern theology. I anticipate the church to mirror this. Through volunteering at the local food pantry, I have a connection with him and some of their members, so I expect to see familiar faces.

I park near the door. Only later do I realize they leave the prime spaces for visitors, with the regulars parking further away. The facility is fresh and inviting, the opposite of what we saw last Sunday. In fact, everything today contrasts sharply with last week's visit.

A man stands by the entrance, opening the door for everyone. He passes us a "worship folder." Beaming, he pumps my hand. "Welcome, folks. Have you ever been here before?"

"Only to your open house, when you opened this facility — three years ago."

"A lot has changed since then." We chat some more and then go inside. While news of a reconfiguration doesn't seem noteworthy, we immediately see a difference. The new layout feels more accommodating.

Scores of people mill about, all engaged in conversation. I spot several folks from the food pantry, but I fail to make eye contact. We mosey in, giving time for someone to notice us. When this doesn't happen, we sit down. Had anyone seemed available, I'd have sucked in a gulp of courage and approached them.

I'm surprised to spot a neighbor. The last I knew, she went to a different church. She waves hi and chats briefly with Candy. It's good to be in church with a neighbor. This hasn't happened in years.

Intended as retail space, the rectangular room is narrow and three to four times as deep. Smartly decorated, the focal point isn't the end of the space but the side, which allows everyone to sit close to the action. There isn't a stage per se, but more of a staging area, with their four guiding principles painted on the wall behind it. Above hang two large monitors, poised to provide information throughout the morning. To the side stands a wooden cross.

The minister welcomes everyone to start the service. "The church's guiding goal," he says, "is to grow deeper, not wider." Spiritual growth is more important to them than numeric growth. This confirms why the church has so many volunteers at the food pantry. They put their faith into action.

He gives two short announcements and calls up an elder. Noting it's only two days past their third birthday, the elder shows a chart of steady numeric growth, now averaging 150, and sometimes spiking much higher. This taxes their facility, and leadership is considering options. The pastor's workload has mushroomed too. They want to hire another staff person to help meet growing needs.

Next, their finance guy reviews donations and expenses. For the past three years they've kept costs within budget, while giving has exceeded projections. They're in a fine position to hire an associate pastor. After introducing the candidate, they review the evaluation process. This takes ten to fifteen minutes and, while exciting, this isn't why we're here.

The minister returns, reiterating the elders' desire to be transparent in the hiring process, to keep everyone informed, and that members will make the final decision using a carefully designed evaluation tool. He segues into the next part of the service with a reading from Esther, using the English Standard Version (ESV).

It's a more literal translation than the popular New International Version (NIV) I use for much of my Bible reading and study. The ESV is a most comfortable rendering. I appreciate the nuances it offers. With copies in every seat, he encourages visitors to take one. Although tempting, I don't. I use a computer for most of my Bible study and the ESV is readily available online.[9]

The pastor's practice is to focus on one book of the Bible, methodically working through it over several months. He briefly reviews the prior weeks' teachings on Esther and gives some opening remarks.

Then the worship team comes forward. Two play electric guitars, with other musicians on bass, keyboard, and an electronic drum kit. The sixth instrument is out of place in this otherwise electrified ensemble: a cello. Although sporting a mic, I can't pick out its sound. Of the six musicians, three use mics, though all six sing.

We sing two worship songs, with the words displayed on the monitors. I estimate attendance at about ten times Church #1

9 I use http://www.biblegateway.com.

(A Friendly Place with a Homey Feel). The people dress casually. Jeans and T-shirts abound, while no one wears ties and dresses. It's also a much younger crowd. This week we're on the older end of the age spectrum. Excitement permeates the place. Life abounds.

After the second song, there's a break for "connection time," an informal opportunity to mingle, get a coffee refill, or grab another doughnut hole. I knew about the refreshments, but I forgot, and no one mentioned it. Candy, the coffee drinker in our household, goes to snag a cup of Joe. The couple in front of me turns around. They're food pantry volunteers and confused at seeing me. I point out our connection and we chat for a while. When the conversation wanes, I excuse myself.

Candy spots a friend from a group she was involved with some twenty years ago, as well as other moms she knows from when our kids were in school. I can't find my neighbor, but I do spot "Bible Bill," a longtime acquaintance and an elder here. As Candy talks with his wife, Bill and I exchange pleasantries, but we don't have time for much more. A former high school classmate of our daughter walks up, but the music resumes, so we'll have to catch up with him later. We scurry back to our seats. There's another song and then the minister launches into his message on Esther, chapter three.

He's an insightful Bible teacher and an engaging speaker, although not polished to the point of stale perfection. He pulls details out of the text, reminding me of them, and adding fresh perspectives. He points out that Haman, the Agagite could have literally been a descendant of King Agag, mentioned in 1 Samuel 15, or Agagite could be a label meaning anti-Semitic. He opts for the second. So do I. It adds an interesting nuance to the Esther story. He speaks for about an hour, but it doesn't seem nearly so long.

After the message, they serve Communion. Communion is open to all who acknowledge their saving faith in Jesus. They pass the bread (oyster crackers) and the juice in swift succession. Some partake quickly, and others wait. *What should I do?* In trying to figure out what to do and when to do it, I fail to focus on why. But I think Jesus understands, and I know he forgives my distraction.

There's a closing prayer, and the service ends. They never take an offering. Aside from the opening presentation, they don't mention money.

There are more people to talk to, acquaintances from other places, and some who are new to us. No one knows if we're first-timers, and some even wonder if we're regulars. For all we know, we may be talking to other visitors.

The minister thanks me for coming. We talk about the food pantry and briefly about my home church. I give him a sincere compliment about his teaching. As Candy and I move our conversation from one person to the next, the crowd thins. Soon we're some of the last ones there.

We drop off the completed guest card we found in the worship folder — which also contained a donation envelope — and pick up our complimentary travel cup complete with the church's logo. We already have plenty, but Candy wants this memento. Two and a half hours have passed since we walked through the doors. Time moves quickly when you're enjoying the company of engaging people.

Today was as easy as last week was hard. Frankly, I'd just as soon return here next Sunday and skip Church #3. Knowing what awaits us, I expect next week will require more effort.

Takeaway for Members: Leaving open parking spots near the door and having an outgoing, friendly greeter makes a positive first impression, forming the basis for the rest of the time in church. However, greeting isn't one person's job. It's important for everyone to welcome visitors.

Church #3:

It Only Hurts When You Care

This week we're visiting our second church with "Baptist" in its name. Despite that, I expect little similarity to Church #1 (A Friendly Place with a Homey Feel).

Although they have a website, many pages are "under construction" or "coming soon." This includes the "about" and "what we believe" sections, as well as the page about their worship service. For the most part, they've finished the sections relating to members, while the pages for visitors are incomplete. The lack of visitor-friendly information frustrates me. All I can learn about their Sunday service is from their events calendar: "Traditional Service—Music & Message." Once again, we head off to church braced for the unknown.

The brick building is about fifty years old. It's the first one that looks like a church. Next door is the school I attended for eight years. Some of my classmates went to this church, and I wonder if any of them still do. I also work with some of their members at the food pantry, so I expect to know a few people.

When we arrive, the parking lot is filling up, yet there are available spaces near the building. Whether or not we park close to the entrance, however, is speculation, as there are several doors, all unmarked. We get out of our car and follow the flow of people.

These folks dress up for church. As the only adult in shorts, I'm grossly underdressed—and that's after I again skipped my typical T-shirt for a polo shirt. My clothes don't bother me, but my observation does. I want visitors to feel comfortable with their attire, but at this church, they wouldn't. As for myself, if I err in my wardrobe, I prefer comfort over confinement.

Like last Sunday, there's a greeter holding the door open and passing out bulletins. He welcomes us, and we have a brief exchange. But there's no time to linger. We're blocking the entrance. The greeter manages to distribute bulletins as others squeeze by, all the while talking to us. We soon move inside.

A friend from high school spots us. Confident, she strides up with a broad smile, "Hi, DeHaans . . . fifty-two churches!" While I fully expected that one Sunday our mission would precede us, I never thought it would happen this soon. I've not yet prepared a response, so I just smile. At least I know someone's reading my blog posts. "Please be nice to us," her eyes dance with mirth, "and don't judge us too harshly."

"Don't worry." Although lighthearted, her words remind me this isn't a trivial exercise. I could hurt people if my words are careless. *Perhaps I should review what I wrote for the first two churches.*

Her tone grows suddenly somber. "This won't be a typical service."

I cock my head and furrow my brows.

"On Thursday, one of our deacons committed suicide," she whispers. "We talked about it in Sunday school, but some people weren't there and so not everyone knows yet. This service will be quite different."

"Thanks so much for letting us know." Though appreciative,

28

my heart sinks. I want to leave. Perhaps we can make it in time to Church #4 and return here next week. Yet, God has a reason for us to be here today. I know we must stay.

She thanks us for visiting and excuses herself to join the choir. No one else approaches, and I don't spot anyone not already talking to someone, so we head to the sanctuary. A man waves hi and shakes my hand. He runs a local restaurant. I knew he went here, but seeing him outside our normal context catches me off guard, so all I do is smile.

The well-lit interior, with its white walls, provides an open feel. There's a baptistry behind the platform, with a piano on one side and electric organ on the other. After we sit, two ladies come up in turn to welcome us. Both claim having difficulty remembering names. They say ours repeatedly, as if trying to imprint them into their minds.

The service begins normally enough: a chorus from the hymnal, a number from the choir, a few hymns, greeting time — during which we meet a few more people — an offering, and a woman's trio performing a special music number. We know some of the songs, though all the tunes have a vague familiarity.

A choir is something I've not seen in years. This one numbers twenty-six, with women outnumbering men six to one. But they make it work.

The pastor stands to give his message. He uses a small lectern on our level, not the bulky dais on the platform. Until now, his public persona has been warm and inviting, abounding with smiles and most engaging. Now subdued, he struggles to release the words welled up in his heart. Fighting to control emotion, he bravely shares the sad news. Ladies dab silent tears from their eyes and stifled sniffles occasionally break the respectful silence. Today we need "to remind ourselves who God is." He adds that the salvation message of Jesus will appropriately be the theme for this service.

He shares four basic truths: 1) We are frail creatures, 2) We need God, 3) He is faithful, and 4) There is a future. It's a message of comfort, abounding in hope. Our response to this tragedy is simple: To pray, weep, and help those who grieve.

We sing a closing hymn, and he ends the service. My friend returns, and we talk some more. Our paths have occasionally crossed in the years since graduation, but we never had much time to talk. The church begins to empty, and we say our goodbyes. Candy and I head for the door and meet the minister. Shaking hands, I affirm his adept handling of an emotional situation. I remind him of what he already knows. "If you didn't care, it wouldn't hurt." My wife gives him an informal blessing for the challenging task ahead. He gratefully receives it.

I now realize my purpose for being here today. It's so I can pray for this church community and its godly leader in the days and weeks ahead. This close-knit congregation deeply cares about each other. They celebrate together and mourn together. Today is one of mourning. This is what true community is and what true church should be.

I may return one day to attend a typical service, but today's visit reveals their character and shows me God at work. *Thank you, God!*

Takeaway for Everyone: When a service will contain difficult topics or unusual situations, alerting visitors beforehand is a nice gesture and keeps them from jarring surprises.

Church #4:

— ❖ —

Successfully Melding Contemporary and Traditional

Next on our list is a church we've visited before, when our church cancelled services due to a snowstorm. I've known the minister since I was ten. He would have been thirteen, the older brother of my best friend. My other connection with the church is through the local food pantry. Though now a broad-based community effort, the pantry is an outgrowth of this church's internal efforts. Many of the pantry's volunteers hail from this church, as do some of our clients. I expect to see many familiar faces.

The church recently changed their name, which used to include "congregational" and now proclaims "community." Their tagline is "your community, your church, your home." They don't have a website, but I learn all the information I seek from a well-maintained Facebook page. Their "services are informal with a blend of hymns and contemporary music." They're "evangelical" and "all sermons are Bible-based."

The facility is a traditional church building with an addition, well-maintained and stately. There's ample parking across the street. The morning is sunny and the temperature, mild. It's a perfect day to go to church. Just inside they greet us. Someone hands us a small tote containing information and a logo-emblazoned travel mug. We spot a couple from the food pantry. They're pleased to see us, and we chat briefly about the pantry and church. Unaware that we know the pastor, they introduce us to him.

The well-lit sanctuary has a high, flat ceiling. Though not a large room, it's open and inviting. In the front is a simple cross, a bit on the small side. It's not rugged but smooth and nicely finished. Above is a beautiful stained-glass window, the first we've seen on our adventure. On each side of the platform stands a flag.

The stage, elevated by a couple of steps, borders on being crowded. There are empty tables for a bell choir and an assortment of musical instruments, ranging from a drum kit to a baby grand. In the center stands a diminutive pulpit, noteworthy for its simplicity. A projector screen hangs to the left, making the space feel even smaller. I suspect the service will match what I see in the facility, a blending of traditional and contemporary, just as promised online.

The church might seat 120, and the people show a preference to sit in the back. We're only a third of the way in, yet most of the people pack in behind us. There are about seventy-five.

The service begins with several familiar choruses, led by a team of four: the worship leader on guitar, vocalist, keyboard, and the minister on bass. The drums sit idle. They don't use the piano for this opening session, but later we hear it for the prelude, offertory, closing hymn, and postlude.

Our final chorus is "Agnus Dei" (Lamb of God). Though limited and low-key, some people raise their hands. Today is the first time we see a physical display of worship. Yet I follow the majority and keep my hands clasped to restrain them from any spontaneous movement in this otherwise reserved gathering. Yet when the worship leader asks us to raise our hands for a final singing of this song, I gladly comply.

Announcements follow. It's a busy place. The bulletin reveals activity every day of the week. Next is a time to greet those around us. This isn't a token effort, nor is it cut short, allowing time to talk. Many people make a sincere effort to welcome us.

They excuse the children, something done in three of the four churches so far.[10] For the first time on our sojourn, the minister leads us in a congregational prayer. Even though this isn't a staple of my home church, it's not a new concept, either. Unfortunately, I tuned out such things in my youth and never broke that habit. The offering follows, accompanied by an impressive piano performance. The piece lasts longer than the collection, and at the concluding measure, enthusiastic applause ensues. I'm uncomfortable, wondering if we're worshiping the God who created music or praising an accomplished performer.

The minister is in the second week of a series from 1 John. He summarizes week one, and we stand for today's scripture. Standing to read the Bible isn't typical in my church practices, but this is the third time we've done so in four weeks. Though he will teach from a longer section, he reads 1 John 2:15–18.

In a delightful bit of Bible trivia, he notes the word "know" occurs forty-two times in this brief five-chapter book.[11] The purpose of John's letter is so that we will know about our faith. Also significant are nine appearances of the endearing

---

10 Church #1 (A Friendly Place with a Homey Feel) had no children — except for two toddlers.

11 Later, I investigate and find thirty-two times in the NIV.

phrase "dear children." John cares deeply for his audience and wants them to fully appreciate their standing with God.

Using an expository preaching style — going through the passage verse by verse — the minister guides us through the text. He pulls in supporting verses to expand certain sections and dips into other translations — the King James Version (KJV) and The Message — for added clarity. As he moves toward the end of the selection, he zeroes in on verse sixteen, which is the basis for his sermon title, "Pollution Free." We need to guard against the lust of the flesh, the lust of the eyes, and the pride of life — thereby controlling the pollution in our lives.

We conclude the service by singing a well-known hymn from the hymnal, with the words also displayed overhead. After three verses, there's an invitation to stay for coffee and cookies. Following the benediction, we stand to sing verse four.

Folks quickly exit the sanctuary, moving with intention toward their snack. With many people to talk to, we're the last to leave the sanctuary, enjoying an extended discussion with the minister on the way out. These conversations take so long that the time for coffee and cookies is now over. Although disappointed, I didn't need a cookie anyway. Plus, the meaningful conversations more than make up for missing the snack.[12]

Overall, they impress me with their successful mix of hymns and choruses, melding the old with the new, worshiping God with ease and without apology. I relish the experience and am glad to be here.

Next week, we'll go to the Catholic church next door. This will

---

12 This reminds me of John 4:32, where Jesus talks with the Samaritan woman and doesn't feel a need to eat.

be a huge stretch for me, and I'm already worried. It would be much easier to return here.

Takeaway for Everyone: Most churches that try to combine traditional with contemporary, do so awkwardly. This church proves it's possible. The key is good leadership and an accepting congregation.

Church #5:

❖

Catholics are Christians Too

When I tell people we're visiting area churches, I specify *Christian*, but they often comprehend *Protestant*. It surprises these folks to learn we'll visit Catholic gatherings too. Their responses range from suspicion to support. As they readjust their understanding of our quest, some overreach, asking if we'll also go to synagogues, temples, and mosques. Again, I emphasize the word *Christian*, at which point they either understand or stop asking questions.

Today we're going to the first Roman Catholic church on our list. It's next door to Church #4 (Melding Contemporary and Traditional). According to their website—the most comprehensive one so far—they offer three service times, with Saturday Mass at 4:30 p.m. and Sunday Mass at 8:00 and 11:00 a.m. Apparently, the priest oversees two parishes, holding a 9:30 a.m. service in a nearby town. He'll have a busy day, and we'll attend his final service.

I've only been to Catholic churches three times, all special events: a wedding, a baptism, and a funeral. The first two were comfortable enough, but the third was confusing, with traditions and practices we didn't understand.[13]

---

13 In this third instance, "we" refers to a female co-worker and I who were there to support another co-worker marking the end of his mother's life on earth. Toward the end of the service, the priest utters something we don't understand. The couple in front of us turns and kisses. My co-worker and I glance at each other and with weak smiles simultaneously whisper, "not going to happen."

Tradition, custom, and ritual all repel me, and I expect to witness all three today. I must guard against a rebellious spirit and seek to receive what this church offers with an open mind, ready for a fresh spiritual encounter, which is why we're visiting fifty-two churches. I approach this day with dread and excitement, but I'm happy that the morning brings less apprehension and more anticipation.

As a final thought before leaving for church, I wonder if I should bring my "Protestant" NIV Bible or a version containing the Apocrypha, the fuller "Catholic" text, such as the New American Bible (NAB) or The New Jerusalem Bible. I opt for the NAB, but it's unnecessary. Though they read the Bible several times during the service, they seldom cite the chapter and never state the verse. This makes it impossible to follow along.

The facility is two connected buildings of distinctive styles. Each has its own entrance and parking lot. People don't head to the larger building but the smaller one. This changes where I will park, so I veer away from the larger lot at the last moment, entering the smaller one via the exit. There are two open spaces close to the door. Narcissistic, I assume these are for visitors and pick the nearest one. I'm nervous, perhaps even more than on the first Sunday of our journey. Shaky and sweaty, my fear of the unknown threatens to overwhelm me.

As I walk in, a friend from the food pantry greets me. It's nice to see a familiar face. She reintroduces me to her kids, but I forget to reintroduce her to Candy, who fortunately doesn't feel slighted by my oversight. As my friend readies the children for a special flower processional, she takes a moment to chat with me.

When we're done talking, we find a seat because there's little room to stand. For the first time in our adventure, we see kneeling rails. In my only other attempt to use them, they presented a challenge to unfold, at least for my friends and me, all of us unfamiliar with their operation. After a few humorous attempts, we gave up. Should I try again today? As a non-Catholic, should I partake in this ritual, or would that offend others? I never conclude my wonderings, as other things soon distract me.

Most noticeable is an ornate crucifix, front and center, with scores of other crosses of varying sizes scattered throughout the sanctuary. They range from the most basic to extremely intricate. The building is newer, with simple cement block construction and an open steel-beam roof that slants from right to left. The walls and ceiling are white. Though the ceiling isn't high, the room has an open feel.

Wood-carved plaques, depicting the Stations of the Cross, hang on the side walls. The side walls also have sets of simple awning-style windows, with each pane sporting a single color of stained glass. The space is longer and narrower than most sanctuaries I've been in. With our seats toward the rear, it's hard to make out much detail up front.

The sparse crowd is casually dressed but not to the point of T-shirts. There are no suits or ties on the men, but a few women wear dresses. I suspect the building seats a couple hundred. With a flurry of arrivals at the starting time and slightly after, the seats end up being over half-full.

Today is Mother's Day. Perhaps because of that, they feature Mary, the mother of Jesus, throughout the service. Most of the hymns focus on her. "Mary is the 'Magnificat' or magnifying glass to Jesus," says the layperson who opens the service. She reads from John 19. She shares the process for the upcoming processional, where the children will present flowers, the May Crowning, in honor of Mary. I'm so focused on how it will happen that I miss the explanation of why. There's also a reference about praying to Mary, who will then intercede to Jesus on our behalf. This surprises me. I didn't know they did that anymore.

Next is a reading from Acts, and then 1 John. Afterward I find these in today's lectionary, number 56, the sixth Sunday of Easter. Later in the service, we read from the Gospel of John, but if we read the prescribed responsive passage from Psalms, I missed it.[14]

Throughout the service, I'm pleased to see laypeople take part. Unfortunately, some attendees disrespect the service, measuring their way through the morning with casual indifference and whispered conversation. The children remain with us the entire time. There's no kid's activity and presumably no nursery. With a nice range of ages present, I see no visible demographic gaps.

It's hard to follow the service. Multiple times a congregational response is required, but we never know what to say or do. About halfway through, we find some of this information in the front section of a book called the missal.[15]

After the service, my friend apologizes for not pointing out a card in the pew racks that would have helped us follow the liturgy. Regardless, the proceedings aren't hospitable to

---

14 The readings for the sixth Sunday of Easter, Lectionary 56, includes Acts 10:25-26, 34-35, 44-48, Psalm 98:1, 2-3, 3-4, 1 John 4:7-10, and John 15:9-17. The initial reading from John 19 is not part of the lectionary passages.

15 A missal is a book with all the prayers and responses for mass for the year. The one we use doubles as a hymnal, containing several hundred songs.

the uninitiated — or as some in the church growth movement would say, not "seeker-sensitive."

The lone musical instrument is a keyboard, which I can't spot. It often sounds like an organ, but it occasionally veers toward piano. (After the service, I notice it tucked in the back corner. There's a strategically-placed vocal mic for the keyboardist, so I presume he was also the song leader.) A choir sits in the back. For one song, they sing the verses and the congregation — at least those aware of the words — sing back in response. I appreciate positioning the singers and musician behind us. This removes attention from them, making it less like a performance and more reverent. This is how it should be.

I'm surprised when the priest leads us in reciting the Apostles' Creed.[16] I assumed it was only a Protestant practice, but obviously it's not. We also recite the Lord's Prayer. Though I'm aware Roman Catholics don't say the final line that most Protestants do,[17] I almost call attention to myself by uttering them out of habit. Interestingly, in his comments after the prayer, the priest recites these extra words.

The priest exudes a gentle persona, affable from the distance that exists between pulpit and pew. However, his English carries a heavy accent, making his words hard to understand. I fear I miss almost as much as I comprehend.

---

16 One phrase in the Apostles' Creed often raises questions: "[I believe in] the holy catholic Church." Small "c" catholic — as rendered in most versions of the Creed — is an improper noun, referring to the universal church or the entire Christian church. To eliminate confusion, some groups replaced "catholic" with "universal" or "Christian." Big "C" Catholic, a proper noun, references the Roman Catholic Church.

17 Some later manuscripts of the Bible end the Lord's Prayer, as found in Matthew 6:9–13, with "for yours is the kingdom and the power and the glory forever. Amen" (NIV).

He begins his message with a series of humorous anecdotes about moms and motherhood. Just when I fear funny stories will be the sum of his message, he segues into love: reciprocal love, romantic love, and love-your-enemies love. I'm perplexed how a priest—one who doesn't marry and is celibate—can address the complexities of romantic love, yet he does so quite well. More important, I'd never considered Jesus's death on the cross as a love-your-enemies type of love. I appreciate the priest pointing this out.

The message is short, by far the shortest yet. Though they call the entire service "Mass," the mass part—what I call communion and they call the celebration of the Eucharist, Holy Eucharist, or simply Eucharist—doesn't occur until the second half. The priest calls it "a memorial service" for Jesus. I like that.

There's much ritual activity, but I'm not close enough to make out the details. Several people go forward immediately and receive the elements from the priest. Then the rest of the congregation—or at least, most of the rest—go up row by row. It's a quick and orderly procession.

Even though we don't partake,[18] I know I should spend this time in contemplation of what Jesus did for us through his sacrificial death and resurrection. But I'm too distracted—repelled—by their use of a shared communion cup. Though the attendant wipes the cup after each use, he uses the same cloth. Doesn't this just remove the saliva of one person and effectively replace it with the collective germs of everyone else? I shudder at this but not as much as my wife. Even

---

18 At Roman Catholic Churches only members may partake in the Eucharist. Some Protestant churches—more typically traditional mainline or high churches—also follow this practice of "closed communion," that is closed to nonmembers.

if communion were available to us, I doubt we would take part.

Afterward follows more responsive liturgy and singing. Then the priest announces that mass is over. The people dart out, with little interaction. Apparently they don't value community. Though I recognize several people, they scatter before I can catch their eye. On the way out, someone hands us a bulletin, albeit too late to do us much good. It resembles a newsletter, complete with coupons for local businesses.

At the exit stands the priest. We shake hands. His eyes dart from Candy to me and then back again. Finally, he blurts out what he's been pondering, "Should I know you?"

I shake my head, but before I can say more, he continues.

"Is this your first time here?"

I smile. "Yes, it is."

"What are your names?"

"I'm Peter DeHaan, and this is my wife, Candy."

An awkward quiet settles. After too much time has passed, I crumble under the pressure. "We liked the service." Inside I shudder. *I just lied to a priest.*

He smiles and nods. He wants to say more, but when the words don't come, I again break the silence, "Ah, well, good-bye." He nods again.

Then we head to a now nearly-empty parking lot. It's exactly one hour after the service began. We drive home with much to contemplate, all the while glad that next week's church will offer a more accessible service.

Takeaway for Everyone: A church that wants to attract visitors and help people connect with God needs to make it easy for people to follow their service and engage in worship. To attract visitors and grow may require letting go of some cherished traditions.

Church #6:

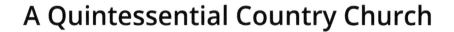

A Quintessential Country Church

The first five weeks of our journey took us to churches in or next to the small village near where we live—and included four of the five churches involved with the food pantry.[19] Today we head in the opposite direction, to a small quintessential country church, our third with a Baptist label. This church didn't come up in our online research. We know of it simply because we sometimes drive past it. They have no online presence, and all we know is from their sign: their name and service time. For all we know, they may not be meeting anymore. If that's the case, we have a backup plan. We'll make a U-turn and arrive at next week's selection in plenty of time. Candy expects they're closed. I anticipate a small gathering.

To my relief, I see several cars when we drive up. I pull into one of the few open spaces. A wheelchair ramp is the focal point and appears to be the way inside. We make our way up the ramp and are surprised when it doesn't connect with the main entrance, but instead it ends at a small side door. It looks tightly shut, so I don't even try it. We retrace our steps, discovering a narrow sidewalk that goes to the main steps and double-door entrance. I smile as I recall Jesus's words about the narrow way that leads to life.[20]

---

19 It won't be until week 44 that we make it to the fifth church.
20 Matthew 7:13–14. Also see Luke 13:24.

Once inside the tiny narthex, a couple of strides take us into the sanctuary. It's smaller than I expected. Several people mill about. Though we won't end up being the youngest people there, we are at this time. One lady greets us, while another scurries off to fetch us a bulletin. It's the simplest of documents but contains all the information we need. She also hands us a visitor card. The card is important to them. Three more people will offer us one before we leave.

Candy fills out the card as I take in the facility. Her handwriting is neat while mine is barely legible — even to me. In awe, I point to the curvature of the ceiling, noting it as a type of construction seldom attempted anymore. Even more impressive is the plaster with a neat pattern of smooth arcing swirls. She feigns interest.

To our left is a large mural, taking up most of the wall. It's an idyllic woodlands scene, with a series of gently cascading waterfalls. I recall the Twenty-third Psalm, even though it mentions "still waters"[21] and not flowing waters. Nevertheless, the effect is the same: calming and serene. People continue to introduce themselves, thanking us for visiting. It's the friendliest church we've been to so far and the opposite of last week.

There's the simplest of crosses in the front, mounted over a curtain, which likely covers the baptistry. On the walls hang several pictures, including two needlepoint hangings, one of the Lord's Prayer and the other of the Ten Commandments. A plaque shows last week's attendance at twenty-nine, which we will surpass this week by a few. The weekly budget is a minuscule $447 — not enough to support a pastor — with last week's giving even lower, at $277. Most of the members are

---

21 Psalm 23:2.

senior citizens, many likely on fixed incomes, so this isn't surprising, but it is sad—for both the people and the church.

With their low attendance, it's surprising that four people
have birthdays this week. We sing "Happy Birthday." I'm
prepared to sing a second verse, like at Church #1 (A Friendly Place with a Homey Feel), but we don't. There are also four
anniversaries. We sing to them, too, using the same tune but
with slightly different words.

The church has a piano and organ, but the pianist is on vacation, so the organ is our only instrument today—except for
the boombox the soloist uses for her special music number, a
gospel number chronicling Jesus's healing power.

After a few songs there's an extended greeting time when
we meet even more people. But we're boxed in, so we can't
roam about as most people do. Given our lack of mobility, the
greeting time lasts far too long. We can do nothing but smile
uncomfortably and squirm. Then the pastor rings a bell, sending people scurrying back to their seats.

He updates everyone on the congregational needs he's aware
of and then others chime in with their prayer requests. Many
mention health concerns, some ask for safe travels, and a few
are for job interviews. I've often sensed that sharing needs
focuses more on the news than on praying, which is one small
step away from gossip. Not so with this group. They have a
genuine concern for each other. Then the minister calls on a
member, who is more than eager to pray.

Today's text is Mark 8:34–38. The pastor focuses on three action words in verse 34: deny, take, and follow. Though he
doesn't look it, he's eighty and likely a contemporary with
most of the congregation. A recurring theme is that they're

nearing the end of life on earth. None of us, regardless of age, has a guarantee for our next breath. We must make the best use of our remaining time.

The pastor has a quirky sense of humor, which he acknowledges, and the congregation accepts. Even so, one quip elicits groans from the ladies. "I'd rather do a funeral than a wedding, because the man has a better chance for happiness at a funeral."

Acknowledging that everyone present is following God, he gives a low-key altar call anyway, but no one responds. He also mentions "the other church" and will head there to lead another service after this one.

Many people invite us to stay for refreshments. In addition to coffee, there's an assortment of snacks and some fruit. Unlike Church #4 (Melding Contemporary and Traditional) where the after-church fellowship was a quick affair, this is an extended one. We talk with the minister a bit, too, before he scurries off to do the service at the second church.

We sit at tables, decorated as if for a party. There are gift bags for the birthday people. One lady goes through her bag with much glee—just like a kid on Christmas. She's pleased to be honored. Another lady says she'll be out of town on her birthday and hopes they'll remember her when she returns. I doubt that will be a problem.

More people greet us. Surely we've met everyone by now. This friendly church cares for each other, happy to linger in one another's company. They thank us for visiting and invite us back but without being pushy. I really like them, but don't want to give them false hope, so I simply say, "It's good to be here today."

Yet I wonder about the church's prospects, with an aging congregation and extremely low giving, their future is in doubt. How many more years does this church have?

Takeaway for Everyone: Be sure to unlock the church doors. Guide people to the right entrance, and help them find their way around the facility.

Church #7:

The New Church

Today we visit last Sunday's backup church. They meet in a shared-tenant business building, but that oversells the space. It's run down, bordering on abandoned. We've been here before, visiting a different church several years ago. The prior church knocked down several interior walls, providing an open worship space.[22]

Their incomplete website, copyrighted last year, too often states, "We are in the process of developing this page." What I do find says they have a "multi-generational contemporary worship service" and have opted for a nondenominational label "because God has called all believers to unity." I fully support their perspective.[23]

They've occupied this space for seven months. Their Facebook page goes back twenty-one months, displaying many older posts but few newer ones. With a twenty-one-month online history, I surmise they're less than two years old.

Next to the door stands a cross. It's rugged and riddled with nails. I imagine a service that invited people to symbolically nail their struggles to this cross. I don't know if my guess is correct, but it seems plausible.

---

22 The original church moved to a more conducive environment. We'll visit them in a couple of months for Church #16.

23 I wrote my dissertation on this subject and am passionate about it.

We walk in. People mingle about. Several soon introduce themselves in a friendly, yet unassuming, way. One person offers us coffee and hot chocolate. It's in the seventies outside, with a predicted high in the mid-nineties, which is probably why the A/C is cranked down. Feeling chilly, hot chocolate calls me. Uncharacteristically, I accept their offer. My wife, a social coffee drinker, seldom passes on a cup. This gives us time to talk with our new friend. Of all the churches we've visited, this one is the most effective at interacting with visitors before the service.

They're only using part of the space occupied by the prior church. The room they use features royal blue walls on the sides, with a dark gray, almost black, wall behind the stage area. There's a solitary wall hanging, a church covenant signed by about twenty people and reminiscent of the US Declaration of Independence. For the second time on our sojourn, we don't sit in pews but enjoy padded chairs instead.[24]

The twenty-four by forty feet room[25] seats fifty-five, but I only count twenty-four people. It's Memorial Day weekend, so I shouldn't be surprised at the low attendance.

"We're often near capacity," boasts one of our new friends, as if reading my mind. "On Easter we maxed out."

This isn't the first time, nor will it be the last, that people felt a need to explain their low attendance, while recalling other Sundays that boasted many more people.

"In a week or two we'll be moving. It's in a small strip mall

---

24 Church #2 (Growing Deeper, Not Wider) also had padded chairs. They were a three-year-old church and also nondenominational.

25 A standard ceiling tile is two feet by four feet. Count the tiles and do the math. I don't know if others have this peculiar habit, but I do.

and a much nicer place." She tells me where. It's even closer to our house. "It will seat 160." She beams. "We'll fill up the space!" I'm not sure if this is godly confidence or a human boast, so I just nod to show I heard.

To start the service, three ladies lead us in singing several contemporary praise and worship songs. The only instrument present, a drum kit, sits unused. Instead of live music, they play recorded accompaniment tracks, another first for our journey. Although it's less inviting, we're not here for a concert but to praise God. If you need high-quality music to connect with the Almighty, surely something is amiss. They don't use songbooks, instead displaying the words on a monitor.

As the music set winds down, we see the pastor for the first time. He looks familiar. There's some informal dialogue between him and a member who picks that moment to ask a question. He segues from her query into a series of announcements, but I zone out, trying to determine if I know him.

The pastor doesn't have a Bible text to kick off his message, which is more akin to teaching than a sermon. He is well into his talk before he mentions any verses. When he does, the passages appear on the monitor. This is needed because they don't provide Bibles, and few people brought their own. He's in week two of a series. Last Sunday he covered God's sovereignty, and this week is about God's providence. He delves into some tough questions, which many preachers would skip. He points out that some people view God as powerful but not too loving, while others see him as loving but not too powerful. The correct understanding is that God is both loving and powerful, but it takes faith to accept this.

When he's done speaking, he prays. The service is over, but there's no formal end or dismissal. We all remain seated. He chats about preparations for an upcoming dance, when he realizes Candy and I have no idea what he's talking about. Redirecting his attention to us, he explains they're planning a flash mob for an upcoming community event. Then he starts a personal conversation with me — while twenty-two other people listen in. That's when he recognizes me too. We were in a discipleship class some fifteen years ago. This was near the beginning of his spiritual journey. He admits he's changed much since then.

Later we talk one-on-one. He's a tentmaker pastor, like Paul in the Bible, working for a living and sharing Jesus for free. Without him drawing a salary — a source of much joy for him — there are more funds for outreach and ministry. The church, which used to meet in his home, is an outgrowth of a small group he once led. Their goal is to be "a transformational church."

Most attendees, he says, are young in their faith, eager to learn about God. They've come without church baggage and since they don't know how they're expected to act in church, they don't have any bad habits to overcome. This all explains the informal nature of the service, the high degree of socializing before and after, his teaching style, and their arriving without Bibles. Their eagerness to learn is why he embraces difficult concepts in his teaching. He's not interested in numbers but in spiritual growth.

As a church, they're doing quite well. People engage with God and desire to know him more. As is often the case, it's new churches — not established ones — where people are most apt to discover God and grow into a vibrant faith.

Newer is often better — and this church proves it.

Takeaway for Everyone: Unchurched folks don't know how to act in church. Don't let this frustrate you. Instead, examine your practices and expectations to discover what's biblically important and culturally applicable.

An Intriguing Opportunity

Next on our list is a "meditation group of self-realization fellowship." Since our mission is to visit Christian churches, if there's any evidence of this being a Christian community, I'm open to check them out—and if not, we'll skip their service.

According to their website, the Sunday meeting is a "reading service." It includes devotional chanting, short meditations, and readings from the Bible and Bhagavad Gita, which Wikipedia indicates is a "700-verse Hindu scripture."[26] There is also mention on their website of Kriya Yoga.

I conclude they are essentially an Eastern-style religion, with a touch of Bible mixed in. There is seemingly nothing Christian about them, and we decide not to visit.

Nevertheless, I wonder if Christians could attend one of their services and connect with the God revealed in the Bible. I suspect so, but they would need to be intentional with their focus and carefully guard against providing an opening to spiritual forces contrary to Christian faith. My ponderings will likely never go beyond the theoretical, but it is an intriguing opportunity, albeit one we'll skip for now.

---

26 http://en.wikipedia.org/wiki/Bhagavad_Gita

Church #8:

A Grand Experiment

This week we visit another newly-formed church, our third so far. A few years ago, a twenty-five-year-old church shut their doors, redirecting members to their nearest denominational gathering some fifteen miles away, which is a twenty-five-minute drive. That church used this closed facility to restart a different type of meeting, experimenting with an innovative approach, one quite radical from their conservative roots. The relaunch happened two or three years ago.

The website of this new church is inviting—and thankfully complete. Led by a husband-wife team, the church's youth programs are part of Young Life.[27] This means they aren't expending time and money duplicating what currently exists. Instead they partner with an organization that already does youth ministry well. Also, they have two services. This suggests they've grown fast. Interestingly, their website contains no mention of them being part of a denomination.

We pull into a semi-full parking lot twelve minutes before the

---

27 Young Life is a non-denominational youth ministry for junior high and high school students, which taps college students as leaders. Young Life organizes around school systems, allowing students to connect with like-minded classmates from other churches. Ecumenically-minded churches and churches with small youth groups or no leaders often plug into Young Life.

second service. Some people are still leaving from the first. The entry opens into a large lobby, which functions as a fellowship hall—a busy, noisy one.

We're warmly welcomed by a greeter who devotes quite a bit of time to us, explaining what to expect and not to expect. But it's almost too loud to hear her. I'd like to chat more, but we're standing in the way, so I thank her for the info, and we head further in.

People mingle, sipping coffee and munching cookies. They allow snacks in the sanctuary, but we bypass the treats, snaking our way through the crowd. The décor is by far the nicest we've seen. Everything is new. Nothing is worn or dated. I suspect an architect redesigned the layout and an interior decorator picked the colors and furnishings. It's first-rate. There are several overstuffed leather sectionals and a pool table or two, making the space feel more like a den than a church lobby.

As with most of the churches we've visited, no one else is available to talk with, so we head for the sanctuary. We pass through a doorway that's in an impressive glass wall that separates the sanctuary from the lobby. My positive impression of the facility continues. The worship space is wide and not deep, placing everyone near a slightly-elevated stage. Comfortable padded chairs, arranged in an arc, seat 180, with 110 present by the time the service starts.

There are ten on the worship team, half singing and half playing. Notably, the musicians vary in age from teens to seniors, with most residing somewhere in the middle. Their sound is good, though not top-notch, but the leader excels in exuberance, so it's most engaging. The opening song is like a concert, seemingly for entertainment. With no words provided, no one sings along. But soon lyrics appear overhead and people join in. Some raise their hands in varying displays of physical worship. The opening set is contemporary praise and worship songs with one hymn updated for guitars, drums, and keys.

Then there's a lengthy set of announcements. It's a busy place. Plans are underway for Vacation Bible School, held in partnership with other area churches. I appreciate their ecumenical[28] spirit in working together. The recent high school[29] baccalaureate service was held here, and I applaud their embrace of community events. The pastor shares prayer concerns and then intercedes accordingly, but there's no opportunity for the congregation to add anything. Interestingly, they also sing happy birthday to those celebrating this week.

The children come up for a children's message that previews today's teaching. During this time they stealthily take an offering. Candy drops our completed information card into the basket before sending it on to the next row. After the children's message, the four- and five-year-olds leave for their own lesson and the rest of the kids return to their moms and dads.

The pastor, who played guitar and sang during the worship set, begins a new series on Philippians. A former teacher, he begins by asking, "What does it mean to rejoice?" Then he reads chapter one from the NIV Bible. This is another first for us, even though the NIV is the most widely-used version of the Bible. The arc of the chapter is of Paul in jail, facing almost

---

28 Ecumenical refers to the whole Christian church, with God's various local branches working together in unity, just as Jesus prayed they would in John 17:23. It is a beautiful thing that I believe pleases God greatly.

29 The high school is down the street and visible from church.

certain execution—and rejoicing.

Even though the pastor covers no new ground for me, it's a good message to hear. Earlier this morning I wrote a memorial poem to our first granddaughter, who unsuccessfully entered our world too soon.[30] While there's much to lament over what will never be, my choice is to focus on the joy her brief existence offered. Writing the poem was cathartic, and the pastor's words confirm my decision to seek joy over grief. After a quick expository romp through the chapter, he concludes with the encouragement to "Rejoice in the Lord always. I will say it again: Rejoice!"[31] And I will.

A prayer concludes the message as the worship team reassembles for the closing set. A musical time of reflection gives way to more singing, when a man confuses everyone by coming forward to become a member, even though no one gave an invitation. As the band plays on, some members take initiative to join him and start him on his journey. Another prayer ends the service.

As we leave, we interact briefly with a few more people, but most ignore us. For the first time, we don't have a chance to talk with the minister. While it should be the members' job to welcome and connect with visitors, I'm disappointed over not meeting the pastor, but I'm not critical for him not being available. For all I know the pastor is focusing his attention on the man who came forward.

Giving up on meaningful interaction, we linger by the information table and then turn to amble out the door. Just then a woman our age tentatively approaches. We make our introductions, and her husband soon joins us. We begin sharing.

---

30 My poem, "An Ode to Peanut," later appeared in **Halo Magazine**.
31 Philippians 4:4, NIV.

They're relatively new to that church, with her having had a long desire to worship locally and not drive to another city. Her story is my angst. We have much in common, and I'm drawn to them.

They confirm my understanding of the church's formation, calling it "a grand experiment," but acknowledging not everyone at the founding church is enthusiastic over such a radical departure from the denomination's solemn traditions.

As for me, the grand experiment is wildly successful—and I will rejoice.

Takeaway for Members: Everyone should reach out to visitors, but not everyone does. Fortunately, it takes only a few people to make a difference and help guests feel truly welcomed. Each member should try to be that person and not assume someone else will do it.

Church #9:

❖

Methodists Know How to Cook

This morning I wake up excited, realizing it's Sunday, and I get to go to church. This has been happening a lot lately, and it's a nice feeling. We're headed to a United Methodist church, our first visit to a "name brand" denomination.[32]

Both services are traditional, which is not my preference. But this is good, since one reason for our journey is to stretch me. I wonder if a traditional service equates to dressing up. Their website doesn't answer my question, so I plan to dress casually.

They have a long history. The original part of their building was constructed in 1861. To put this in historical perspective, Abraham Lincoln was president then and slavery hadn't been abolished. The minister listed is female, the first for our sojourn. I'm sad that I seldom see a woman leading a church or preaching a sermon. Though women in ministry are a problem for some, it isn't for me. I applaud the opportunity for all people to use their gifts and skills to serve God in any capacity, including leading and teaching.

The website lists many activities throughout the week: game night, chancel choir, women's group, Bible study, "support the troops," and monthly dinners—which are renowned in

---

32 Some might argue that last week was our first "name brand" church visit, but since they're an outlier church for their denomination, I doubt we had a "name brand" church experience.

the community. The Bible study is a midmorning weekday meeting which, not being conducive to people with jobs or young kids, leads me to wonder if this is an older congregation. Advancing this suspicion is that "large print bulletins and personal amplifiers are available from the ushers." Regardless, I'm expectant for what I will learn and discover — about them, God, and myself.

We pull into their parking lot fifteen minutes before the second service starts. It's well over half-full. There are two visible entrances, with signs directing us to a third, tucked between the original building and an addition. Inside, two greeters hand out preprinted nametags to the regulars. They offer us blank stickers to write our names on. Nametags are another first for our journey. I find them helpful.

The sanctuary has an all-white décor and is a near cube in shape: the depth seems to match the width, with the height not being far behind. It seats about 120. The front wall, architecturally divided, has three sections. The center, outlined in gold-colored trim, prominently features a large, backlit cross. A colorful banner to the right boldly proclaims, "Catch the Spirit."

Their minister is away at meetings this week and another one, also female, fills in. Notable is a farewell potluck for their departing organist. Through a public announcement and many personal invitations, they encourage us to stay for the meal. "Methodists," they say, "know how to cook."

After a ceremonial lighting of two candles, a layperson acting as today's facilitator opens with a short liturgy, Bible reading,[33] and acknowledgment, sans singing, of one birthday and one anniversary. Six kids listen to the children's message, given

---

33 We read from Jonah 3:5–10. I suspected the reading might be from the lectionary, but it wasn't, making the selection even more curious, since the message didn't mention it.

via a hand puppet. In contrast, most of the eighty or so present are in the senior citizen category. A time of sharing "joys and concerns" follows, then the reading of a general prayer, which the minister smoothly delivers, concluding with the congregation reciting the Lord's Prayer.

There's no choir today, but a guest soloist sings a gospel song *a cappella*. He sings again during the offering, this time with piano accompaniment. While I listen, I smile as gifts overflow the offering plates. We sing hymns from two hymnals and the potluck's honored guest deftly switches between organ and keyboard for his final Sunday there. He garners enthusiastic applause for his overture.

We stand as the minister reads Mark 1:14–20 from the NIV. They don't use the Revised Standard Version (RSV) pew Bibles. Candy and I are among a small minority who follow along in our Bibles. The minister's sermon is "Come, Let's Go Fishing." She reads her message. Normally this distracts me but not today. Her delivery is smooth and her message, accessible. She compares fishing for fish with fishing for people, as Jesus asks his followers to do.[34]

Afterward, we sing a closing number — which might pass for an altar call song at a Baptist church, albeit without an invitation to come forward. They ceremonially extinguish the candles, and we make our way to the fellowship hall for the celebratory potluck.

The only open spots are at a table on the fringe. We join three others already seated. Our initial exchanges are awkward, but we soon learn that both the woman sitting across from us and the couple next to me are new to the area. I think our

---

34 Mark 1:17.

conversation helps them become better connected with each other. As promised, the food is ample and delicious. I eat too much, with only a hint of self-condemnation for being a glutton. I tell myself that I overate for the sake of community.

Eventually others join our table, including the woman who first encouraged us to stay. Another man, having retired from two careers, now heads up the renovation project for the sanctuary basement. As the meal wraps up, he asks if I'd like to see the progress. I eagerly accept. The first couple at the table joins us. The husband has also helped with the basement and wants his wife to see their work.

I can see myself joining in on the reconstruction. In fact, for most of the churches we've visited, I've seen areas where I could easily help. Wisely, I don't offer my services, today or ever. If I did I'd quickly become overcommitted.

Having a meal with people is an excellent way to connect with them and form community. The potluck did that for us today. I'm not sure if all Methodists know how to cook, but this congregation sure does.

Takeaway for Everyone: Food is a smart way to celebrate community and make meaningful connections. God can be more present there than during the church service—and I think that's how it should be.

Church #10:

A Special Father's Day Message

In a departure from recent Sundays, I'm not excited about church today. I need extra prayer to have a good attitude. Still in bed, I lift my arms to God, giving him my day and seeking his blessing, but words elude me. Eventually I give up and get up. Today, we'll visit our fourth Baptist church in ten weeks. I never realized there were so many. I desire more variation in our adventure.

I know little about this congregation: they have no website and their Facebook page is nothing more than a listing with a link to the website for American Baptist Churches USA. If the prior three Baptist assemblies are any indication, this will be a traditional service.

With essentially no online presence, their outreach efforts—especially to a younger and increasingly postmodern demographic—are likely nonexistent. I assume they cater to an older, traditional-thinking crowd. I'm not dismissive of their age or disrespectful of their perspective, but their future lacks promise, as members will die off with no one to replace them.

On our drive, we pass other churches from our journey: Churches #2, 7, and 8. I wonder what they're doing. Each is more appealing than where we're headed. *God, I need you to get my head and heart into this, else today will be a bust.*

The building is older, circa 1960, with an aged exterior, exacerbated by neglect. The parking lot needs attention too. With grass growing through the cracks, their minimal car traffic is insufficient to thwart the advance of weeds. Inside is more of the same. They've made updates but in a basic, we're-on-a-tight-budget, way. The sanctuary seats perhaps two hundred, but someone directs us to sit on the right side. He says, "Not many people attend anymore." The pastor and song leader both stand on that side as well.

Several members introduce themselves, and we reciprocate as they make a careful effort to remember our names. But no one goes beyond this to engage in conversation. With about forty-five present, it's an older congregation. We're among the youngest.

Before the service began, a technical glitch had large ramifications. The retractable screen over the baptistry is in the up position and refused to lower itself. Three parts of the service require overhead projection, including a video of an interview with Tony Dungy. I suspect the recording was the service's focal point. Though had he not mentioned this issue, I'd have never known the difference. They adjust, and a meaningful service unfolds despite the problem.

The format is much like the other two small Baptist churches we visited.[35] One new twist for our adventure is an old practice: we sing a chorus as a round. While I enjoy hearing the resulting melding of voices and notes, I find it impossible to participate, especially with Candy singing the opposite part, along with all the other ladies. Another remnant from a bygone era is the song leader directing us, keeping time with the rhythmic movement of his arms. I've seen this before but

---

35 Churches #1 and 6. But this one has about twice the attendance.

not for a long, long time. Though an organ is present, all our singing is with piano accompaniment.

Today is Father's Day, and the service reflects that theme. There's a book for each dad, which we must go forward to receive. Despite being a bibliophile, I'd gladly forgo the gift and avoid the attention, but my refusal would be conspicuous. I reluctantly get up to accept my present. It's *199 Promises of God*, a concise booklet of assurances found in the Bible.[36]

The pastor's message—which I suspect he quickly pulled together to replace the non-viewable video—is "a brief tribute to our Heavenly Father." The minister reads sections of Jesus's Sermon on the Mount[37] and reminds us that God always responds to our prayers. Sometimes he says, "Yes," sometimes, "Wait," and other times, "No." Yet regardless of the answer, it's always for our own good.

He concludes by saying, "God is a father to the fatherless." As a poignant underscore, the minister reveals he's an orphan: his mother deserted him and later his father abandoned him too. God is truly the only father he has ever known. Psalm 27:10 is especially meaningful to him: "When my father and my mother forsake me, then the Lord will take me up," (KJV). His message has put an alternate focus on Father's Day for me, an insight I greatly appreciate.

The service ends without the anticipated altar call. Though we do sing a song of invitation. Then the pastor prays the

---

36 The book, I'm sorry to say, is a most pathetic effort. It's merely a compilation of Bible verses from the KJV. I try to use it as a morning devotional but give up because some verses contain only the vaguest implication of a promise, if that. Though the idea of giving a gift was well-intended, their selection left me with a negative impression.

37 The Sermon on the Mount is in Matthew chapters 5, 6, and 7. Our specific readings are Matthew 6:25–34 and 7:7–11.

"sinner's prayer"[38] for those not yet following Jesus to recite.

Before the day is over, my children both wish me happy Father's Day, despite having seen me the night before. I can't do the same for my dad, as he died a few years ago. Even so, I can redirect my paternal well-wishes to my Heavenly Father, an appropriate gesture I've never considered.

Happy Father's Day, Papa. Thank you for being my good and perfect daddy. I love you.

Takeaway for Everyone: Church services don't always go as planned. Making adjustments — without complaining — is key for turning potential failure into a meaningful experience.

---

38 The "sinner's prayer" is an Evangelical salvation practice. There are many variations of it, with the chief elements being: I'm a sinner, my sin separates me from God, Jesus died for my sins, and I repent of my sins and ask Jesus into my heart.

Church #11:

❖

Charismatic Lite

Today we'll attend a church we didn't know existed until Candy's research. Their trendy website, though complete, gives no indication of their focus or affiliation. In contrast, their Facebook page declares they're charismatic.

I've never been to a charismatic church service, though I have gone to charismatic conferences, so I think I have a general idea of what to expect. Regardless, I anticipate the service will stretch me, which is my goal for visiting fifty-two churches.

At the risk of oversimplification, the pentecostal and charismatic stream of Protestantism places greater emphasis on the work and power of the Holy Spirit, specifically speaking in tongues.[39] Within this reside diverging perspectives. Some proclaim that speaking in tongues is a necessary sign of salvation, while a more inclusive view sees speaking in tongues as an optional, albeit desirable, ability. Between these extremes exists an array of views.

---

39 "Speaking in tongues" is one of many possible "spiritual gifts" God gives to his followers. Sometimes going by the shorthand "tongues," it's comprehended differently by its practitioners. A composite understanding is that speaking in tongues is vocalizing in a language unknown to the speaker. They may or may not understand what they, or other people speaking in that language, are saying. Depending on perspective, their words may be a known (earthly) language or an unknown (spiritual) language.

All my early church experiences downplayed or even ignored the Holy Spirit, much like that eccentric uncle many families have but seldom mention. Despite this, I now embrace the Holy Spirit's role in my life and rely on him for daily guidance. At times he gives me supernatural insights or prophetic words. In that sense, I'm Charismatic. Nevertheless, to the dismay of some, I don't speak in tongues. People have instructed me and prayed I would but without results. Frankly, I'm not even sure if I want this spiritual gift. I've seen it misused too often. God has gifted me in other areas, so why should I seek something else?

Candy and I say our pre-church prayer and hop in the car, finding their location easily. The church is a storefront, much like Church #2 (Growing Deeper, Not Wider). It's also an outgrowth of a small group with a tentmaker pastor, like Church #7 (The New Church).

Inside are seventy-five folding chairs, arranged in an arc. We sit in the third row, which is also the last row. I'm grateful they're padded. A few people come up and introduce themselves. They're friendly, but I'm not connecting with them, perhaps because I don't feel well. This is my first outing since having outpatient surgery four days ago. At one point, I feel dizzy and nauseous, likely from my pain medication. I ask Candy to pray for me, so I can make it through the service.

As we wait for things to start, the pastor spies Candy and comes over. They know each other through her past work at the local Christian radio station and his, as a youth pastor at a large area church.

Eight years ago he resigned from his ministry position to take a job outside the church. "The church had become so big.

Connecting with people was hard," he says, "and I only interacted with people who attended church."

I nod, and Candy agrees, "Experiencing community is hard at large churches."

Then I laugh. "Once I introduced myself to a couple at church. They asked if I was visiting and were shocked to learn I'd gone there six years. They told me they'd been there for eight. I never saw them again."

The pastor smiles and nods. "My wife and I wanted to be part of a much smaller congregation, one where community was a priority. This is the result."

"It's an ideal size for that," I say.

"Many of these people dropped out of other churches. They were disillusioned and discouraged. This has become their sanctuary."

I comprehend all he says, yet I'm surprised that after seven years they have less than thirty people—and then I chastise myself for using size to gauge success. This is a common attitude among today's consumer-driven people and business-focused church leaders. Numbers—attendance, offerings, and budget—do not signal God's blessing and kingdom impact but merely man's view that bigger is better.

Though I don't ask, I wonder if they once had more people. Apparently, they used to also occupy the empty space next door. Their sign is over both entrances, but the second spot is now "for lease."

The service is much like our visits at non-traditional evangelical churches. They start with a song, followed by a short meditation—given by the pastor's wife. Several announcements preview their summer schedule, followed by an impromptu sharing of praise and prayer requests. Next, they have a greeting time and an extended period of singing. Aside from one updated hymn, the songs are all contemporary choruses, though only one is familiar. We sing to pre-recorded music, while the pastor plucks away on his bass guitar. He sings backup while a female vocalist leads us. Then the pastor switches to an acoustic guitar as the only instrumentation. A keyboard sits nearby, but today it serves only as a table.

A couple of times I think I hear people whispering in tongues. As the music ends, one of the worshipers praises God aloud, which morphs into a prayer and then becomes a prophetic word. His actions are a suitable end to our worship time. The only other differences are some adults who are freer with hand raising and offering verbal exultations between songs and during musical bridges, but it's minimal. Interestingly, the younger people are reserved, not following their parents' more demonstrative example.

For the second time in two weeks, there's no effort to obtain our contact information. I'm not sure if this is good or bad. Today's church attendees already have too much of a consumer mindset. Proactively pursuing them only reinforces this. I don't think this is what Jesus had in mind when he said, "Follow me."[40] Nevertheless, many people expect organizations, including churches, to pursue them, and they dismiss those who don't as being uncaring.

---

40 John 1:43 and many others. Often Jesus's instruction to "follow me" comes with another requirement, such as repent and follow, give away your money and follow, take up your cross and follow, and so forth. But sometimes he merely invites others to "follow me." This is his message at its simplest. See my book, **How Big Is Your Tent?** to learn more.

A first for us is having the sermon notes and scripture references on YouVersion.[41] Of those following along, about half use smartphones and half, Bibles. Their preference divides them by age, with all the younger folks going digital and most of the older ones taking the traditional approach.

They're in a series called "Getting Past Your Past." Week one was about the labels we carry (I listened to part of the message online). The next week addressed forgiving others who've hurt us. Today is about seeking forgiveness from those we've hurt. "Be a peacemaker," the pastor instructs after reading Matthew 5:9. His style is casual and easy to listen to as he shares accessible examples and packs in relevant scripture. When he finishes, the service ends abruptly with a quick and quiet passing of the offering plates.

Despite their self-description as charismatic, there were no supernatural manifestations or bizarre behaviors. I'm not sure if I'm relieved or disappointed.

Takeaway for Leaders: Ensure your marketing efforts reflect reality and aren't merely what you hope to become or what you once were. That is, if you say you're charismatic, make sure you really are.

---

41 YouVersion is an online Bible reading and study resource, with a mobile app, http://www.youversion.com.

Church #12:

More Methodists, More Food

Next on our list is another United Methodist Church. We visited our first one three weeks ago (Church #9, Methodists Know How to Cook), with it being a memorable service. I project my fond memories of that church onto this one, all the while aware that churches in the same denomination can vary greatly. Although less than six miles from our house, we never knew it existed until Candy found it during her internet search for churches. It's a rural church and not on the way to anywhere we go, so we've never been by it.

For some reason, I expect little from their website, but they surprise me. It's the most visitor-friendly site we've seen. Notably is a "what to expect" section, addressing the concerns a first-timer might have. Marcia, one of their members, wrote it and includes her picture, saying her face may be the first one we see. She talks about parking and the building, what they offer and don't, and invites us to "come as you are." Described as "a quaint, country church" and now knowing what to expect, I'm even more excited about our visit.

We arrive to a nearly-full parking lot, as their website said might happen. Overflow parking on the grass has begun, but there are still a few available spaces near the door, and I use one of them. We walk inside and, as promised, Marcia welcomes us, giving us a bulletin, a newsletter, and a welcome pack.

We enter the sanctuary. People occupy the back rows, so we end up sitting closer to the front than the rear. This provides less distraction and a better view, but it doesn't allow much opportunity to observe the congregation. Seating 110, about seventy-five are present. It's July 1st, not quite a holiday weekend but almost. Some regulars may be away, with out-of-town relatives visiting others.

The facility layout reminds me of Church #9 (Methodists Know How to Cook), as do the attendee demographics and the service format. Though an organ and piano are present, along with two pew hymnals, this Sunday we sing newer songs to a guitar, with the words displayed overhead.

After an opening song, there's a time to share what God has been doing in our lives. They relate many prayer requests, along with some answers and thanksgiving. Several couples will celebrate anniversaries this week. After they share each item, the minister says "Lord, in your goodness . . . " or "Lord, in your mercy . . . " and sometimes both. The people reply with "Hear our prayers." I like this. The act of sharing is the prayer. They don't need to repeat the people's words to God. Their liturgy reminds me of that.

The children's message has a patriotic theme, with a lesson about the American flag, which stands on our left, compared to the Christian flag, on our right. One of the kids recites the pledge to the US flag. Then the minister shares the pledge to the Christian flag. Though the concept is familiar, the words aren't. With multiple versions of the pledge, this one is older and more liberal.

There's also a presentation for world missions, and two children volunteer to receive donations. The receptacles are hemispheres of a globe, which are most fitting for a world missions offering. Following this is the regular collection, using traditional offering plates. They don't pass the plates along the rows, but the ushers slowly walk down the aisles. It's up to givers to get their donations to the ushers. The plates are handed to the minister. Holding them, she turns and faces the cross, lifting the offerings high in the air, symbolically presenting them to God. Then she prays.

The patriotic theme continues with the message. The introduction is about the Declaration of Independence and the ensuing US Constitution. While granted freedoms by the Constitution, we must balance them with responsibility. The sermon's title is "Do you have a constitution?" Or more directly, "Do you have a *religious* constitution?" Then comes the thought-provoking question, "What does it cover?" She offers several considerations. Her conclusion asks, "Have you ratified your constitution?" Although interesting, I don't catch a single scripture reference during her message. *How biblical is this?*

The time of sharing was lengthy, the mission presentation took up more time, and communion is to follow. This may be why the message was concise, seemingly ending before its time. But with the key point expertly conveyed, we need no additional words.

Communion is open to all who are interested, and for once the minister clearly communicates this. She lifts the bread and then the juice up to God, then symbolically presents them to the congregation, and finally prays over them. As we witnessed at the Roman Catholic Church (Church #5, Catholics are Christians Too), the elements go first to those officiating. Then the rest of us go up by row to partake. The minister gives us the bread. Then we move to the juice, held by a member. Both say something to me. Though I can't make out the words,[42] I receive them as a blessing. I suspect there's a prescribed response, but not knowing it, I just smile and nod. I dip the bread into the juice and eat. Singing occurs throughout the ceremony, some are familiar choruses but not all. We conclude the service singing "God Bless America."

Refreshments follow in the fellowship hall. (We missed their monthly potluck by one week.) Several people invite us to stay. This gives us time to connect with others. Candy makes a passing comment about how tasty the communion bread was. This just happens to be to the person who baked it. Pleased, she offers us the unused portions, saying they never know what to do with the leftovers. We gratefully accept her generosity. When she presents it to us, she explains it isn't holy bread and we're free to eat it as we wish. "If you don't eat it all, feed it to the birds. Don't throw it away."

We later meet the minister who reiterates the same thing. Today she wears an elegant white robe, something she does for Communion and special services. They have different service styles throughout the month, varying in instrumentation and song selection. To fully comprehend how they worship, we'd need to visit for a full month, and if not for *52 Churches*, I'd like to do just that.

We leave with renewed appreciation for our nation and well-fed, both spiritually and physically.

Takeaway for Everyone: Letting visitors know beforehand what to expect takes the edge off any apprehension and makes attending less intimidating. Having a regular, official greeter is a great idea — as long as other members also embrace visitors.

---

42 Candy later enlightens me that the two phrases are "the body of Christ broken for you" and "the blood of Christ shed for you."

❖

Embarking on a Metamorphosis

So far, we've faithfully attended every Christian church[43] on our list, according to their distance from home. As our journey continues, we'll skip some to maximize the breadth of our experience.

The first church we're skipping is an RCA (Reformed Church in America) church. There are two reasons: We've visited this church several times before with a family member. And the church has been struggling and is embarking on an organizational metamorphosis. They are in a time of transition from which a new church will hopefully emerge.

This new gathering will have a fresh perspective, a different pastor, and a new name. They will be reborn. Since this is all in the planning stage, we'll set this church aside. If their transformation progresses, we'll visit later. And if this strategy doesn't work, there will be nothing left to see.

It's a tough time for the faithful few who remain. I pray for a successful metamorphosis.

Takeaway for Everyone: Every church will at some time struggle. Make sure that season doesn't turn away visitors.

---

43 We skipped one church when we determined they weren't exclusively Christian.

Church #13:

A Dedicated Pastor Team

The church we're visiting today has no website and a blank Facebook page. I sigh. With the lack of information on contemporary channels, our experience suggests they're a smaller, aging congregation with a traditional service.[44] Once again I must fight to have a positive attitude, or I might as well stay home.

We arrive ten minutes early and are the sixth car in the lot. The building sits atop a hill, presenting a pleasing panoramic view. The cornerstone on the simple block construction reads 1963.

The pastor is the first person we meet. A younger man, he smiles broadly. He's smartly dressed, wearing a suit and tie, in sharp contrast to my T-shirt and shorts. Perhaps in his thirties, he's not a contemporary of the older parishioners milling about. He looks at Candy, "Are you the one who called about service times?"

She smiles, pleased at the recognition. "Yes, that was me."

He beams even more. "Thank you for visiting. We're so glad you came today." He shakes my hand and then Candy's.

---

44 Churches #1, 6, 9, and 10 fit this pattern, as does the church we skipped today. Although there's a strong empirical connection between the absence of an online presence and the size, demographic, and worship style of the church, the question of causality remains.

His winsome personality draws me to him. I instantly like him, while at the same time, I wonder if he's trying too hard. *They must not have many visitors.*

As we talk more, his wife walks up, holding their youngest son. Later three brothers make their appearance. They sport matching outfits, right down to their ties. We don't meet their fifth child, a daughter, until after the service.

The sanctuary is a thirty by forty-eight foot rectangle[45] with one front corner walled off and labeled "library." The counterpart room, on the other corner, could be an office. The walls have blond paneling. The pews and massive pulpit match each other, with an even lighter finish. Gratefully, the pews have padded seats. There's a KJV Bible in each pew rack, along with a hymnal and supplemental songbook. We end up with about thirty people.

The pastor's wife is the pianist. (She will later sing the special music number). She's accomplished, exuding joy as she plays. An organist later joins in. The pastor leads the singing, both vocally and visually as his hands sway to keep time. He has a beautiful voice—a tenor, says Candy—which he projects with confidence. The words to the hymn, "No Other Plea," resonate with me: "My great Physician heals the sick. The lost he came to save." I appreciate the reminder that Jesus came to both heal and to save. Today most people focus on Jesus's saving power but diminish his healing power. While two millennia ago the crowds clamored for healing, largely missing his intent to save. We must embrace both.

We stand in respect for the reading of God's word: Psalm 7. Prayer follows. The phrase "offering of praise" catches my attention. This is good. Offerings don't need to be monetary.

---

45 Again, I count ceiling tiles and do the math.

We can give our singing to God as an offering. But, lacking musical ability, my attempt may not even qualify as making a "joyful noise."[46] I wonder how God receives it. Even more disconcerting is the lackluster way I tend to offer it.

The message comes from Revelation 21, not Psalm 7. The pastor is teaching a series on the end times. After a lengthy introduction, he begins a detailed expository teaching starting at verse one. Verse six strikes me. God says, "It is done."[47] Completing the things he set out to do, he is pleased. Continuing, God adds, "I am Alpha and Omega, the beginning and the end."[48] In the beginning, God says of creation, "It was very good."[49] Whereas at the end he says, "It is finished."[50] These words from God serve as nice bookends to the rest of the Bible.

Although his detailed discourse interests me, progress is slow. I assume he intends to complete the entire chapter. Wondering how long it will take, I begin to squirm. But after verse seven, he checks his watch and stops. With no fanfare or benediction and without music, the service ends. I assume next week he'll resume with verse eight.

The pastor scoots over to talk as we pick up our Bibles. I enjoy our conversation, but people back up in the aisle behind him. Though they're patient, an air of agitation brews. He's unaware of this, but it preoccupies me. When there's a lull in conversation, I thank him for his time and wish him a good afternoon.

---

46 The phrase appears in several Psalms in several versions of the Bible. Start with Psalm 66:1 in the KJV.

47 Revelation 21:6, KJV.

48 Revelation 21:6, KJV.

49 Genesis 1:31, KJV.

50 John 19:30, KJV.

His wife stands by the exit in her husband's stead, shaking hands and chatting with people as they leave. We have an extended conversation with her. Later, her husband joins her. If not for family coming over, they'd have invited us to their home for lunch. Perhaps this could happen in the future.

The thought honors me. Sharing a meal is a wonderful way to launch a friendship. But I'm also torn. Would I have been disingenuous to accept their invitation, knowing they're offering it in hopes of growing their tiny flock, when we have no plans to return? Today, I'm spared from making that decision, but I must be ready the next time someone invites us to their home for lunch.[51]

However, another observation troubles me more. The only people we interact with all morning are the pastor and his wife. No one in the congregation makes any effort to introduce themselves or even say "Hi." Do these people not care, or do they think this is their minister's job? It's both lazy and shortsighted. If people connect only with the pastor, when he leaves, so will they, but if people connect with the congregation, they will likely remain when their minister moves on.

This young couple, a skilled ministry team, is faithfully serving God by pouring themselves into this tiny church. They work hard, with a congregation content to let them. Their dedication to serve touches my heart. *God, bless them and their ministry. Provide for them and their family.*

Takeaway for Members: If you want your minister to grow a following, let him do all the outreach. If you want your congregation to grow, members need to be the ones to act.

---

51 This is a needless worry, as no one else invites us to their home for dinner after church.

❖

Part One Perspective

We're one-quarter of the way through our journey. It's been more than what I'd hoped for and at the same time, not as much of what I expected. In attending the churches closest to home in our rural, white,[52] middle-class area I expected little racial diversity, and we saw even less. Although I could assume our few local minorities don't go to church, it's more likely they aren't attending the ones nearby. This lack of racial diversity reflects poorly on the nearly all-white churches we've visited.

Despite areas of concern, I liked each of the thirteen churches and, if needed, any one could become my church home, though some would take much more effort than others. But finding a new church isn't our goal. Our mission is to expand our worship of God and meet our extended Christian family. Still, three churches grab my attention:

Church #7 ("The New Church") draws me. I like that they're truly nondenominational and unaffiliated. Even more, I appreciate their many unchurched and under-churched attendees, as well as their goal of growing deeper. As a bonus, they recently moved and are now the third closest church to our home, a scant 1.4 miles away. Their community calls me.

Both United Methodist churches hold an appeal, but the second one, Church #12 ("More Methodists, More Food"), edges out the

---

52 See Appendix 3 for details.

first. This is in part because they're in our rural area, whereas the first, although slightly closer to our home, has more affinity with the nearby city I've become weary of driving to.

I also really like the pastor at Church #12. Her quiet reverence in leading worship guides me into God's presence like nothing I've ever enjoyed at church. However, the United Methodist Church periodically relocates its ministers, and I wonder if I'd still feel drawn to the church once they reassign her. She's already been there six and a half years, and I suspect she'll move on soon.

Church #5 ("Catholics are Christians Too") has a pull for me, likely because they're an enigma. There's much I could learn from them about worshiping God. Unfortunately, their service isn't accessible to outsiders, and it would be hard to make friends there since there's little community.

Additionally, I'd like to make repeat visits to Church #3 ("It Only Hurts When You Care") and Church #8 ("A Grand Experiment"). For the first one, I want to witness a typical service there, whereas for the second, I wonder if I'd still be as interested in their community after a second visit. I fear I wouldn't, so maybe it's best not to return.

Candy says that out of the thirteen, Church #2 ("Growing Deeper, Not Wider") is her preference. It, too, has a strong draw for me. This makes sense as its worship style and age demographics are the most like our home church. My only concern is that their doctrine is much narrower than mine, and I fear I would soon chafe under its teaching.

Overall, and most disconcerting, is the correlation I've seen between the members' age and dress compared to their facility and worship style. If you show me the building and service, I'll predict the audience's age and what they'll wear. Alternately, tell me the age and attire of attendees, and I'll predict the type of service and even the character of the facility.

The question is causality. Does an aging congregation produce a traditional service in a dated facility or does a traditional service in a dated facility attract an older crowd? Conversely, does a younger or multigenerational gathering create a contemporary service in a nontraditional setting or does a contemporary service in a nontraditional setting attract a younger or multigenerational crowd?

Instead of wondering which caused what, the greater insight is to simply note a connection between attendee age and service style. I suspect the two go together.

Older congregations with traditional services face a deadly downward spiral, with one feeding into the other, which only exacerbates the trend. I see no long-term hope for these aging congregations and no realistic way to rejuvenate them—aside from supernatural intervention. Pray that God will intervene.

So far, this adventure has been great. Part of me doesn't want it to end after fifty-two weeks, as there are a couple hundred churches within easy driving distance, but another part of me wonders if I have the stamina to persevere to the end. Added to this are churches that warrant repeat visits. I also wonder what I might learn about Christianity by visiting non-Christian faith gatherings. Despite that, I also miss having regular community with close friends.

With all this in mind, we press on.

Takeaway for Everyone: Many churches operate as they always have, unaware that society has changed and seeks something different. The future of these congregations is in jeopardy.

Part 2:

The Second Quarter

Going forward, we may bypass more churches on our list to vary the scope of our adventure. So far, we've skipped one that wasn't a Christian gathering and another because they were in limbo, pending a turnaround.

The next thirteen churches on our list promise a wider variation of experience. This excites me. I also see some churches we'll exclude because they don't hold much promise for additional variation. Our journey is about growth and discovery, not about thoroughly covering every option in a precise order. Though we have a plan, the plan is flexible.

Takeaway for Everyone: Plan, but be flexible. Fixating on the plan, as well as having no plan, will miss opportunities that arise.

Church #14:

❖

The Pentecostal Perspective

Three weeks ago, at Church #11 (Charismatic Lite), I expected a charismatic church experience. It didn't happen. Today I anticipate it will. The church website doesn't say they're charismatic,[53] but the pastor's bio declares he's a "licensed minister with the United Pentecostal Church." This implies the church's orientation and affiliation. It's the only mention of Pentecostal on their website, though their Facebook page prominently proclaims they're Pentecostal.

The 50-year-old church has three ministry staff, one with the title of Pastor, while the worship leader and youth director use Rev. Also posted are seven sermons; however, they aren't for the last seven weeks but random ones spanning several months. This small sampling features six different speakers: the three staffers and three others, each sporting the title of Rev. Who will we hear today?

Facebook says the service lasts two hours. Though some churches had services this long, we didn't know it beforehand. With this knowledge, I dread what awaits me.

---

53 Here and throughout this book I use charismatic (with a lower case "c") in a generic sense to encompass all Pentecostal movements and the subsequent Charismatic (upper case "C") manifestations that grew from it.

Their website's "About" section shares their doctrinal statement. Salvation, it says, requires repentance, full-immersion water baptism, and Holy Ghost baptism evidenced by speaking in tongues.[54] Candy and I don't speak in tongues, so I assume they'll view us as heathens, or at minimum, second-class Christians. The site also mentions the importance of unity. Unfortunately, their embrace of unity is only with those who believe as they do about the Holy Spirit, while they decry those with different perspectives as promoting disunity.[55]

Though their narrow views on salvation and unity bother me, I realize attendees and even members at many churches don't know their church's doctrinal stance—and would disagree with some aspects of it. Given their constrained theology, I must spend extra time in prayer to get rid of my negativity and embrace what God has for me. Who knows, I may speak in tongues before the service is over.

We leave the house a bit later than I wanted. We pray for our adventure as we drive. After the "amen," we shift to casual conversation, and I miss my turn. This is the first Sunday I didn't drive directly to our destination.

Their newer building is atypical of most churches. The large parking lot is filling with cars, but we find a good spot. People welcome us as we head to the door. Inside, I make a special effort to remember the greeter's name, but I forget it after hearing several more. He's a great ambassador, who will

---

54 This puts them in the second wave of Pentecostalism, a more narrowly focused and dogmatic understanding, circa 1960, in contrast to the present third wave of Pentecostalism.

55 It's a common modern perspective to assume your understanding of truth is correct and everyone else is wrong—and this church is thoroughly modern.

interact with us several more times throughout the morning. He makes a point to introduce us to the pastor's wife, and it's not long before her husband seeks us out.

"Have you ever been to a Pentecostal Church?

I shake my head. "No, we haven't."[56]

He raises his eyebrows, but instead of saying what he's thinking, he merely smiles. "Please keep an open mind."

Several more people welcome us. We've been to many friendly churches, but this one excels at pre-service hospitality, leaving us feeling welcomed and appreciated.

The large rectangular room[57] has a simple elegance. With 240 padded chairs, it's slightly more than half-full with people of all ages, including many children. I'm encouraged to see the next generation of the church. Though I've stopped looking for crosses during our visits, this church lacks one. In a couple of months they'll celebrate their fiftieth anniversary. Today the founding pastor is present, along with some missionaries and a traveling seminary group. We're not the only visitors.

With nine on the worship team, they produce a full sound, ably led by the worship director, who also plays the keyboard. The words to their contemporary songs appear on the front wall as we sing along. There's some hand raising but not much. Aside from that, the service better matches my experi-

---

56 While we've never been to a Pentecostal church service, we have attended multi-church gatherings with a charismatic flare, and I've been to several conferences that focused on the supernatural and the work of the Holy Spirit, so whatever happens today shouldn't shock me.

57 There are too many ceiling tiles to count. The width is approximately 66 feet and the length must be half again as much. With a 14-foot ceiling and smart décor, the room has an open feel to it.

ence of Baptist than my expectation of Pentecostal.

The ushers stand in front for the offering, and the people come forward to drop in their gifts. This solves the issue of feeling obligated to give when they pass the plates, but this practice encourages image-conscious people to go forward for show.[58]

The pastor delivers his message with conviction and passion, which is a polite euphemism for loud. At one point, the high volume threatens to spawn a headache, but thankfully the feeling subsides. His message is on commitment, starting with Romans 12:1 and then bouncing around the Bible. He weaves in verse after verse about commitment to God or the lack thereof, as exemplified by Paul, Jacob, Isaiah, John Mark, Luke, and Demas, plus a few more I missed.

He encourages us to clap our praise to God or demonstrate agreement. He asks for, and we hear "amens" but not as frequently. At one point there's a time for corporate prayer where everyone simultaneously prays aloud.[59] The words I can make out are English, but I assume some pray in tongues.

The pastor winds down the sermon. I avoid checking the time but suspect the service lasts another thirty minutes. He moves into what seems to be an altar call, asking people to respond to his message of commitment. Virtually everyone goes forward. Only we and four others don't respond. This leaves me feeling more like an observer than a participant. Once, the pastor says a brief phrase in tongues, but I'm not sure if his

---

58 Consider Jesus's warning in Matthew 6:1–3. Also related is Luke 21:1–4 and Matthew 6:1–3.

59 I've witnessed this practice but am not in favor of it. For me, the words of others distract me from forming my own. Then there is Paul's teaching to do everything in an orderly manner (1 Corinthians 14:23 and 26–33). I can't get past these two problems.

next words in English are the interpretation or not.[60]

The focus shifts to water baptism, full-immersion.[61] Today, they'll baptize a twelve-year-old boy, symbolically showing the washing away of our sins.[62] After the immersion, the minister tells the lad to raise his hands and pray for the Holy Spirit to fill him so he can speak in tongues. What's the implication if he can't? What pressure the boy must face.

When he comes up from the water, family and friends lay hands on him and pray. The focus shifts to singing, but I keep watching the boy. Eventually, I hear a repeating guttural sound. I've heard many people speak in tongues but nothing like this. Though phonetically unaltered with each iteration, it increases in conviction. Satisfied with the outcome, his smiling supporters return to their seats.

The service ends soon thereafter, and we talk more with others, some for the first time and several for the second or third time. This includes former neighbors as well as acquaintances of our kids. We tarry in our conversations and are among the last to leave—two and a half hours after the service started.

Several invite us back for the evening service, the first non-Baptist church to have one. "Please come back tonight," says a young acquaintance, half our age. She flashes an earnest smile. "That's when we Pentecostals get really wild." Her eyes twinkle as she shimmers with excitement.

---

60 According to 1 Corinthians 14:27, there must be an interpretation of the tongue.

61 Specifying "full-immersion" is important to them, but I'm not sure why, because "partial-immersion" is an oxymoron.

62 An alternate symbolism of baptism is the death, burial, and resurrection of Jesus. I'm okay with either.

"I'd like to come back sometime, but we can't tonight." I really mean it.

Her countenance dims in disappointment but rebounds quickly. "I hope you do. Then you can have the full pentecostal experience."

I'm disappointed. I expected a pentecostal encounter this morning. Some Sunday night we may join them again, but tonight we already have plans, so a return visit will need to wait for a different day.

She smiles some more, and the twinkle returns to her eyes. We head toward the door, and she introduces us to her dad, the greeter who welcomed us so well when we arrived.

Takeaway for Everyone: Make sure your church's theology doesn't divide Jesus's church. Instead, it should unite us, just as Jesus prayed.[63]

---

63 John 17:23.

Church #15:

An Outlier Congregation

Next on our list is a church we visited a few years ago. My impulse is to skip them and go to the next one, but they've moved and have a different pastoral team. I desire a fresh look.

Quietly affiliated with the United Methodist Church, this one is nothing like the other two we've visited (Church #9, Methodists Know How to Cook and #12, More Methodists, More Food). Based on those visits, this one isn't typical of their denomination.[64] I consider them an outlier congregation: unlike the norm, an enigma to leadership but embraced because of their potential or results. They could be a short-lived anomaly or a glimpse into the future.[65]

Their website says we'll find "a laid-back, coffeehouse atmosphere" with "an unconventional setting where a blend of people, of all ages, from all walks of life, can gather and feel at home." That's my kind of church.

---

64 This assumption may not be true as the pastor says she's firmly Charismatic, and there's a charismatic movement within the denomination. See http://aldersgaterenewal.org/who-we-are/what-we-believe/196-guidelines-the-united-methodist-church-and-the-charismatic-movement.

65 I consider my home church to be an outlier in the RCA denomination. Another outlier church would be Church #8 ("A Grand Experiment"), part of the CRC.

Weather permitting, the service will be outdoors. I'm excited for a chance to worship in nature, but I'm disappointed I won't witness their typical service. The predicted weather for 10 a.m. is eighty-one degrees, 57 percent humidity, with a 10 percent chance of rain, so I expect we'll meet outside. I throw two beach chairs in the car in case we need them, but I forget the sunscreen.[66]

We arrive and see no hint of an outdoor service. We later learn that yesterday, based on today's forecast for ninety-three degrees, they decided to meet inside. It's just as well, for today's cloudless sky and higher humidity would make for a hot, sweaty, sticky church service.

The building is the former headquarters for a credit union. Designed for business and not church, they've smartly adapted the space for their use. Their prior location was in a small strip mall. At several times the size, this stand-alone building is spacious. Smartly decorated, there are numerous classrooms and offices forming a U-shaped perimeter around the sanctuary. There's seating for perhaps 150, with forty to forty-five people present. I remind myself that summer attendance drops off at most churches, especially between the Fourth of July and Labor Day, so we're likely seeing one of their lower attended Sundays.

The service starts with a video. It's an allegory that shows the importance of churches maintaining their original purpose: focusing outward and avoiding the snare of self-centeredness or adopting an inward preoccupation. As the video finishes, attention moves to the worship team. Standing on a platform, elevated by three steps, they're easy to see, without coming

---

66 In prior outdoor services, you sit on the grass unless you bring your own chairs. And given Michigan's summer sun, sunburn is a likely outcome, warranting the generous use of sunscreen.

off as a stage performance. The music comes from a guitar and bass, with three women vocalists. A drum kit and keyboard sit idle.

They lead us in two contemporary songs. With minimal instrumentation, it's a simple sound, allowing me to contemplate the words I sing. Two projectors display the lyrics. The ministers, a husband and wife duo, sit in the front row, raising their hands at various points, but no one else does. How should I respond? I want to follow their lead, but don't want to make others uncomfortable. I clasp my hands to keep them from impulsive movement, all the while feeling guilty for it.

Another video follows. It's a present-day setting, interviewing survivors from a near-disaster at sea. The ancient parallel is Jesus asleep in the boat during a storm while his disciples fear certain death. This introduces today's message: "Summer Storms."

We all have storms in our lives. They come from stress and change and death, from poverty and suffering and evil in the world. Churches have storms too. This church is in a tropical depression, real and needing attention. With a new building and having just received their conference's permission to officially organize—both arduous tasks—the people are tired. The church stands at a crossroad. Some want to take a break, while others desire to press forward. The minister calls this a spiritual drought.

I've seen churches go through this: Leaders cast a grand vision. It's demanding, requires much effort, and the outcome is uncertain. Once they reach their goal, some people desire to coast. Others want to press forward, building on their momentum.

This church is at that juncture. To move forward, they must reject apathy. Everyone must become involved and contribute. The risk of inaction is not closing but of failing to respond to opportunities. So ends the message.

Next is a time for healing prayer, another first on our journey—and a most welcome one. A music video about healing rain provides an inviting atmosphere for people to come forward. With two prayer teams and plenty of takers, needs are privately shared and addressed. The prayer teams anoint them with oil as they minister to each person. Hugs of gratitude are a typical response. Lasting several minutes, it's beautiful, and I'm glad to witness it.[67]

Praying for and anointing a mission team—the youth group and their leaders—who will head to Oklahoma next Saturday comes next. As a congregation, we extend our hands in agreement and bless them.

During the concluding worship set, several people raise their hands in praise and some clap. The congregation brings their tithes and offerings forward during the final song, placing them in a basket. I'm still uncomfortable with this practice. The people who go forward call attention to themselves, while the people who remain seated show they didn't give. Perhaps there's no ideal way to receive an offering.

After the service we linger to talk, catching up with friends. We're not the only visitors today. We receive a tour of the facility, with ample time to chat and ask questions.

At multiple times we interact with both ministers. As the morning winds down, I talk briefly, but intentionally, with the minister who spoke today. She's different from the other

---

67 At my home church, I'm part of the prayer team. I miss having the privilege of praying for others.

Methodist ministers I've met. I sense a theological kinship. I feel the Holy Spirit's nudge, perceiving she's exhausted from the journey and concerned over the congregation's future. I try to offer her encouragement but am unsuccessful. I silently pray for her, her husband, and the church they lead.

Will this church be content to coast, or will they continue to advance God's kingdom? *God, bless them. Bless them indeed!*[68]

Takeaway for Everyone: Don't be content with the status quo. Yearn for more. Seek to advance. Never coast—not even for a season.

---

68 This is a paraphrase from the prayer of Jabez in 1 Chronicles 4:9–10 as rendered in the KJV and several others.

Church #16:

Something's Missing

Just like last week, the next church on our list is one we visited a few years ago. At that time, God prompted me to take a month to check out four churches. I wondered if he'd tell us to change worship locations. He didn't. Instead, he affirmed we were already at the right place.

When we first visited this church, it was new. They met in, and later vacated, the same space now used by Church #7 ("The New Church").[69] The leadership was successful in attracting their target audience—those who didn't attend church—but it was a passive crowd. Today we'll learn if that has changed.

This nondenominational church now meets in a public-school auditorium. In some parts of the United States it's unheard of for a church to gather in a government building but not in our area. Though some would claim overreach, citing "separation of church and state," I think it's smart: using a public building for the public, generating revenue for the school, and saving the church from purchasing and maintaining a facility.

We briefly interact with a young couple as we arrive. They're visiting too. At the main entrance stands a greeter, who gives us a quick rundown on where to go and what to expect, concluding with a heartfelt welcome. Lastly, the two pastors give us a quick "Hi." As one pastor introduces himself, I'm

---

69 They, too, have since moved, but then Church #27 moved in.

shocked when the other one remembers us from our single visit a couple years ago. Our conversation is brief, for the service is about to start, so I don't fault them for rushing away.

Unfortunately, this is the extent of our interaction, despite many people bustling about. Candy fills out the guest card and drops it off at the information table, but there's no one there for her to talk to.

It's an older building, but the updated auditorium features theater seating, complete with movable armrests and cup holders. Beverages and snacks are part of their gathering. The auditorium has a sloped floor for easy viewing. The main level seats about 225 and is almost full. I'm not sure about the balcony. The people dress casually. Kids through fifth grade have their own activities, so we don't see them during the service, while most of the high school students are off on a mission trip. This leaves us with junior high students and adults.

During announcements, we learn that people wearing green nametags are greeters and available to answer questions. I look around but can't find anyone with a green nametag.

There's more technology in use than we've seen so far. When not displaying song lyrics, Bible verses, or videos, they project the pastor's image on the large screen behind him. Three stationary cameras, mounted on the front face of the balcony, provide views from different angles. Though they can't pan or zoom, the camera shots are a nice addition and, I suspect, provide a welcomed alternate view from the balcony.

They show a video from Samaritan's Purse about Operation Christmas Child, in which people pack shoeboxes with Christmas gifts for impoverished children. The church wants to fill and donate one hundred boxes this year. Everyone can help with this project, which will provide Christmas joy for kids who would otherwise go without. As a side benefit, the church will build community as they work on this project.

The worship team is much like that of other contemporary services. As for the teaching, it's more informal. The pastor sits on a stool as he teaches from James 1:22–25, weaving pop culture into his message and bantering a bit with some people in front. "We are educated two years beyond our obedience," he quips. "There's more [to Christianity] than passive church attendance."

We worship God, just like each week, and we hear a worthy message, just like each week, but unlike prior Sundays, we have minimal contact with others. They don't even have a time in the service to greet one another.

We stand at the service's conclusion, but I don't move. I hope someone will approach us. I try in vain to make eye contact with someone, anyone. Candy says, "We're standing here like pathetic lost puppies and should get moving." She's right, of course, but I still long to talk to someone. I finally spot a man with a green nametag, but he rushes by in haste.

As we shuffle out, I think God tells me to reach out to the couple we met when we arrived. Wondering how I'd ever find them in this mass of people, I spot them right away, standing by one of the nurseries to pick up their child. I suspect that's the connection God wants me to make today, but I tell myself it's a bad idea and walk past them.

There are many things I like about this church: the service, the pastor, and the message, but I'm empty inside. Although this feeling isn't new to me, it's a first for our sojourn.[70] It's not a

---

70 We also had minimal interaction at Church #5 ("Catholics are Christians Too"), but for some reason, I didn't feel empty when we left.

sentiment Candy shares, but she understands my angst and patiently listens as I vent my disappointment on the drive home.

Although social interaction provides emotional satisfaction, I'm dismayed that a lack of human interaction produced a spiritual emptiness in me. Is my spiritual contentment dependent on people? Am I that superficial? I hope not.

Then I realize I don't need social interaction, but I do crave meaningful spiritual conversation. That's what I missed this week. That's what I desire. For me, spirituality isn't an introspective state that silently exists between God and me. Instead, my faith emerges as a persistent life reality that I yearn to share with others.

The leadership at this church is doing the right things to foster spiritual connection, but the people aren't following. They're passive, coming to church, doing the church thing, and then going home.

Yet, I did the same thing. God prompted me to seek out the young family we met on the way in, to see if they wanted to go to lunch or maybe hang out. But I told myself they wouldn't be interested or would think I was creepy. So I ignored them, just like everyone else ignored me.

I feel empty, and it's my fault.

Takeaway for Members: If you're a "greeter," make sure it's your priority. If you're not a "greeter," make sure you do it anyway.

Church #17:

A Doubleheader

When we started our quest, we decided that for churches with multiple Sunday morning services, we'd attend the final one. This has happened three times,[71] but today is different. This Lutheran church has a 9 a.m. contemporary service followed by an 11:15 traditional one, with Sunday school in between. We decide to attend both services.

Like the Roman Catholic Church (Church #5, Catholics are Christians Too), this will be another high church experience,[72] and I'm looking forward to it—not because I expect to enjoy it, but because I know it will stretch me. Coincident or not, the sanctuary reminds me of the Catholic Church we visited three months ago: long and narrow, but instead of a low ceiling, this one has a steeply-pitched roof. There's an impressive display of stained glass behind the platform, depicting a huge cross in multi-color splendor.

In a first for us, there's a sign language interpreter for the hearing impaired, who sit in the first three rows. It's a treat to watch these folks sing with their hands and sign interactive portions of the service.

---

71 In addition to this one, Churches #5, 8, and 9.

72 High church originally applied to the Anglican church, but it's now generically understood to refer to any more formal, liturgically-focused church tradition. The opposite is low church, which is less formal and liturgical. Virtually all of Candy's early church experiences, and some of mine, are low church.

Right away, I realize their idea of *contemporary* is vastly different from mine, with this service being one of the more reserved ones we've attended. Though the contemporary elements are there: current songs, guitars, bass, piano, and drums, it exudes a stiff formality. The half dozen vocalists are more like a choir than song leaders. I characterize it as "formal contemporary," while Candy simply says "sterile."

Part of the pre-service meditation is the "gathering song," with the congregation somewhat listening but not singing. Next is the welcome and announcements, followed by a "confession and absolution" liturgy. For the rest of the songs, we sing along, following words printed in the bulletin. From a facility standpoint, there's no way to integrate a projection system into the sanctuary.

We read three lectionary texts,[73] standing for the third one, from John. There's a prayer and then the message. The church is without a regular minister, with a retiree filling in, but he's gone this week. Covering for him is the denomination's campus pastor. For his sermon, he recounts service projects he's gone on with students. Although interesting, it's a rambling narrative with no purpose I can discern.

Following the message, the minister reads the "prayers for the day." He concludes each petition with "Lord, in your mercy . . ." and we add, "Hear our prayer." Then there's an offering, followed by the Lord's Prayer.

For communion there's no invitation for visitors to partake. I whisper to Candy that it's best we not participate. Released by row, the congregation walks up the center aisle, individually receiving and eating the bread, followed by the juice.

---

73 They read Exodus 16:2–4, 9–15, Ephesians 4:1–16, John 6:24–35, but they don't read the other three prescribed texts.

They return to their pews via the side aisles. When the usher motions us to go up, he assures us communion is open to all. As my wife pointed out in the bulletin, I know the minister will say "May the peace of the Lord be with you always" and I'm to respond, "and also with you." I say my line as prescribed. The "bread" is a thin wafer. It's dry and flavorless. I struggle to swallow.

Next is the juice, in tiny plastic communion cups, with two colors. I pick the closest one, purple. The man holding the tray says something I don't understand, beyond realizing it's different from what the minister said. Unsure if "and also with you" is a proper response, I just give him a weak smile and nod. Then I drink the juice. Only it's not grape juice, it's wine, and I'm quite unprepared for it. It's not the soothing sip I anticipated to wash down the crumbs stuck in my throat. Although I went through the motions of communion, I forgot God in the process.[74]

We return to our seats, join in singing the final song, and the minister dismisses us. Aside from the usher, no one talks to us the entire time. During a scheduled greeting, people only exchange rote hellos, with virtually no eye contact or more communication.

* * *

No one mentions it, but there are coffee and donuts in the fellowship area. Next to each is a donation basket. I feel guilty for grabbing a treat without feeding the fund, but that doesn't stop me from enjoying a donut. There are several round tables, all with open spots, but no one motions for us to sit. I pick a friendly-looking couple and ask if we may join them. They graciously agree.

---

74 This is a common dilemma for me during 52 Churches, where I become fixated on the "how" of communion and miss focusing on the "why."

They're visitors of sorts, having returned to the area for summer vacation and connecting with this congregation. Long-time Lutherans, they note this church has the most formal contemporary service they've ever seen. Skipping Sunday school, we talk for the next hour. When they excuse themselves to leave, we return to the sanctuary for the second service.

* * *

Upon re-entering, the usher gives us a different bulletin. This one is void of song lyrics and full of liturgy. There's the same "confession and absolution," during which the bulletin says we can sit or kneel. In expectation, I study the mechanics of the kneeling rail but am relieved when no one uses them. There's also a processional hymn, during which we're supposed to face the cross as it moves down the aisle. No one does this either.

The sanctuary seats over two hundred and was nearly full the first service. This time there's less than fifty and most are older. The instrumentation is an organ and we sing plodding hymns from the *Lutheran Service Book*. The lectionary reading is the same. Afterward we stand to recite the Nicene Creed.[75] There are again "prayers for the day," followed by the Lord's Prayer, and the same sermon, which is even less engaging the second time.

For communion, the ushers release people on the outside aisles and they go forward, kneeling to receive the elements. Some partake individually and some with their group. The

---

75 The Nicene Creed (http://www.reformed.org/documents/nicene. html) is longer than the Apostle's Creed. Though I'm quite familiar with the Apostle's Creed, I'm only somewhat aware of the Nicene Creed.

minister gives them a blessing, and they return to their seats via the center aisle. It's a more solemn event this time, and several people don't go forward. Could it be this service has a closed communion? Or perhaps we misunderstood last time. The usher pauses only briefly at our row, glances at me, and with little hesitation proceeds to the next. With a bit of encouragement, I might have gone again, this time to try the drink in the white cup.

The service ends, and the ushers ceremonially release us by row, just like at a wedding. We shake hands and make brief comments to the minister. As we saunter to our car, no one makes eye contact or any effort to talk. If not for our exchange with the other visitors between services, I would have left feeling empty, just like last week.

Regardless, I do have much to contemplate about worshiping God in a more formal, liturgical manner—and that's why we came.

Takeaway for Members: It's understandable that people want to talk with friends at church, but it's also selfish. Search out visitors and outsiders first. Then seek friends.

Revisiting Roman Catholicism

Today we make our second visit to a Roman Catholic Church. I'm excited, wondering how it will be different and how it will match our first experience (Church #5, Catholics are Christians Too). They have 8 a.m. mass every day and on Sundays a second one at 11 a.m. Their schedule calls it "Mass Pro Populo." I don't know what that means and worry we're getting into something weird.[76] After some online research, I conclude it's from the Latin phrase *Missa pro populo,* which means "Mass of the people" or "parochial Mass." I assume they use the phrase to distinguish Sunday mass from daily mass.

Their website mentions the Knights of Columbus, which surprises me, launching an unrelated, but interesting, investigation. I'm surprised to discover their mission is to support the work of the Roman Catholic Church. It's open to men over eighteen. I like the idea of a group working together for the common good of their church and community, but I'm torn at it being gender exclusive. Although, there are apparently auxiliaries for women.

Their website reminds me that Roman Catholics have seven sacraments, whereas Protestants have two. We have in common communion and baptism, which I've participated

---

76 It's human nature to fear the unknown. I am human.

in at many Protestant gatherings and witnessed at Catholic churches. The remaining five sacraments are penance, holy orders, matrimony, anointing of the sick, and confirmation. This, too, is worthy of investigation — later.

This church is two blocks away from Church #16 ("Something's Missing"), and I wonder about their service as we drive by. Today's church facility is large. I miss the first parking lot, so I drive around the building to enter a second one. Many people park on the streets, even though both lots have plenty of room. We follow the flow of people and enter via a back door that takes us to a side entrance of the sanctuary. Mounted by the door is a vessel of water. A woman in front of us dips her finger in and touches her forehead. *Should I follow her example?* I don't know the meaning of the ritual, so I walk by.

I'm struck by the size of the sanctuary. It's grand without being ostentatious. Contemporary and airy, it seats several hundred and is the largest we've seen so far. It's close to full by the time the service begins. Pews are in four sections, each angled toward the front. Behind the platform is an impressive marble-looking wall, with a huge crucifix in the center. On the side, at floor level, is a wooden statue of Mary. Along the side walls are plaques portraying the Stations of the Cross, along with some stained-glass windows.

It's interesting to watch people enter. Most dip their fingers in the water and touch their foreheads. Some then turn toward the crucifix, bowing slightly. Many, once they arrive at their desired row, drop to one knee in the aisle. It seems their goal is to do this as fast as possible. Once seated, about half of them flip down the kneeling rail to pray. Some do this as a quick ritual, while others linger in pious contemplation. For each of these rituals, making the sign of the cross seems to be a common conclusion.

Perhaps our memories of Church #5 (Catholics are Christians Too) have faded, but this Roman Catholic Church seems even more steeped in ritual, with a service that's harder to follow. There are two hymnals, but today we only use one, *Choral Praise*. While the hymns are always announced — and displayed on placards on each side of the platform — the rest of the liturgy proceeds without direction. We think we're prepared, but we aren't. Some of the service uses a "Mass Prayer and Response" card and some uses "Today's Missal," located in the pew rack in front of us, while much seems to follow neither, though perhaps we're just not looking in the right place at the right time.

A layperson reads two of the day's scripture passages, while the priest reads the third.[77] English is his second language, and he's hard to understand. His message is short, beginning with a joke and followed by an anecdote of a nun not recognizing a visiting priest because he wasn't what she expected. When Jesus came to earth, many didn't recognize him either — because he wasn't what they expected. The priest's concluding words are, "We need to recognize God in the people we meet in daily life."

Then we stand to recite the Nicene Creed, they take the offering, and next is mass. Ritual surrounds the presentation of the Eucharist. The priest mentions no restrictions for partaking, but I understand non-Catholics may not. There are four communion stations, one for each section. As prompted by ush-

---

77 According to the Revised Common Lectionary, the prescribed readings are 2 Samuel 18:5-9, 15, 31-33, Psalm 130, 1 Kings 19:4-8, Psalm 34:1-8, Ephesians 4:25-5:2, and John 6:35, 41-51. We hear the 2 Kings, Ephesians, and John passages.

ers, the congregation goes up by row to partake. The process flows smoothly. I assume they use wine and am surprised to see children drinking it. Though the attendant wipes the chalice after each person, all I can think of is the germs accumulating on the linen cloth, which in effect returns them back to this community goblet. Once again, I'm so fixated on the process that I miss meditating on its meaning.

Afterward is a ritual where we exchange the greeting "peace be with you" to those around us. This is the only interaction we have with anyone. They recite the prayer of St. Augustine[78], followed by announcements. Then the priest dismisses us. The people exit quickly, and we make our way to the car. At exactly twelve o'clock we head home.

For the third week in a row I feel empty. Today I'm also angry. Though their traditions have meaning to those who understand them, they serve as a roadblock to someone who lacks a Catholic background. Manmade rituals kept me from connecting with God today.

I fill with righteous indignation. Then I recall the priest's teaching: "the people didn't recognize Jesus, because he wasn't what they expected." My anger subsides. Was it their traditions that kept me from seeing Jesus or my own expectations?

Takeaway for Everyone: Will people see Jesus at your church? Will they see Jesus in you?

---

78 Catholic.org says the Prayer of St. Augustine is "Breathe in me, O Holy Spirit, that my thoughts may all be holy. Act in me, O Holy Spirit, that my work, too, may be holy. Draw my heart, O Holy Spirit, that I love but what is holy. Strengthen me, O Holy Spirit, to defend all that is holy. Guard me, then, O Holy Spirit, that I always may be holy. Amen," (https://www.catholic.org/prayers/prayer.php?p=81).

Church #19:

❖

A Near Miss

With no website and a phone line that doesn't work,[79] we assume this church, listed only in a computer-compiled online directory, either never existed or maybe once did but no longer does. Unsure, Candy drives to the address on Saturday. There at the specified location stands a pristine church, white and petite, with a freshly-trimmed lawn. Tomorrow we'll be there, hopeful to find a gathering but with a backup plan in case we're wrong: Church #22 and 23 are both nearby and have the same starting time.

The sign in front of their building is the only reason we know the service time, just as with Church #6 ("A Quintessential Country Church"). Based only on the building's appearance and no online presence, I suspect we'll find a small, older evangelical congregation that enjoys a traditional service.

When we arrive on Sunday, I'm pleased to see other cars and people headed toward the doors. Inside there's a greeter, who's surprised to see two visitors. With slight apprehension, she asks if we're open to sign the visitor registry, prominently displayed just inside the entrance. We do, permanently recording our presence.

Matching the smallness of Church #1 ("A Friendly Place with

---

79 Calling multiple times over several days reached a recording to "enter your security code."

a Homey Feel"), there are seventeen people present. Some are away on vacation, including the organist and pianist. It's an older crowd. The service is traditional, but informally so. There's no liturgy. What perplexes me is at times it seems evangelical and other times mainline, with periodic hints of Charismatic. It might just be the ideal blend of all three streams of Christianity.[80]

The service begins by lighting two candles,[81] an opening prayer, and a time for greeting, during which there are almost as many hugs as handshakes. Surely everyone greets everyone else. We share items of praise, followed by concerns. Then we sing three contemporary songs to accompaniment tracks. After this is a short congregational prayer, preceding the sermon. It's an expository message from Acts 22 and part of 23. The theme is truth. "Two people can hear the same thing," says the minister, "but they understand differently. So it was when God spoke to Paul on the road to Damascus."

At the sermon's conclusion we sing a hymn a cappella, leading us into communion. Without the covering of music, we can't miss the words, which provides a meaningful path to the communion table. In the most insightful invitation I've ever heard, the pastor affirms that all who are in relationship with God are free to participate, regardless of church status or affiliation.

"We do not know your hearts to reject you," he says, "or

---

80 Christian A. Schwarz establishes the foundational teaching for this in his profound booklet The Threefold Art of Experiencing God.

81 We've seen this practice at the United Methodist Churches (#9, 12, and 15), the Roman Catholic Churches (#5 and 18), and the Lutheran Church (#17). In all instances, two candles were lit to start the service and extinguished at the end. I suspect there's a reason why it's always two, but it's a mystery to me.

know your hearts to accept you." He concludes with, "Only God knows your heart. This is between you and him." Children of any age may participate when they're ready to and understand. In this, he concisely covers all that communion should be: community-centered, family-focused, and God-oriented.

We go forward together to partake of the elements, which consist of broken crackers and grape juice in plastic communion cups. To conclude the service, we sing from the hymnal, as a member fingers the basic tune on the piano.

Afterward we congregate in the lobby to enjoy some cake, along with a prolonged time of community. In talking with the minister, I learn he's a tentmaker pastor,[82] who works as an electrician during the week. He also ministers at the local jail, which is two blocks away.

After meeting several other people, I end up talking with two members at length. I eventually ask a curiosity question, "Is your church independent or part of a denomination?" I ask because I seek some perspective to better comprehend the style of their service.

One lady shrugs. Apparently, the thought never occurred to her. "You, know, I'm not really sure." She looks to her friend for help.

"No." Then she pauses. "Well, I don't think so. Maybe." She thinks some more. "Perhaps we are."

She looks back at the first person, who shakes her head but then adds, "Well, I think I remember some talk about that

---

82 Consider Paul's example of working his trade to provide for ministry in Acts 18:2–3.

once, but I'm not really sure." They glance around, looking for someone else to ask, but no one is available. "Maybe Pastor knows."

"Yeah, I guess you need to ask him. He should know."

I smile and nod. I'm amused at how flummoxed these ladies were at my question. At the same time, I'm pleased denominational affiliation is a nonissue for them. Personally, I oppose denominations. By design, they divide the church and are the antithesis of Christian unity.[83]

Eventually, I'm able to talk with the minister again. "I asked two of your members if you were part of a denomination, but they weren't sure."

He smiles, hesitates, and finally explains. "I don't talk about this much, but we are indeed part of a denomination. Most people here don't know that."

I nod to show I'm listening and to encourage an explanation.

"Most of the denomination has skewed liberal, and I can't stomach it. But they pretty much leave us alone, as long as we adhere to three essential elements of faith."

He runs through the list, and I nod my agreement with each one.

"We have a 150-year history with them, and I don't want to throw it away. As long as they let us do our thing and don't interfere, we'll stay with them."

As he continues to share, I'm drawn to his heart. With their small numbers, they've considered closing, but he feels God's

---

83 See 1 Corinthians 1:10–13.

call to persist and for him to remain their leader—despite the many times he's asked God to release him. He smiles at this and so do I, both amused at the mysterious ways God works and knowing not to question his wisdom.

Their mission is to help people advance in their faith journey, connecting them with other churches that match their needs and preferences. If they happen to pick up members along the way, that's a bonus, but it's not their goal. Although it took a while, all the members eventually agreed on this counter-cultural mission.

He admits they considered canceling services today, so they could instead worship at the nearby Presbyterian church (Church #23). He's good friends with their minister, and today is that pastor's last Sunday there. In fact, this pastor will head over there once things wrap up here, so he can be part of the farewell celebration for his friend.

This pastor, serving in anonymity, will never receive acclaim for his work, but the church Jesus founded needs more leaders like him and more churches with this one's perspective. As we leave, he blesses us, and I do the same to him, asking God to richly provide for him, his ministry, and the church.

We almost missed this church, and I'm so glad we didn't.

Takeaway for Leaders: If you want to reach others, make it easy for them to find your church and to learn about you, your format, and service times.

Church #20:

Different Language, Same God

This week is another doubleheader. Church #17 (A Doubleheader) was the first. This week, instead of traditional and contemporary options, today is a service in Mandarin followed by one in English. Their schedule is simple: At 10 a.m. is a Mandarin worship service with English Sunday school. At 11:30 it's the opposite, with an English worship service and Mandarin Sunday school.

Not wanting to cause offense, we email to ask if non-Chinese are welcome. We are. Some non-Chinese, the email informs us, opt to attend the Mandarin service. I sense God will have something to teach us if we go to both. I'm not worried about us possibly being the only white people there, but I am concerned about the language. However, just because people attend the Mandarin service, doesn't mean they only speak Mandarin.

We intentionally arrive at 10 a.m., not wanting much idle time before the service. Three people, each in turn and with varying degrees of English proficiency, try steering us to the English Sunday school. They correctly assume we don't speak Mandarin, but they're incorrect that we seek an English worship service.

The sanctuary is much wider than deep, allowing everyone to be close to the front. With chairs for about one hundred, they'll use most before the service is over. I remind myself it's August, and some people are likely on vacation. Surely, they'll pack the place in the fall. Desiring to be as unobtrusive as possible in a room full of Asian faces, we sit at the end of the back row.

The worship team numbers eight, with four vocalists, a guitarist—who also sings backup vocals, bass guitarist, drummer, and keyboardist. They project the words overhead in Mandarin, with the English translation underneath.[84] I read the words in English as I enjoy the melodic beauty of a different tongue. As they sing, and I listen, God's presence engulfs me. There's an occasional raised hand, but at times arms erupt with widespread participation. I wonder if it's okay for me to follow their example, even though I don't know why. It's a question I can't answer, so my arms remain at my side.

A prayer follows. I comprehend not one word until the final one: "Amen." Next is the scripture text, read in unison—in Mandarin. The woman in front of me has a parallel bilingual Bible, so I know they're reading from Exodus 19 or 20. Later, the projector displays "20:3–17" surrounded by Asian characters. I turn to Exodus 20:3–17 and find the Ten Commandments.

Until now, the laity has led the service. Now we see the minister for the first time. Speaking in Mandarin, he's dynamic, animated, and at times funny. I find myself chuckling with everyone else even though I don't know why. Laughter, I re-

---

84 The translation appears to be word for word, with one English word matching each Chinese character. In one of the more perplexing examples, a Chinese symbol is translated "tacitness," which sends me to the dictionary when I get home. Tacitness is a noun and its root word, tacit, means silent or not spoken. Though I can't recall the exact wording, the context is the tacitness of God.

alize, is a universal language.

I don't expect to understand the teaching, but I do expect the Holy Spirit will speak to me, about either the message or the adventure. He doesn't—or perhaps he did, and I wasn't listening. I know the sermon is over when I hear the familiar "Amen."

More words in Mandarin follow, informal instructions, it seems. Then a woman at the far end stands and shares using a handheld microphone, perhaps it's a prayer request. When she finishes, everyone applauds. Maybe she reported on an answered prayer. This continues as the mic weaves its way through the audience. After several people share, the minister looks in our direction and speaks, but I know not what he's saying. Suddenly I hear English, "Will you please stand and introduce yourselves?"

Someone thrusts the microphone in my hands. I stand, trying to mask my panic. My goal is to be concise and sit down. *Will they even understand my English words?* But English is all I have, so I state my name and with a gesture, introduce Candy. "We're visiting area churches," I explain, "to learn how others worship God and to worship with them. We'll attend both your services today." I sit down to supportive applause, which seems louder than for the other visitors. As my racing heart returns to a more normal pace, Candy assures me I communicated well.

We sing the "Doxology." The tune is familiar, but the words are Mandarin. I consider their English equivalents as others sing. The service concludes with the "Threefold Amen." Though I didn't feel isolated or dismayed with their Mandarin service, I'm overjoyed at being able to sing along for the first time this morning.

Without a break, about two dozen children join us. Vacation Bible School (VBS) has just concluded for the summer, and there's a short program. They sing a couple songs, perform a skit, show pictures, and share key verses. To my delight, this is all in English. When the program finishes, it's past time for the next service to start. We slip out for a quick restroom break, and the second service begins before we return.

This time we sit in the middle of the sanctuary. The crowd is about half the size. Part of the worship team is back, along with some new members, but the song set is different. It's contemporary, though we do sing one hymn to organ accompaniment. The scripture text is the same, and I presume the sermon is too, except in English. Focusing on the command to not make graven images, the minister offers an expanded teaching. His three points are to not make an image for God, for self, or for others. Initially I'm apprehensive, but as he explains, I appreciate the meaningful truths he shares.

As this service wraps up, there are again visitor introductions. Since I did this once, I hope for a reprieve. But when the minister asks me to do it "again," I smile and comply. We sing the "Doxology," this time in English, followed by the "Threefold Amen."

As we stand to leave, several people invite us to stay for lunch. They do this every Sunday. "Sharing a meal is important to us," one lady explains. I nod in agreement. The churches where we've enjoyed the greatest connections and best community all had food in common.[85]

---

85 Interestingly, communion was originally a shared meal at home, not the sip of wine or juice and a bit of bread or cracker at church that most Christians have turned it into.

As we wait in line for our meal, Candy looks at a jar with Asian writing. As she wonders about its contents, the lady behind me explains, "It's hot sauce." As we nod our thanks, she adds, "It's really hot," as if that's a selling point.

"We no like hot," says Candy, who surprises me by picking up their speech patterns. I hope this didn't offend our new friend. Perhaps she didn't notice.

We gratefully accept our food, minus the hot sauce, and sit down to eat, making two new friends as we share a meal.

Today is a wonderful day at church. Although our only language isn't their primary one, we manage just fine. Our time with them is a delight, as it should always be when God is the focus.

Takeaway for Everyone: We must follow Jesus's example to accept all people, especially those who are different: people who look different, talk different, dress different, and act different.

Church #21:

A New Kind of Church

Based on their website, today will be most unusual, maybe even freaky.[86] I'm excited for what I pray will happen, while at the same time fearful of the unknown.

We have their address but can't find them. We drive back and forth looking for the street number, their sign, or anything resembling a church. Frustration surges. I'm upset I can't locate them and angry they're so hard to find.

There are two other churches within a quarter of a mile and the same starting time. I want to give up and go to one of them, but God prompts me to look once more. I pull into the parking lot where I think they should be. Only then does Candy spot an 8½ by 11-inch flyer on an office building door. Things don't look promising. There's only one car in the lot, and it's time for the service to start. Fear bubbles up. The impulse to flee threatens to take control, but again the Holy Spirit prods me to press on.

With chairs for twenty, only three people mill about. I remember it's Labor Day weekend. They offer us coffee, and we talk a bit. The leaders are a husband and wife team, commissioned as apostles. The fifth person is their teenage son, present but

---

86 The website is full of Christian jargon with hints of Messianic Judaism, but we infer a New Age or eastern vibe. They may even be a cult. Our son-in-law jokes, "If you disappear, we'll know where to look." In retrospect, the only thing worse than no website is a bad one.

not engaged in what's happening.

The bulk of their ministry occurs on Saturday, so most of the people were here yesterday. The Sunday service is for those they meet during their Wednesday evening street ministry, as well as for some of their flock who live close by. They give a brief overview of the service: it will be informal, we are free to move around, and it's okay to praise God in tongues, but if given a word for others, there must be an interpreter. I'm pleased with this biblically-accurate instruction.

This church is primarily a training center, helping those who follow Jesus to step into all he calls them to be. Their goal isn't to build a local body but to equip people and release them back into their community for ministry. Their focus is Saturday gatherings, not the Sunday service. There are two events each Saturday and three on the first Saturday of the month. Yesterday was the first Saturday, and some people drove two hours to be there. They started at 2 p.m., with a scheduled end at 8:30. Instead they continued until two in the morning. No one wanted to leave.

The pastors start the service by sounding the shofar.[87] Then we sing one song a cappella. We know the tune, which is good since there are only five of us. The lead pastor carries us with her strong voice. Then she begins the teaching, interspersed with dialogue.

We turn to Hebrews 6 for the text of today's message, but as she establishes the foundation for her lesson, the Holy Spirit sends her to Ephesians 4. We go through most of that chapter,

---

87 A shofar is a trumpet traditionally made from a ram's horn and used in the Old Testament during various festivals and also as a signal in battle. In this case, their shofars were Yemeni shofars, made from kudu horns, which look much more impressive than ram horns.

focusing on verse 11. We never make it back to Hebrews.

For people who like to stick with a plan, this unexpected redirection could cause frustration. Though I embrace structure, I'm used to meetings where the Holy Spirit is in charge, so a God-directed change is neither surprising nor disconcerting. I admire her sensitivity to his leading and that she can teach for an extended time without specific preparation.

I think the Holy Spirit should lead all our meetings. I'm dismayed this is the first time it's happened in twenty-one weeks. Are today's services so tightly controlled that there's no room for the Holy Spirit to move? Or perhaps leaders stick to the plan because the laity complains. Then I have a more disconcerting thought. What if most ministers can't hear the Holy Spirit?

I'm not sure what the teaching from Hebrews 6 would have been, but I know Ephesians 4 was what God wanted us to hear. It helped us better understand their ministry and connect us to them in the process. Plus, I can share this with a friend who's been seeking deeper meaning from this passage.

We discuss how the message applies to us. Although most church services are one person dispensing information with the rest receiving it, mutual interaction is helpful, building community in the process. When offered, we stand to receive a spiritual impartation relating to our gifts and calling.

God prompts me to bless our teacher. I feel presumptuous for suggesting it, but she gladly receives the words God gave me to say.

Ninety minutes have passed, but it doesn't seem like it. Assuming the service is over, we head toward the door, but instead she invites us to stay to praise God. Walking down the hall, curtains part to reveal a special room. Inside is a re-creation of the Ark of the Covenant. I feel we've entered the Holy of Holies.[88] It's a small room with a couple dozen chairs, a small projector and screen for song lyrics, a keyboard, and an assortment of percussion instruments. We're invited to pick up a drum but neither of us does. We're also given freedom to worship God, moving and dancing as we wish.

Not only is the pastor a gifted teacher, she's also a talented worship leader. She brings us into God's presence. We only sing two songs. The first one lasts twenty minutes. Although Candy tires of the repetition, I'm drawn in. I kneel in reverence and then bow low in awe of God. Tears form, threatening to escape my eyes.

We know the second song, and it's shorter. She wraps up with a typical benediction given directly to us, but instead of leaving, we talk some more and then sit down again. Although I'd like to linger, I'm aware they had a late night and not much sleep, so I suggest we wrap up with a prayer.

If you view church in a traditional manner, then we didn't go today. If you understand church as two or more people gathered in the presence of God, then today offered much. This wasn't a typical church visit, but it was my most significant one yet.

Takeaway for Leaders: Follow the Holy Spirit's leading. Be ready to change plans—even in mid-sermon—regardless of what people may think or say.

---

88 Read the summary of the "Holy of Holies" or "Most Holy Place" in Hebrews 9:3-4. The original details are in Exodus, Leviticus, and Numbers, such as in Exodus 26:33-34.

Church #22:

❖

A Caring Community

L ast month I met the pastor of today's church when he joined our writers group. The piece I shared that evening was the opening chapter of this book. As a result, he knows about our sojourn. Afterward, someone asks if his church is on our list. It is.

Perhaps I said too much. "Would it distract you to look up some Sunday and see me there?" He considers this and then assures me it will not. I hope he's correct. In a few minutes we'll find out.

This church was a backup option last week. In looking for that church, we came upon this one. It was tempting to go here instead. Today, we will.

It's a newer building, contemporary and smart in appearance. It's most inviting. Many people introduce themselves. Their genuine interest—without being pushy—is refreshing. Names are important to them. Many people repeat ours, with deliberate care. When they share theirs, they pause, giving us time to truly hear and remember. Unlike prior weeks, today I recall most of the names and the faces they go with.

Though the edifice is new, they didn't build it. Another church did, but the bank repossessed it during the bad economy. They celebrate having this grand facility, yet also grieve with the church that lost it.[89] It seats about 170 and will be half-full when the service starts, but not much before then. This is because there's a bustle of activity in the lobby.

Much like Church #5 ("Catholics are Christians Too"), I'm glad to see member involvement in the service: giving announcements, reading scripture, announcing the offering, praying, and leading worship. There are five on the team: vocals, guitars, drums, and keyboard. They have a soft pop sound, circa 1990. It was perhaps progressive two or three decades ago. But now it's tired. Candy calls it "safe contemporary." I remind myself it's not about the music. It's about worshiping God—and we do. Worship is what matters.

My friend steps up to give the message. Though I can't tell it, he says he's losing his voice and considered finding a replacement. I'm glad he didn't. The title of the message is "Living with one another in a countercultural world." They're in a series about loving with great purpose. Today the focus is on loving the world. He reels off a series of scripture references: we are the salt of the earth,[90] a light to the world.[91] We are to love one another and let it be our example.[92] Our unity is our witness.[93]

To save his voice, he lets the congregation finish the sermon. He invites them to share their stories of what others have done for them, how people showed love and provided care. I've too often seen efforts like this fail, either because amid long, awkward silences too few people share or because the

---

89 Though they don't identify which church, I later figure it out. We'll visit them (Church #32) in a few months.

90 Matthew 5:13.

91 Matthew 5:14–16.

92 John 13:34–35.

93 John 17:20–23.

time becomes hijacked by people who talk too much, go off topic, have an agenda, or all three.

This congregation, however, does this well. Each example is relevant, heartfelt, and often poignant, sometimes shared with halting voices and occasionally, tears. Acts of kindness, once done in anonymity, receive public recognition. This happens without calling undue attention to the person who's sharing or the person they're honoring. It's done to affirm community and confirm how to truly care for one another, praising God in the process.

This congregation is a genuine community. They prove it in the quiet ways they help each other. "Caring for community," concludes the pastor, "is a witness."

We sing a final song. After the closing prayer, he invites everyone to stay for cake to celebrate the fiftieth wedding anniversary of two members.

The open community atmosphere, present before the service and confirmed during it, continues afterward. We renew past acquaintances and continue to make new ones. The pastor chats with us briefly and even tells those standing nearby that I'm writing a book about the churches we visit. Then he quietly excuses himself. He fades away, perhaps because he doesn't feel well, but more likely because he doesn't need to be a visible presence. The congregation envelops us into their community.

Takeaway for Everyone: In a healthy church, the congregation should take the lead in embracing visitors.

Church #23:

They'll Be Fine

In three of the past four weeks, we've been within a couple blocks of this church. For two of those weeks this church was our backup plan, but today it's our only plan. It's Presbyterian, so I expect a high church service. I'm a bit reluctant because I'm not used to liturgical services, but I'm also excited, because I know God has much to teach me if I am willing to push through and listen for his lesson.

For the first time during our trek, I lose track of the time, which is understandable since we have a different schedule every Sunday. We hurry out the door. Candy prays as I drive. One of her petitions is that I'll calm down. *Is she concerned with my driving?*

It's mid-September, and today is the final Sunday for their "summer" schedule: a 10 a.m. contemporary service. Next week they'll switch to their "winter" format: an 8:30 a.m. traditional service, an 11 a.m. contemporary one, with Sunday school between. Had we known this, we might have made different plans today and come back for a doubleheader next Sunday.

We rush in at ten, but in the few seconds it takes them to make our nametags—as at Church #9 ("Methodists Know How to Cook")—the service begins without us. We mouth quick hellos to friends we see in the back before heading to one of the few remaining open pews. The sanctuary is box shaped,[94] a white décor, with high ceilings. Colorful banners hang around the perimeter. The carpeted aisles give way to hardwood floors beneath the well-worn pews. Padded cushions, which shift each time I do, provide some comfort. It seats about 175 and is perhaps 80 percent full. All ages are present, but the casually-dressed congregation skews older, comprised largely of the senior citizen demographic.

After introductory remarks is a time to greet one another. This is friendly and not faked or forced — both of which we've seen elsewhere. Afterward, the congregation shares multiple announcements, including two about Young Life.[95] Then there's a contemplative prelude, followed by lighting two candles.

Throughout this, a person mills about: occasionally sitting and sometimes murmuring. She appears homeless.[96] She acts mentally ill.[97] Although her antics distract me, I'm pleased no one confronts her odd behavior or removes her from God's house. Everyone accepts her presence and her demeanor, so I suspect she's a normal fixture.

They ran out of bulletins. This is a problem because it contains the liturgy. The projection system is having issues, so we miss this part of the service. I fight a spirit of rejection and am unable to participate.

---

94 Judging from the ceiling tiles, it's roughly thirty-two by sixty-two.

95 Church #8 ("A Grand Experiment") was also part of Young Life. With them being in the same school district, the kids from both churches likely connect with each other through Young Life.

96 When we leave the service, I spot her several blocks away, pushing a shopping cart, full of her belongings.

97 As I mentioned before, this is an unqualified assessment, as I lack the training to make such a diagnosis.

Next we sing some choruses. The song leader plays the keyboard, with the background vocalist — who is also the Young Life leader — on guitar. There's a bass guitar and drums rounding out the sound. Following a reading, we sing another song with piano accompaniment. There's no song leader. The music and words display overhead. A sacredness fills the sanctuary. A "Prayer of Illumination" follows.

Next is the first reading of Psalm 46 from the New Living Translation (NLT). I'm surprised, since the pew Bible is the New Revised Standard Version (NRSV).[98] Following this, the guitar-playing Young Life leader gives the children's message. Five kids come forward to learn about the parable of the sower.

The second reading is from Matthew 13:1-17, covering the same parable. This is the text for the sermon, "Listening to God." The interim minister gives the message. Today is his first official day on the job. Their esteemed leader[99] of twelve years left a few weeks ago, and they're in a time of transition. The interim minister is their "in-between pastor." He's not a candidate to become their regular one. Notably, he also filled this role here fourteen years ago, after their minister of thirty years left. He served in that capacity for two years, with the implication it could take that long again.

His message addresses the season the church is in, providing instruction and encouragement to members. First, he says, this is not a time to coast until a replacement arrives. It will be "business as usual." While most "congregations are too pas-

---

98 We don't use the NRSV during the services. Nor do we use the two hymnals in the pew racks. I assume the traditional service favors both the Bibles and hymnals.

99 Most everyone we talk to says this. In addition, leaders at two nearby churches mentioned their profound respect for this man. I wish I could have met him.

tor-dependent," their former leader trained this group to not depend on him. They are ready to make this transition well. "Your new pastor should find us fully engaged" when he arrives. "In the interim, we will listen to God." Just as Jesus's parables contain unexpected twists, so too should be the attitude during this time.

He speaks for an hour, but it doesn't seem like it. He apologizes for his longer-than-anticipated sermon and assures us he'll be briefer in the future. He then prays, and more congregational singing follows.

Next is the "Prayers of the People." After each person shares their request, the congregation responds in unison with "Lord, hear our prayers." I like the rhythm. It's solemn and simple. Following this is a time of silent prayer, with reverent background music, during which they receive offerings in the back. We conclude by reciting the Lord's Prayer.

There's a brief congregational meeting afterward to confirm the pastoral selection committee. Nonmembers may stay and observe. They present a team of ten. By age and gender, they're a great cross-section of the congregation. Then someone asks how many of them regularly attend the traditional service. Only two do. I fear this could become a major item of contention, but it's dropped. With no nominations from the floor, a voice vote approves the slate, albeit with a few dissensions but no apparent rancor. The meeting adjourns.

Afterward is a time of fellowship. We enjoy some punch and a snack as we make new acquaintances. We spend most of our time talking with two longtime members. They confirm that their former minister prepared them to function without him. They have much respect for him, as well as for their interim pastor. They expect to do just fine.

"When you switch to two services next week, which one will you go to?" I ask.

"We don't attend the same one," says one person. "I go to the contemporary one and he goes to the traditional one."

"So, you won't see each other again for nine months," I joke.

"Oh, no," they say in unison.

"We'll see each other at Monday night Bible study," says one.

"And at Wednesday potlucks," adds the other. "You're welcome to come too." They give the times. To be polite, I make notes of each. I'm tempted by the potluck, but I make no promises. "Sunday school starts next week. It's between services. There are classes for adults."

During this fellowship time, two tables have games for kids. An adult sits at each table. They seem to have as much fun as their charges.

Throughout the morning, many people welcome us and invite us back. When I say we're visiting area churches to learn how others worship God, they don't seem to hear and instead respond, "We hope you'll come back."

As we leave, we meet three more people, who confirm what we've just learned: this congregation is prepared for transition and will navigate it well. I heartily agree.

Takeaway for Leaders: Although it's practical to conduct church business on Sunday, when members are already there, this isn't good for visitors, especially if conflict arises.

Church #24:

Good but Not Typical

Today we visit a church that's part of a small conservative denomination common in our area. Church #8 ("A Grand Experiment"), although part of the denomination, is an outlier congregation and not representative. Today I expect a more typical service.[100]

This church resulted when three churches merged a quarter century ago.[101] The building, constructed two years after their formation, is contemporary and in pristine condition, looking younger than its age. The sanctuary is a hexagon. Pews are arranged in four sections, with the outer two angled by forty-five degrees to face the front. It can accommodate perhaps four hundred, but today there's less than a quarter of that number, who sit only in the center sections.

Behind the stage hangs the massive pipes of the organ. Impressive and grand, they fill the space. Crosses, ubiquitous in the beginning of our journey, no longer attract my attention, but today the absence of one is conspicuous. This isn't an issue for me, but for many it is. The cross is a prime emblem of

---

100 Two of the churches I've attended in the past were part of the Christian Reformed Church, the first one with my parents and the second with Candy early in our marriage. Together, they represent thirteen years of CRC church attendance, almost one-fourth of my life.

101 One of these three churches was the church of my youth. As such, I won't be surprised if I see people who look vaguely familiar.

Christian faith, but we must remember it's only a symbol.

The congregation is predominantly senior citizens, with few children present. The worship team gathers onstage, all teenagers. Three play guitars, with one on percussion. Offstage is a pianist, the church's worship leader and only non-teen in the ensemble. There are a couple vocalists, while two guitarists also sing. We don't use the two hymnals, and the pipe organ sits idle.

The teens lead us in contemporary songs, with the words displayed overhead on either side of the pipes. Accomplished, without being assuming, their sound is a safe contemporary and is most conducive for worship. They point me to God. It's a wondrous time. I stand in awe, so taken that I forget to sing.

Worship styles, as with musical tastes, are a personal preference, with one being no better than another, only different. Though today's musical style is not my preferred choice, I find it compelling. They play and sing with joy. Their worship is pure. I'm ushered into God's presence.

This group is good at what they do, confident and poised, but without calling attention to themselves. Their focus is praising God. This part of the service is unexpected, an anomaly inserted into a traditional order of worship, with its formal labels and established structure. The service is easy to follow, though, courtesy of the overhead projection, flowing from one element to the next.

The pastor is in the middle of a sermon series: "For a Life of Wisdom." Today's message is on "Friendship," featuring relevant verses from Proverbs. He introduces the topic with a reference to Facebook and how the social media juggernaut has redefined the meaning of "friend." This produces a false sense of community. His Facebook reference amuses me. He explains Facebook to this older congregation, though his description wouldn't help anyone unfamiliar with it.

True friendship, he says, requires constancy, honesty, and wise counsel. Quoting an unnamed source, he adds, "A true friend always lets you in and never lets you down."[102] Jesus, he reminds us, is the ultimate friend.

To end the service, the worship team leads us in singing the "New Doxology" and then reprises their prelude for the postlude. Again, they draw me back to worship. I want to sit and listen, to take it in, but everyone else is leaving. I don't want to appear rude should someone wish to talk, so I too turn and exit.

They invite us to stay for "fellowship." There's Sunday school too. To my relief no one invites us to that. Though Sunday school might just be for kids, there aren't too many of them around.

I learn that only one of the teens leading worship attends this church. The rest came for the day. The worship leader occasionally does this to vary their worship style and offer a blended worship service. Ironically, that's what I liked the most.

Both before and after the service, people repeatedly say, "Thank you for visiting." No one wonders if we're visitors, they all know. For the first time, their conversations with us aren't so much to share faith, as much as to entice us back. One woman works hard to establish common ground. No

---

102 Several online sources attribute this to Tim Keller, circa 2007.

matter how I restate our intent, she doesn't understand — nor does anyone else.

They're anxious to grow. Though Candy later reminds me they're not as desperate as some of the other churches we visited.

Takeaway for Everyone: Listen to what visitors tell you and react accordingly. Don't make assumptions about their intentions. Trying too hard to pull them in can push them away.

Church #25:

Embarking on a Metamorphosis, Part 2

This church meets in a school building, just like Church #16 ("Something's Missing"). Their service starts at eleven, later than most, likely to allow time for setup. The contemporary website of this four-year-old church shows captivating photos of their worship team. I expect an exciting time where they musically push the limits with high energy and an edgy sound. I anticipate what I'll see.

We head for the school and spot a temporary church sign by the road, confirming we're at the right place, but once we park, we don't know where to go. With no people to follow, we head toward the main entrance. We're almost there when we spot someone to ask. They redirect us to a side door.

Inside waits a team of greeters. One spots my T-shirt, which says, "The Armor of God" and references Ephesians 6:10–18. He gets excited. "Did you wear that shirt on purpose today?"

I'm confused, so I smile as I try to figure out what to say.

"The message today is about the armor of God! Did you know?"

"No, I didn't."

"What a happy coincidence."

I start to agree, but then say, "With God there are no coincidences." In uncharacteristic deliberation this morning, this wasn't the first T-shirt I considered wearing but the third. God knew.

Everyone has an adhesive nametag, and we make our own. Unlike prior churches with nametags, where members wear permanent ones and visitors use temporary ones, everyone here wears a handwritten nametag. Even though they know we're visitors, our nametags don't single us out.

People mill about, even though the service should begin at any moment. After a few minutes someone calls out, "We're about ready to begin," and we find our seats. There are perhaps eighty to one hundred folding chairs set up, with maybe fifty or sixty people to fill them. A couple we know invites us to sit with them. This is a comforting gesture. Despite knowing people at most of the two dozen churches we've visited, no one's asked us to sit with them. We're used to sitting alone. Though we don't need this affable act to put us at ease, a typical visitor might appreciate it.

The worship team is far different from what their website portrayed. There's no high-energy, edgy worship band, but a laid-back team of two. The worship leader plays an acoustic guitar while the pastor pats a conga. There's nothing wrong with their simple sound, but I expected something quite different, and it takes me awhile to realign my thinking. Even so, I'm disappointed.

To wrap up the singing, the pastor's wife guides a team of girls, who lead us in a kid-friendly song about Jesus, complete with visual aids and audience participation. This segues into the children's message, given most capably by one of the friends we're sitting with. She engages the kids, while teaching the adults. Her lesson introduces the pastor's teaching and matches the message on my T-shirt.

The minister's words are a concise reminder of the six elements of the Armor of God, with a review of their purpose. He moves into an update for their church. Several people told us to expect an important announcement. They're anxious to hear it.

Three months ago, we skipped a church on our list (Embarking on a Metamorphosis). Visiting them would have not advanced our journey. Today we learn the future of that church and this one will intertwine. The first church needs more members and this one would like a building, but it's not a merger. Many details remain undecided, but they give a timetable. Two other churches will also send people to this endeavor. In many ways, it's a church plant.[103]

In a few months, both churches will cease their Sunday meetings, while remaining connected in other ways. They'll visit other churches, meet in small groups, and prepare their future facility and organizational structure for a joint relaunch. Although the timetable is aggressive, they aim for Easter, in six months.[104] This pastor will lead the new group, but they'll have a new name, a different board, and a renewed focus.

---

103 A "church plant" or planting a church, is a process of establishing a new congregation. It's done by the intentional effort of another church or a denomination to form a new gathering that will eventually function on its own, independent from its founding organization, but often still affiliated with it. Church #2 ("Growing Deeper, Not Wider") and Church #8 ("A Grand Experiment") are recent church plants. Church #15 ("An Outlier Congregation") was also a church plant, but that occurred a few years ago.

104 They were off by six months. Although they held a few practice services in the summer, the official opening didn't occur until mid-September.

Generally people have apprehension over a change that lacks details, yet the overall mood here is excitement. Several years ago, we were part of a church plant, and I know how invigorating it can be.

Afterward, we linger to talk, and this group is eager to share. Eventually they stow their gear, readying the facility for school on Monday. They're fortunate they can store their equipment onsite, eliminating the need to haul it away each week. Though there's much to do, with many people helping, it proceeds quickly.

I'm excited for the future of this group of believers and pray for a wildly successful future.

Takeaway for Everyone: There are advantages to not having a church building. Aside from avoiding mortgage payments and building maintenance, there's significant community and camaraderie when setting up for the service and tearing down afterward. If you don't own a church building, don't be in a rush to buy one.

Church #26:

❖

An Unknown Situation

As our journey progresses, we discover more churches. Today we're visiting one a friend mentioned. She calls it African-American[105] and knows only two other things about it: the location and its age, about three months. Tucked into a back corner of an L-shaped strip mall, it's only 5.4 miles away and is the thirteenth closest. There's no sign other than what's on the door: their name and service times, but no phone number or website. Their Sunday service schedule is for two and a half hours. Though we've spent this much time at many churches, knowing this in advance is a bit unsettling.

A Google search of their name matches a denomination birthed in Nigeria fifty years ago. Today, it has a worldwide reach, with six hundred parishes in North America. I search their website for churches in our area and don't see any. Is there a connection between this church and the denomination?

We arrive ten minutes early and find only four people. A man plays a keyboard but stops to greet us. His oldest son is readying the A/V equipment, while the younger son plays a handheld video game as his sister provokes him. At ten o'clock only nine people are present. Apparently the starting time is only a guideline. A few more trickle in and eventually the service begins. There's an opening prayer and then

---

105 A more correct label, it turns out, is simply an African church.

singing. Words appear on a screen in the corner of the room as we sing with recorded music, first a Third Day song and then a lot of Kirk Franklin—whose style is more agreeable to this dark-skinned congregation. In addition to the keyboard, there's also a drum kit and double conga, but they go unused.

Worship occurs organically, so naturally that I don't realize there's no song leader. Hands often rise in praise to God, and I'm glad to shed the constraint of physical worship that's been present at many of the other churches. Though I don't match their demonstrative expressions of worship, I'm glad to enjoy freedom of movement as I sing.

People continue to trickle in, with the last wave arriving at 10:35. Our number eventually swells to twenty-seven, half filling the fifty-five padded chairs squeezed into the room. Candy and I comprise two of the three people with pale skin. We're also among the oldest, as well as the most casually dressed adults. Several men wear suits, and most women have on nice dresses or professional attire. One couple sports traditional African garb.

The many kids wear jeans and T-shirts. They're mobile throughout the service, especially during worship, bouncing from chair to chair and migrating from friend to friend.

Tambourines are a big part of their worship. Since rhythm eludes me, I pass the one next to me to another worshiper. However, they don't use these instruments to keep time—or at least to any beat I can discern—but shake them with vigor to emphasize words and phrases or as an extended exclamation at the end of a song or chorus. I'm pleased at their use to accentuate worship. This involvement transitions us from audience to participants, but after an hour, my ears desire a break.

Everyone is friendly, abounding in smiles. During the greeting time, we surely shake hands with every adult—sometimes more than once—and even a few of the braver kids. Most adults speak accented English. My wife characterizes it as Jamaican, a lilt she is familiar with and professes to understand, courtesy of a Jamaican co-worker she once had. I think her assessment is simplistic and could be stereotypical. Instead, I suspect they hail from various African heritages. I want to ask, but to avoid possible offense I keep my question to myself. Later, I overhear one lady ask a visitor what country she's from. It's easily asked and casually answered. Yet even with her example to guide me, I don't think I can pull it off and don't try.

We witness a baby dedication, the first for their new church. The pastor wonders aloud if there will be more, laughing as the couples of childbearing age avoid eye contact. He declares a blessing on the child. His words are intentional and more fervent than for any other infant dedication or baptism I've ever witnessed. The pastor's prayer is passionate as he proclaims protection, favor, and God's grace on the child. This isn't a request but a declaration. I like his spiritual confidence, making a mental note to follow his example.

The bold proclamation of blessings repeats throughout the service. We see it next as we recognize three children with October birthdays. The minister places his hand on the head of each child, giving each one their own impartation. We extend our hands toward the kids, nodding and voicing our affirmation. It's powerful. I'm confident these children will enjoy a better future because of the words spoken over them today.

Though the room is small, and we hear the pastor fine, he uses a microphone anyway. His amplified words reverberate, as if we're in a large auditorium. He reads 1 Peter 2:9–10. We are "a peculiar people," as stated in the King James Version. The pastor spends the next hour unpacking that phrase. We are a chosen people, a royal priesthood, a holy nation, but this does not apply to everyone. We are not to "impose our peculiarity on the general population."

He jumps from one scripture verse to the next. I work hard to keep up, as I strive to pull words from his accent. "The people you are around," he adds, "determine your expectations." For example, if you were to be around the president of the United States, you'd wear your best clothes. I know not if he said it, implied it, or I inferred it, but the same applies when we're around God. I'm mildly embarrassed over what I'm wearing, but my practice of dressing casually for church is to help visitors feel comfortable. I don't want my attire to offend the unchurched, though I'm not so worried about those in the church. As for God, he knows my motives, and so far, he's not told me to dress differently.

The service ends at the appointed time with a prayer of cleansing and another blessing powerfully pronounced on us and our schools, work, city, and county. Afterward the pastor's wife, our only white compatriot, asks if we have any questions. I do, but they form a jumbled mess in my mind, and I'm unable to voice any. Instead, I shake my head.

After the service, they share a meal to celebrate the baby's dedication. They invite us to stay, and we gladly do. The minister makes a point to inform us about the food. "The meat is spicy. The rice is not."

I don't do spicy—not at all. "Thanks, I really appreciate knowing that." I select the rice, while Candy takes one small piece of meat to add to her plate.

As we return to our chairs with our food, they begin congregating in groups. No one joins us or invites us to join them, and I don't see a graceful way to insert myself into their clusters. They aren't being rude but merely gravitating toward their friends and those they're comfortable with.

I'm not angry or hurt, just lonely. I can't fault them. I've surely done the same thing to minority visitors. I welcome them, smile, and shake their hands, but then retreat to the comfort of who I know. I have much to learn about relating to people of other backgrounds and especially how I interact with visitors at church. *God forgive me for my errors. May I do better in the future.*

I thank the minister. His message gave me much to think about, his bold prayers are an example to follow, and their worship of God inspires me. We give our best to the new mom and compliment her beautiful child.

As we reach the door to leave, the minister thanks us for visiting, invites us back, and asks where we live. He's dismayed we live across the county line, an area his blessing didn't cover. I assure him we weren't offended, but he's compelled to correct his omission. Taking our hands, he proclaims abundance and blessing for our locale. His vision for a better future and his bold pronouncements encourage me. We thank him and head for our car. We may be the first to leave, but our visit will stay with us for a long time.

Takeaway for Members: Being outgoing and friendly is a great start, but be sure to embrace visitors, especially during social times. Give extra care to visitors who look, dress, or act differently.

❖

Part Two Perspective

We're half done with our journey. For the past twenty-six weeks we've sought to expand our understanding of how others worship God. I blog about our visit each Monday morning, but friends frequently ask for more.

"What are you learning?"

"That God's church is more diverse and varied than I ever imagined."

"Is your journey changing?"

"No. We're still planning to return to our home church when we're done."

"Do you want to revisit any of the churches?"

"Yes." I start to reel off a list along with my reasons, but they don't seem interested in the details. *Why do they ask if they don't care about the answers?*

Aside from these questions, a sobering realization is that church is not about the teaching or the music. It's about community.

We've heard messages from gifted speakers and those not-so-talented, the formally trained and the self-taught.

We've heard deep thoughts and entertaining fluff. But in all cases, we received a worthwhile word from God. I suspect if we pray expectantly and are open to hear, we will.

Similarly, we've sung traditional hymns, modern songs, and contemporary praise choruses. Accomplished vocalists, struggling crooners, and everything in between have led us in worship. There have been worship bands, pipe organs and pianos, accompaniment tracks, recorded songs, and even a cappella. If we focus on the words, we praise God regardless of musical style.

Nonetheless, message and music, I'm sad to report, aren't important — not really. The big variable is community. Aside from that often-awkward official greeting time during the service, community is a meaningful time of spiritual interaction with others. When we make connections with others, we share Jesus. God is more present in these informal exchanges before and after the service than during the planned and prepped moments of the service.

A few churches have no community. People come, people sit, and people leave, without saying a word. This is not church as God intended. Church #18 ("Revisiting Roman Catholicism") had no community. Church #17 ("A Doubleheader") and Church #16 ("Something's Missing") had minimal community. They gave us no reason to return.

Fortunately, most churches allow community to some degree and a few excel at it. I want to revisit these churches. Community is church at its best. Four churches stood out in their embrace of us. Though our visit could have been an anomaly, I suspect all visitors would receive a similar welcome.

Many churches have an official greeter or two and most have a couple of outgoing people who reach out to visitors, but at Church #22 ("A Caring Community") it seemed everyone reached out to us. We met so many people who were truly interested in getting to know us. They were sincere, accepting, and engaging.

At Church #25 ("Embarking on a Metamorphosis, Part 2"), we enjoyed many friendly conversations beforehand, had people invite us to sit with them, and enjoyed significant interaction afterward.

The after-church community at Church #19 ("A Near Miss") was also great. We talked with many people, made connections, and learned about their church, ministry philosophy, and vision. It felt as if we were at a family reunion with extended relatives.

At Church #14 ("The Pentecostal Perspective") many members of the congregation were friendly. We felt welcomed before and during the service, enjoying spiritually-significant conversations. Unfortunately, their narrow theology placed us on the outside. They would never fully accept us into their community.

Receiving honorable mention are the two minority congregations: Church #26 ("An Unknown Situation") and Church #20 ("Different Language, Same God"). Both were extremely friendly, but we failed to make deep connections with anyone at either church. For the first, this was due to language differences and for the second, cultural differences, though I should note, we weren't in the target demographic at either church.

A second observation also stems from the preaching and singing. Consumerism is rampant in the modern church. The mantra of many churches, especially the larger ones, is "excellence in everything." Doing whatever God calls us to do to the best of our abilities — that is, with excellence — is God-honoring. He deserves nothing less. Unfortunately, pursuing excellence feeds into a consumer mentality.

Many people seek a church with the most engaging speaker and professional musicians. When they find it, they join that church — and stay there until a better preacher or music comes along. They are church consumers, looking for the best value. They forget about community and never ask what they can give to a church.

I'm not being overly critical. How many times have you heard someone leave a church because "I'm just not being fed anymore"? I've heard it, and I've even said it. Its cousin is "it's just not meeting my needs." Although both complaints sound sincerely spiritual, they reveal a consumer mindset: "What will church do for me? If this church can't meet my needs, I'll find one that does." The result is church shopping and church hopping. This isn't God-honoring, and we should be ashamed.

A third item is church size. Size does matter and bigger isn't better. There's a progression: Excellence in preaching and music triggers a consumer reaction, so churches that excel in these areas attract bigger crowds. They grow and may even become a megachurch.

From the perspective of structure, resources, programs, staff, and efficiency, bigger churches have a huge advantage. This plays well in modern society, but it isn't the purpose of church. Church is to connect people with God and with each other. This is hard, if not impossible, to do with any degree of intimacy and integrity at a large church. That's why they form small groups,[106] promoting smallness within the structure of largeness.

At the churches with, say, more than two hundred people, no one knows if you're a visitor and few care. If you want to get lost in a crowd, go to a big church. If you want community, seek a smaller one.

These are the three key insights God showed me in the past six months. Our church visits confirm it. I'm not down on church, but I wonder if today's church has lost its way.

Contemplating this, I recently blogged, "Church isn't about message or music. Those are often distractions or settling for less than the best. True church is about community, where we are all priests, with each one giving and receiving, mutually edifying and encouraging one another on our faith journey."

I'm sure we'll learn more on the second half of our journey. I can't wait for what else God has planned for us.

Takeaway for Everyone: True church is about community. The message and music are secondary—and may even distract from what really matters.

---

106 I'm using "small groups" in a generic sense. The actual names vary: small groups, life groups, Bible studies, pods, service teams, and fellowship groups.

Part 3:

The Halfway Point

We live on the eastern edge of a rural county, near a small village of a couple thousand. The first five churches were in or near this village. To the west is a larger village and to the east, in the adjacent county, lies the area's largest city. After our fifth Sunday, we've alternated between driving west to attend churches in the adjacent village (Churches #7, 8, 10, 12, 14, 16, 17, 18, 19, 21, 22, and 23) and east to broach the perimeter of the city (Churches #6, 9, 11, 13, 15, 20, 24, 25, and 26). This is because we picked churches based on the driving distance from our home.

It was also disconcerting, like being a tennis ball at a match, bouncing back and forth. Churches to the west have a rural culture, while those to the east, a more metropolitan vibe. As strange as it sounds to say it, I can't keep this up any longer. I need a different approach to avoid encountering this jarring contrast each week. I adjust my plan.

We'll continue visiting churches within ten miles of our house, but for the next part of our journey, we'll do so by area. First we'll cover the remaining churches around the village to our west, with ten more to visit.

A few miles southwest sits a third village. We haven't visited any of those five churches. They'll come next.

Third is the three remaining churches in our local school district, which covers a large geographic area. Churches #1 through 6 are in the district and Church #7 ("The New Church") recently relocated here. These three remaining churches are on the school's eastern border.

Takeaway for Leaders: If what you planned no longer makes sense, change your plan.

Church #27:

A Charismatic Experience

Today we head to a building we've been in twice before—each time for a different church. We were here for Church #7 (The New Church)—which since relocated—and a few years ago for Church #16 (Something's Missing) before they moved. The first two churches rented the space, but this one bought the building.

It's a long structure, built for shared-tenant use. All the exterior entrances remain, but most of the interior walls are gone. We don't know which door to use. We wait in our car for others to arrive, so we can follow them.

Each time we've been here, we entered by a different door and each time they met in a different place. This time we walk in toward the rear of the building and turn right to face the stage. There are six rows of padded chairs, enough for a hundred people, with open space behind them for a couple hundred more if needed.

We're greeted soon after we walk in, but the conversation is confusing. Eventually we discover our new acquaintance is visiting too. He knows the pastor and introduces us to him. The minister is a gregarious man, easy to talk to. With effort he locates a bulletin for us. Then, giving a commanding gesture toward the worship area, he tells us to have a seat, but no one else is sitting down. Not wanting to isolate ourselves, we stand awkwardly in the jumble of people milling about.

On the wall opposite the door there's a snack bar, complete with posted prices. As I try to figure out their intent, Candy glances at the bulletin. A woman comes up and shares her first name. Candy connects this with what she's just read, asking if our new friend is the pastor's wife. She is. We make small talk as we learn about each other. She mentions there's no coffee and points to an empty instant coffee maker sitting next to the sound booth. Someone works on brewing a pot.

By now some people are sitting down, so we join them. I pick a row near the back and move toward the end. An unpleasant odor assaults my nose. Candy can't smell it and gives me a you're-just-imagining-it look. Soon I grow used to it but never like it. As we wait for the service to start, one more man introduces himself, but most people ignore us. I've learned to expect this at bigger churches but not at smaller ones.

A youthful praise team assembles on "stage," a platform elevated a mere eight inches. The low ceiling allows for little more. In addition to three on guitar, there's one on bass, a drummer, and two backup singers. The lead vocalist doubles as one of the guitarists. They're accomplished but without a showy polish. They play and sing with energy and are some of the best worship leaders we've seen.

They encourage us to worship any way we wish, be it to dance, to raise our arms, to kneel, or even to prostrate ourselves. For the second time in the last two weeks, a young child sings loudly and off-key[107] but with unabashed passion. I love it and hope no one ever squashes his zeal for praising God.

The three-song set lasts about thirty minutes, and Candy grows weary of the repetition, the repetition, the repetition. Though I understand her angst, this is also a visual worship

---

107 If I can tell they're off-key, it must be bad.

experience for me. Many children and a couple of wom-
en dance in the aisle and a few approach the stage. Theirs
is an exuberant expression of joy, which I vicariously enjoy
through them.

One of the backup vocalists, perhaps in middle school, jumps
and dances with abandon as she sings, full of energy and passion and joy. With an occasional arm raised heavenward and
an effervescent smile of endless delight, she often looks up as
she praises God. It's as if she sees Jesus and is smiling at him.
Her angelic face ushers me into God's presence. It's a beautiful thing, and I don't want it to end.

Worship segues into a time for "testimony and prayer." One
couple comes forward to share. Weepy and weary, they beck-
on their family to join them. Soon three generations assemble to form a tight huddle, beset with unspoken turmoil. The
family's matriarch tearfully proclaims she will give no more
attention to the devil for what he has done and will instead
praise Jesus for the deliverance he will provide. The pastor
prays for them as some church members surround this family, showing support and voicing agreement. One woman
grabs her Bible and boldly proclaims a Psalm of deliverance.
Others follow with more prayers and declarations.

Each person who prays does so loudly, to the point of shouting.
I've never understood this. God can hear our faintest whisper.
He knows every thought. We don't need to yell for him to hear.
Perhaps the high volume is to encourage each other or maybe
it's simply what someone modeled for them. Of course, the opposite extreme is whispering a passionless monologue short on
meaning and devoid of feeling. I seek the middle ground.

Another person comes forward to give testimony via song
and we soon join in as she sings "Amazing Grace." A third

person has a word to "share with someone present." Next is the offering.

An hour into the service, the sermon starts. The minister is functioning on little sleep. He and his wife returned from vacation yesterday, but due to a flight delay, they didn't get home until 2 a.m.

His springboard text is Joshua 1:8–9. Holding up his Bible, the minister says, "This is enough." He gives a series of devastating scenarios — such as a divorce or terminal illness — concluding each one with, "the Bible is enough."[108] He follows with several related biblical texts, though I'm not quite sure of his theme or overall intent.

At one point, he chastises us: "Forty percent of you did not worship God today." His tone is unequivocal. "You were preoccupied." Contrary to what he said earlier, apparently there *are* expectations in worshiping God however we want. Implicitly, he desires outward expressions and judged our worship as inadequate.[109]

He continues his criticism, noting this church lacks in the five-fold ministry.[110] Before this thought is fully articulated, he di-

---

108 At times on our journey I've disagreed with things pastors have said. Yes, the Bible is of critical importance, but sometimes we need more. It would have been more correct for him to say, "God is enough" or "Jesus is enough," but let's not elevate the Bible to the level of the God who inspired it.

109 My home church suffers from this same contradiction. They uphold "freedom in worship" as a virtuous goal, but the leadership has specific expectations of what that freedom does and doesn't include. If we fall short, we're criticized for not fully engaging in our worship of God.

110 I think he's referring to Ephesians 4:11, and I suspect his point is that no one is operating as an apostle.

gresses. Some people are "addicted to prophecy and others are addicted to a word of knowledge and others . . . " I can't write fast enough.

He concludes with a time for public confession, and some people tearfully request — and receive — forgiveness from others. The minister launches into what I suspect will be an altar call, making me squirm with his frequent mentions of visitors, but then he meanders for an extended time, never issuing a challenge or giving a call to action. The service ends. No one approaches us, and no one is available for us to talk to, so we leave.

Despite this church's many shortcomings, the kingdom of God powerfully advanced today, and the Holy Spirit was active. Though I want to return for more worship, the lack of interaction and confusing message discourages me.

Takeaway for Leaders: It's okay to publicly address visitors to celebrate them, but it's bad to confront them or cause them to feel condemned.

Church #28:

❖

Intriguing and Liturgical

We almost missed this church. They didn't come up in our online search. We learned of them only recently when we spotted their name in a church directory in the local paper. Even once we knew they existed, it was hard to confirm their meeting time.

They're part of the Celtic Episcopal Church, whose website proclaims, "Western Orthodoxy for the Third Millennium." It lists seven churches, with most scattered throughout the eastern United States. Based on the website, we expect a traditional, liturgical service. They're located just around the corner from Church #12 ("More Methodists, More Food"). We pull into the parking lot eight minutes early. There are only two other cars.

We walk inside, and two ladies are sitting down. One stands to introduce herself. She's the minister's wife. She shares some basic information about the liturgy for today's service. Without her help, we'd have been lost. The liturgy is from the *Book of Services: The Celtic Episcopal Church*.

The sanctuary has four rows of pews, replacing the padded chairs they once had.[111] It could accommodate about sixty

---

111 I know this from their denomination's website, the church's only on-line presence. From this website, we learn the names and see pictures of their minister and deaconess. The only other information is a se-

people. The simple thirty-two by twenty-four square foot room oozes color and symbolism. Along with several lit candles, incense burns. I'm sensitive to scents and wonder if I'll make it through the service without succumbing to a hacking, teary-eyed reaction. Thankfully, I'm okay, but the smell remains an uncomfortable presence throughout the service.

An organ sits in the front corner. It's covered and not accessible. Soft background music plays, courtesy of a CD. It's an instrumental selection, soothing and worshipful. At the appointed time, the music stops, and the opening liturgy starts. The minister reads the selection from outside the sanctuary. Then he enters, followed by the church's deaconess, who assists with the service. A series of rituals follow, perhaps preparing the altar for worship. We don't know the meaning of these rites, but they have a mystical aura that is both comforting and intriguing.

Our leaders are ornately attired. Their garments strike me as a combination of what a priest and a rabbi would wear during their respective services.[112] The liturgy progresses, and we follow along in the *Book of Services*. As we bounce from section to section, each time our new friend slides up behind us, whispering the page numbers. We're grateful for her assistance. Because of her, we're able to follow along and participate.

---

ries of photos of their church and sanctuary. An early picture shows their chairs and a later one proclaims, "our new pews." This is interesting, since many churches replace pews with chairs, not the other way around. We later learn the photos are of their prior building and sanctuary. Because I have the image of their old building in my mind, I drive past their new one and must turn around.

112 I've only been to mass twice and have never visited a synagogue, so my assessment must be from TV and movies.

In addition to guiding us, she also operates the music via remote control and strikes the chimes at the appropriate times. For the parts in the liturgy requiring a congregational response, hers is the voice that carries us. Candy and I are tentative and though a fifth person joins us, our other two co-worshipers are passive.

As part of the liturgy, the minister reads a prescribed prayer. It's specific, holistically covering various facets of faith. After each stanza, we reply, "Lord, hear our prayer." Next are two readings from today's lectionary: Galatians 2:16–20 and Luke 8:5–15.

The message follows, and the minister looks at us for the first time. He smiles, suddenly affable. So far, the service has been solemn, but now it becomes casual. In a conversational manner, he instructs us, merging the two scripture readings into today's teaching. The sudden switch from the formal to informal presents a jarring dichotomy I can't fully grasp.

With only five sets of eyes for him to connect with, it seems he's often talking directly to Candy and me. I'm uncomfortable with his eye contact, preferring to visually keep him at a respectful distance. Yet I know looking at him communicates interest, encouraging him as he speaks.

The sermon is short, lasting only ten minutes. I jot down "Judaizing" to look up later, but I forget the context. Then I note, "The apostles will judge the twelve tribes" and "Jesus will judge us." These are my only notes, and I fail to grasp his point. I think my struggles with eye contact presented too much of a distraction.

Of his words directed specifically to us, the first set is an attempt to explain the low attendance. The second, to forewarn us that later in the service we will greet each other with a holy kiss. Though I appreciate the warning, it's still an uncomfortable exchange, but at least low attendance means I only need to do this a few times. The third is instructions about the Eucharist.

From the platform he determines we're eligible to receive communion and invites us to do so. They have a shared communion cup, which from a sanitary perspective I'm uncomfortable with and my wife even more.[113] Had it been a large gathering, we could have skipped going forward, but not so when we make up 40 percent of the congregation.

There's more liturgy to conclude the sacrament, reverting to the reserved manner that opened the meeting. Without any singing,[114] the service concludes an hour after it started.

We follow everyone across the hall into a small fellowship area. Once there, they offer us coffee and pie. A neighbor and her dog join us. Though she missed the service, she's a welcomed part of their group.

The minister is gregarious and a great storyteller. He's also a history buff with much to share. They trace their church to 37 AD and Joseph of Arimathea. After ninety minutes of sharing, people begin to trickle out. We leave thirty minutes later, having been there for three hours.

This tiny church and their strange worship intrigue me. I want to learn the meaning behind their rituals, understand the history of their practices, and discover the rhythm of their

---

113 Afterward we're told that intinction – dipping the wafer into the wine – is an acceptable alternative.

114 Last week Candy was dismayed at how long we sang. This week she's disappointed we didn't sing at all. For my part, I didn't mind the absence of song.

liturgy. It's there but would take repeated visits for me to first grasp and then embrace it. Though they worship God differently than I do, it's no less viable and offers much. I want to learn more.

Takeaway for Everyone: Examine all your church practices. Do they make sense? How will visitors feel? If it's creepy, stop it.

Church #29:

Led by Laity

As we drive to church today, our fourth United Methodist visit, we pass several places we've already attended. I recall memories from each. When we arrive at today's destination, the building looks familiar. That's when we realize our daughter attended preschool here, over a quarter century ago.

There's minimal parking in front, so we drive around back. The lot is huge, more than the building requires. We see another couple, older than us and dressed more formally. We talk as we follow them inside.

In the narthex, greeters welcome us and offer a bulletin. We amble down a short corridor to the sanctuary. As we do, one woman approaches us and then mutters, "Where's the guest registry?" She moves toward an ornate wooden stand, stationed next to the center aisle. It holds nothing. As she searches for the missing book, I decide to ignore her comment.

Walking past her and the empty stand, we enter the sanctuary. It has a warm feel. Likely constructed in the sixties, it's half again deep as wide, with a tall, steep roof. There are ten rows of pews, with padded seats, likely able to accommodate 150, plus whatever the small balcony holds. The windows are stained glass, with contemporary geometric shapes. Two banners in front proclaim, "Come Holy Spirit" and "Live by the Spirit." Elevated between them is a cross.

To begin the service, they light three candles.[115] The minister is gone and a lay[116] speaker is filling in. She begins by sharing announcements. We sing an opening hymn with organ accompaniment. Another layperson leads us in a liturgical call to worship. Displayed on a screen on the right of the sanctuary are the song lyrics and the liturgy. Some people refer to it, whereas others follow along in the bulletin or hymnals. They have three hymnals, distinguishable by color: red, black, and green. Then we sing a second song.

A bell choir is up next, a first for our journey. Then is a time of greeting. Many people flash wide smiles and give warm handshakes, but only two share their names, and no one asks ours. The scripture reading is next, with two selections from today's lectionary: Job 42:1–6, 10–17 and Mark 10:46–52.[117] Prior to each, the reader explains the passage's context.[118] Though the pew Bibles are the NRSV, he doesn't use that version.

Afterward we sing a children's chorus, beckoning the kids to come forward for the children's message. The only problem is that I don't see any. Finally, a group of five emerges from the balcony and makes their way forward. Though the song is appropriate for preschoolers, this pack is much older: later elementary, junior high, and even high school. They dutifully sit down in front to hear the kid's message, based on the reading from Mark. Though geared for a younger crowd, all five listen without apparent resentment.

---

115 If a church lights candles, there have always been two. This is the only time we see three.

116 Part of the laity, not clergy.

117 They don't use the other three passages from the lectionary.

118 I appreciate this. A concern over the lectionary is that people who have a steady diet of it have difficulty placing each passage in its proper context.

The chancel choir is next. Two of the singers were in the bell choir and came for the children's message. This perplexes me. They're treated as children but also functioning in adult roles.

The message, called "Blind Faith (Trust)," is next. Our speaker connects the two readings, which she ties in with a poignant personal story of a motorcycle accident as a teen, the lifelong aftereffects, and God's provision. She has written out her presentation and reads most of it. Though not an accomplished speaker, I applaud what she's doing. The entire service, led solely by church members, proceeds without trained clergy. This is how it should be, and I wonder why it seldom happens.

During the message, the person on our left passes a clipboard and sign-in sheet to Candy. With members already listed, they simply check a box next to their name. Candy adds ours to the bottom and marks "visitor." As she wonders what to do next, someone motions to the row ahead. She leans forward and hands off the clipboard. Amused, I watch the clipboard as it passes from person to person. Fixated on this unusual practice, I'm distracted from the message. I never do reconnect with our speaker, missing her concluding words. In fact, I've taken no notes and know only that she shared her story of God's work in her life.

After her message, she reads a list of member concerns and joys. Then other people stand to share theirs. When they're done, she reads a liturgical prayer, and we agree with a collective "Amen." The bell choir plays during the offering. The congregation applauds, which they also did for the chancel choir and the lay speaker. They're a supportive group.

To wrap up the service, we sing the Doxology, say a prayer of dedication, and sing a hymn of commitment, followed by the benediction. Though the service began with organ accompaniment, it ends with piano.

We talk with a friend as we exit, and someone invites us to stay for coffee. The refreshments are in the narthex, not the fellowship hall. It's crowded, and there aren't enough chairs. The treats are ample, left over from a funeral. We stand alone off to the side, nibbling on our snacks. Eventually a few people approach us. Each time the pattern is the same. They introduce themselves, thank us for visiting, and invite us back. Then they squirm and excuse themselves. They're not rude. They just don't know how to welcome visitors, but at least they try.

The service lasted an hour and we stay another fifteen minutes. Most people linger, but we see no reason to tarry, so we head for the door. In the parking lot, there's another invitation to return and several people smile as they wave goodbye. They're a friendly church but socially awkward. Despite this, my lasting impression is that laity led the entire service. For that, I salute them and praise God.

Takeaway for Everyone: Involve members in the service. Don't expect paid staff to do all the work and be the only ones to lead.[119]

119 Consider 1 Peter 2:4–5, 9.

Church #30:

Misdirected and Frustrated

The sparsely-attended service proceeds normally enough: an opening prayer and song, sharing prayer requests, an offering, a greeting time, and a sermon, with more singing and prayer interspersed.

The older crowd is friendly but awkward. During the greeting time we shake hands with each of the twelve people present, sometimes more than once. The message is about parables, perhaps introducing a series. Although well-prepared—with ample scripture references and a couple of points inserted in the middle—it lacks clarity. I learn nothing, and I'm exhausted for what I've endured.

Fifty minutes later the service concludes. I'm glad. Bored and tired, I'm ready to go home. Then they drop a bomb on us. "Thanks for coming. The service will start in about ten minutes." That's when we realize we've just endured Sunday school—a really bad one.

When Candy asked about the service time, the pastor confirmed what their website said, 10 a.m. Neither mentioned Sunday school. The bulletin concurs with this ruse. They should be upfront: Sunday school is at ten and church starts at eleven.

No one explained Sunday school when we arrived. They just handed us a visitor card and told us to "sit anywhere."

I suspect they think they're clever, but I feel manipulated. In sales, they call this "the bait and switch" — and only the sleaziest use this deplorable tactic. They duped us.

Mentally, I'm not prepared for another service. I should use this time to pray, asking God to clear my mind and restore my focus, but I'm so frustrated I don't even think of it.

One member tells us the church started thirty-five years ago, a split from another congregation over their bus ministry. I didn't know anyone did a bus ministry anymore, but this church still does, having two small buses that pick up area kids and adults needing transportation.

As people drift in, excitement mounts. Anticipation surrounds us. A few more welcome us, but, unable to shake the prior hour from memory, it's hard for me to fully receive their greetings. The church seats about 150, with perhaps seventy present, although their milling about makes it appear fuller. Most men wear coats and ties, with women in dresses. All age groups are present.

A choir of eleven opens the service. Although having a near equal mix of male and female voices, they sing in unison, not in parts. They sing with gusto. Soon we sing too, old-time hymns with piano accompaniment. The organ sits idle, as the organist is gone this week. They sing with vigor and slowly draw me in. Our collective volume makes our number feel much larger. These folks enjoy their hymns, singing with more energy than I can ever recall.

There are several gift bags up front, which the minister disperses in a playful, yet honoring, manner. I assume these may be birthday gifts, like Church #6 ("A Quintessential Country Church"), but the lady in front turns around, whispering,

"They're secret pal gifts."[120] We nod our comprehension, but I think it's odd to dole them out during the service.

There's a time of greeting, and we shake even more hands. Most people thank us for visiting, but only a few share their names or ask ours. Names seems trivial, especially since it's unlikely anyone will remember, but I've come to realize what an important gesture this is. When the greeting is over, the kids leave, apparently for a children's activity.

After more singing, we stay standing for the scripture. In a first for us, we read it in unison. Our NIV Bibles are of no use, and Candy scrambles for the lone pew Bible in our row, the KJV.[121] We read Hebrews 12:12–17 about bitterness. The minister likens the root of bitterness to the tenacity of a yucca plant, for which he has great disdain.

He's a gifted speaker, dynamic and entertaining. His message shares four characteristics of bitterness, followed with steps to rid ourselves of this destructive trait, and ends with Paul's instruction to forgive one another.[122] He leaves us with the parting reminder that "Forgiveness removes transgression but doesn't automatically restore fellowship."

Nevertheless, the minister has a quirk that annoys me. Candy tunes it out, but it's a constant distraction for me. He ends many sentences with "Amen," voiced in the form of a question. I've heard this before, but he takes it to the extreme. "God is good, amen? The good book, amen?, says he loves us like children, amen?"

---

120 "Secret Pals" is a practice at some churches. Ladies who wish to participate are secretly assigned another person from the group to encourage throughout the year through small gifts and notes. At the end of the year, the identity of each secret pal is revealed at a banquet.

121 All the Baptist churches we've gone to use the KJV.

122 Ephesians 4:31–32.

One deacon did something similar when he prayed before the offering: "Lord, we thank you, Lord, for your gifts, Lord. And Lord, we seek your help, Lord, in our trials today, Lord. And dear Lord . . . " I begin counting. He averages one "Lord" for every four words.

As the minister wraps up his message, he launches into a typical Baptist altar call, "with every eye closed and every head bowed . . ." But just as I'm tuning out the familiar,[123] he mixes it up. "If you're one hundred percent sure you'll go to heaven when you die, raise your hand." I don't feel like playing along, but if I don't he'll conclude there's a sinner in his midst who needs saving. I raise my hand at the last moment.

Then he asks anyone who's not one hundred percent sure to raise their hands. He gives time for people to respond while the music plays. I grow anxious and eventually peek. A few people kneel on the stage steps. As the song concludes, they scurry back to their seats. The service ends.

Afterward, one of the church leaders comes up to chat. He sports a red and white lapel pin, matching an unfamiliar flag on the stage.

"What does it represent?" I ask. "I've never seen it before."

"It's a Baptist flag," he proclaims, as if I'm ignorant for asking. "The four sections say Baptist, the Book, the blood, and the blessed hope." He beams as if he's just shared something profound, but elevating Baptist to the level of the Bible doesn't sit well with me.

---

123 Early in our marriage, Candy and I attended a conservative Baptist church for five years. We heard over five hundred altar calls, with little variation and much repetition. Much like Pavlov who conditioned his dog to salivate when he heard a bell, I became conditioned to stop listening when the altar call began.

"I'm used to seeing the Christian flag at churches."

He's quick to denounce it. "We'd never have that flag in our church. It's dangerous and not biblical." I'm sure he thinks his pin is a conversation starter. Instead, he drives a wedge between us. He's not being mean, just passionate to a dogmatic extreme. I can't wait to end our conversation and escape.

More people greet and invite us back. To each I respond with "thank you." To me this means, "I hear you and appreciate the invitation" without making a promise I won't keep, but I'm not sure what my words mean to them.

Today we heard a powerful message, one of the best in the past thirty weeks. We worshiped God with people passionate about singing to him and who truly enjoy each other's company, but I struggle to appreciate any of this. Tricking us into attending Sunday school remains my key memory.

Takeaway for Everyone: Be sure you're not misleading visitors. If you do, they won't come back.

Church #31:

A Day of Contrasts

It's Saturday, and we head to church, a Seventh Day Adventist gathering. I've always wondered why most Christians don't worship on the Sabbath as practiced in the Bible. Though Sunday meetings became the preferred practice many centuries ago, I've never found a biblical reason why. Going to church on Saturday seems right, even though it feels strange.

I'm busy most Saturdays, so it took a couple of weeks to schedule this. I now realize why the unchurched often find it a challenge to attend services even when they want to. They already have a full day. Fitting in church requires a shift in priorities. Despite good intentions, existing schedules are hard to change.

On the way, we disagree on the route. The easiest path is not the shortest or the quickest. The driver prevails, and his passenger sulks a bit, but we find the church easily. There are six visitor parking spaces near the door. I feel guilty for using one, but they're intended for us.

Stationed at the entrance, two greeters welcome us. One opens the door and the other hands us a tote bag and bulletin. With people milling about, there's no obvious traffic flow. One greeter confirms my guess on which way to head.

We weave our way through the throng to the sanctuary, which seats about 230. I estimate 150 people, mostly older and dressed up.

The architecture captures my attention. The focal point is a large stained-glass array behind the pulpit. It portrays an abstract arm extended heavenward, with a dove upon an open hand. I'm not sure if the dove is being held, released, or presented to God. I ponder the spiritual implications. Isn't that the point of art?

To the right of the stained glass hang the organ pipes, prominent but not ostentatious. Next to them, on an angled wall, hangs a large flat-panel monitor. Smartly designed announcements loop as the display counts down the time to the scheduled start. The service is one of the most technologically integrated ones we've seen so far and certainly the most professional with its application.

.The contemporary ambiance contrasts with several traditional elements of the service: singing hymns, the pipe organ, and a male chorus. In addition to the organ and hymns, we hear the piano a couple of times, as well as two contemporary tunes, albeit from the 1980s. In the pew racks sits a *Seventh Day Adventist Hymnal*, but it remains unused.

At one point, the leader asks everyone who is able, to kneel. There are no kneeling benches. It hurts to kneel, but I do so anyway. Focused on my discomfort, I miss the words they pray. I wished I'd stayed seated, even though no one else did. The prayer begins and ends with singing "God is So Good." Used throughout the morning, the monitor displays song lyrics as well as video of the service, which they stream live and will post on YouTube.

It's World Kindness Week, and today's service revolves around that theme. It starts with two young girls reading about the Good Samaritan.[124] The first reads in Spanish.[125] Though I know not what they mean, her words have a beautiful flow. She draws me in. The second reads from the KJV, even though the pew Bibles are the more understandable New King James Version (NKJV).

Next, middle school students perform a skit showing present-day scenarios about helping others. They do an excellent job. In an abbreviated message, titled "Giving at a Cost," the guest minister starts with the Good Samaritan and ends with a story from Native American lore, poignantly illustrating the importance of helping those in need.

The reason for the guest speaker and abbreviated message is that today is a special celebration. They recently paid off the loan for their addition. They have a note burning ceremony and a litany[126] of dedication. Afterward will be a Thanksgiving potluck.

Publicly they invite all to join them, but no one personally asks us. Aside from the two greeters at the door, no one talks to us all morning, not before, during, or after the service. With no greeting time and no effort to collect our contact information, I wonder if anyone cares we're there. After the service, I try to make eye contact with someone, anyone, but fail. I'm invisible and fight to hold back tears.

---

124 Luke 10:33–37.

125 No other parts of the service are in Spanish. Though the county is 11.6 percent Hispanic, we've not heard Spanish in other church services.

126 A litany is a liturgical prayer where the congregation offers a fixed response to the leader. But what they did, didn't sound like a prayer. Perhaps the speaker misspoke, or maybe a litany means something different to him.

The service presented an ideal melding of the traditional with contemporary. Its professional execution, engaging presenters, and compelling content draws me to their worship. Unfortunately, with no interaction from anyone, nothing draws me to their community. They ignore us, but perhaps today's festivities distract them from reaching out.

Candy has plans for the day, but she delayed them to attend this service. I'm surprised when she doesn't head straight to our car, that she's contemplating staying for the meal: "If we walk slowly, maybe someone will ask us to stay."

No one does.

Takeaway for Everyone: The official greeter shouldn't be the only one to welcome visitors.

Church #32:

❖

Commitment Sunday and Celebration

Today we visit the area's only Episcopal church. For the past year, they've met in the Seventh Day Adventist facility, where we were yesterday.[127] I knew they bought a building and understood they'd move in a few weeks, but last night a friend tells me they already have. Last week they celebrated their first Sunday in their new facility, at least one new to them. The cornerstone says 1956.

We arrive ten minutes early and pull into the next-to-last parking space. This is a good sign.[128] Bubbling with exuberance, a young girl greets us at the door. Several people give heartfelt welcomes and one asks us to sign their visitor book. Another asks, somewhat awkwardly, if we're visiting or wish to join. She quickly clarifies. Today is commitment Sunday, with contribution pledges sought for the upcoming year. She's embarrassed that our first visit falls on their annual plea for money.

Typical of the architecture of its day, we stand on a landing. A few steps descend to the basement, and others ascend to

---

127 This church built, but then lost, the building now used by Church #22 (A Caring Community). It's a sad part of their 167-year history. No one hides this from us, but I had pieced this together before arriving.

128 While some would find a lack of parking troublesome, I'm thrilled to visit a church with this problem. Too many churches have had nearly empty parking lots — and sanctuaries.

the sanctuary. Several in this older congregation struggle to navigate the stairs.

As we climb the steps, a gregarious woman approaches. "Thank you for visiting." She wears a white vestment with a clerical collar underneath. Yet despite the formality, no church has received us so cordially. "Are you familiar with the Episcopal church?"

We shake our heads. "This is our first time."

She's delighted. "What is your church background?"

This should be an easy question, yet I fumble for an answer. Eventually, she understands we're not used to liturgical services.

She smiles broadly, "Here's what I'm going to do." She quickly scans the sanctuary. "Our services can be hard to follow if you're not used to them, so I'm going to seat you next to someone who can guide you."

"Thank you so much." The simple gesture touches me. It makes so much sense, but no one's ever done this for us before.[129] "That's a really great idea." She introduces us to a couple our age and explains the situation. I sit next to the husband, and he's eager to help. He takes his assignment seriously and performs it admirably.

The sanctuary is spartan, though roomy and most-inviting. There's a simple crucifix behind the communion table and a banner on the side. The lone musical instrument is a piano. With the simple setting, there's nothing grand or gaudy to

---

129 Church #28 (Intriguing and Liturgical), where the minister's wife would whisper us cues, accomplished the same thing, but to pair us with someone to guide us is extraordinary.

distract. Our purpose is to worship God, and we will do so with little to interfere.

We sit in padded chairs. I estimate fifty people. Had the choir not remained up front, we'd be quite crowded. But I've sat in too many sparsely-attended churches in the past seven months, so crowded feels good.[130]

A choir of five starts our service and eventually their number grows to eight. My new friend cues me to the liturgy as we bounce between two books, often in quick succession. We also sing one song from the bulletin. Only once do I lose my place, but that's my fault, not his. Unlike other liturgical churches we've visited, their bulletin is an ample guide, but it's one more item to juggle, so we appreciate his assistance. The priest[131] also provides verbal direction when possible. I'm not sure if this is for our benefit or her normal practice, but it's also helpful.

The guest speaker gives a brief message, albeit without any scripture references. He acknowledges their recent journey. Although arduous, the outcome is good. He affirms their commitment and their community, quoting JR Woodward, "Bigger is no longer better in the church world."[132] Then he adds, "Smaller is where the work will be done." He's so right.

---

130 Church growth experts teach that when a sanctuary is 80 percent full, visitors feel there's not enough room for them and will be uncomfortable. Today the percentage exceeds 90 percent, but they can solve this with a few more chairs. Thankfully there's room to add them.

131 Her official title is "The Very Reverend" and more informally, "Mother." In later conversation, she refers to herself as a "priest," but the people lovingly call her by her first name, without any title.

132 http://churchnext.tv/2012/11/09/jr-woodward-the-latest-trend-is-smaller-churches/.

They receive his message well, but his main purpose is to secure pledges for the next year. In only three weeks, they collected enough money to buy the building for cash. Now the focus is raising enough funds to keep their shepherd on full time. Without emotional appeals or being pushy, he asks each person to consider stepping up their pledge for the next year, be it moving closer to a tithe (giving ten percent), up to a tithe, or beyond a tithe. The members fill out their pledge cards, which they bring forward as an offering to God.

The Holy Eucharist follows. I assume it's closed to visitors, as at the Roman Catholic churches we visited, but it isn't. The minister thoroughly explains the process and invites us to participate. When we go up, if we just want to receive a blessing, we cross our arms over our chest and the priest will bless us. To partake in the Eucharist, we receive the bread—and it really is bread, not a cracker. Then we proceed to the wine, where we can dip the bread or drink from the cup. Most dip their bread and so do we. I'm still not used to wine.

Afterward is a brunch to celebrate God's provision. Many invite us to stay, and to one I respond, "But we don't want to intrude on your celebration."

Her response removes all doubt, "*You* are one of the reasons we're celebrating."

As we mingle and wait in line for our meal, we talk with many people. They're a wonderful community, a close faith family. Each person I talk to rejoices over the new building. Though it's nothing like their prior facility, no one complains and most express joy over not having any debt. Now they can focus on reaching out to the community.

We enjoy the food and, even more so, the conversation as we learn more about their church. With the pledges tallied, they share the results. They met their goal, providing a fitting end to their celebration.

I feel a deep connection, an affinity that's hard to explain. They invite us to return. Part of me wants to, but next week our journey will take us to another church. We're learning much on our sojourn, but it doesn't offer us the opportunity to tarry. That's the one sad downside to our adventure—saying goodbye to friends we've just met.

Takeaway for Everyone: If your service is hard for guests to follow, members can guide visitors.

Church #33:

A Shepherd Cares for His Flock

We only recently learn of this church, discovering them in a printed directory of churches. Aside from a spartan Facebook page, they have no online presence. They meet in a converted airplane hangar, resembling half of a metal tube lying on the ground. The inside boasts nicely finished walls and a vaulted ceiling. Though the building lacks windows, white walls and ample lighting provide an open feel.

Sunday school is wrapping up. The minister greets us. He and Candy exchanged email messages in recent weeks as we tried to pinpoint their location. Online maps — including the one on their Facebook page — and his initial directions were wrong.

To our left is the fellowship area. Both their Sunday evening service and Wednesday night meeting involve sharing a meal. Rectangular tables are already set up. Behind them and along the opposite side are smaller rooms and offices. To our right is the worship space. There are six rows of padded chairs and in the back row sit a couple of recliners.

The minister, a lay preacher, once attended a different church. When a local tragedy occurred, he helped neighbors cope and invited them to church. His fellow parishioners didn't appreciate the demeanor of these new folks. As a result, he and the people his church rejected began meeting in a trailer park. A year later, they transitioned to their current location. Having worked in industry for forty-one years, the last dozen also as this assembly's leader, he recently retired to focus on this tiny church.

The name of the original church isn't shared, but I suspect I know which one it is. They could now use extra members to bolster their shrinking size. Sadly, this parallels the formation for Church #30 ("Misdirected and Frustrated").

There's seating for sixty and I count twenty-one; one third are elementary-aged children. The kids sit in the front two rows, excited and behaving — for the most part. The frontmost rows consist of seven child-sized wooden chairs. Simple in construction and brightly painted, they possess a throne-like quality. The church celebrates the kids' presence and includes them in the service — until they leave after the children's message.

With two other visitors today, the numbers would have been even smaller. But some regulars are missing: a few ill and others traveling. The pastor's clan, with four generations represented, makes up half the church. They function as family, and I'm not sure who's related and who they've assimilated.

We struggle as we sing hymns. The organist learned to play because no one else could, and the minister isn't adept in leading singing. Eventually he recruits a member with a strong voice to come forward and guide our worship. The pastor's wife is sick today, and we wonder if she would normally do this.

The scripture text is from Habakkuk 3:17–19. With no pew Bibles and no projector, the bulletin includes today's reading, as found in the KJV. Verse 17 recaps the dire conditions of the day, with a transition occurring in verse 18 when the prophet proclaims, "Yet I will rejoice in the Lord," and a verse later he affirms, "The Lord is my strength."

Four days before Thanksgiving, the minister's message "Thanksgiving Anyhow!" takes the same tone as Habakkuk. The people of this rural congregation struggle with the implication that some will only eat one or two meals today. The pastor asks who's had breakfast. For those who didn't raise their hands—my wife included—he assumes it's because of a lack of food. In Candy's instance, she often skips her morning meal. I'm not sure about the others, but two ladies are regulars at the food pantry.[133]

The message offers many suggestions on how to help those in need. This isn't to call attention to the giver but to show how this church family takes care of one another. Behind the church is a sizable garden, planted for their church community. "When God blesses you," the pastor says, "you need to pass it on." Though the growing season is over, there are still onions and potatoes in the ground should anyone need them.

Deer hunting season began a few days ago and the pastor has already bagged two. If anyone lacks meat for Thanksgiving, he offers venison. He owns twenty acres nearby, from which he cuts firewood for those needing wood for heat. His property also includes two acres of fruit trees. He normally shares the produce, but this year, due to an early spring and late freeze, the harvest was nil. He refers to Habakkuk's mention of no fruit. "Yet I will rejoice," he repeats.

We must "be thankful in hard times and be thankful for our salvation." He shares more verses and additional stories of

---

133 I've recognized food pantry clients at five of the churches we've visited.

need and provision. "In everything, give thanks—even on your bad days."

Even though this church is only nine miles from our house, the contrast between their lives and ours is stark. I seldom think of being in need and only at the Food Pantry do I realize how much some people struggle to eat. Yet the reality of these people's lives puts an exclamation point on being in need and going without. As followers of Jesus, we need to do more. We need to help people in need.

Today at church we struggled with our singing, but no one cared. They are with their church community, their extended family. Being together is what matters. This minister takes care of his tiny flock. He loves them, and they, him. He is their good shepherd.

Takeaway for Everyone: There are people in need all around us. We must help them in Jesus's name.

Church #34:

— ❖ —

Acts Chapter Two

Today's destination is a charismatic church just down the street from Church #31 ("A Day of Contrasts"). We've not been to many charismatic churches (#11, Charismatic Lite; #14, The Pentecostal Experience; and #27, A Charismatic Experience), so I'm excited for what we'll find.

As planned, we arrive ten minutes early. With only two cars in the parking lot, my anticipation sags. We walk in, surprising six people who aren't expecting visitors. There's an older couple, a younger woman, and her three kids.

We're flabbergasted to learn they're not expecting anyone else. Their pastor resigned a few months ago and some families left too. Three couples now rotate in planning each service. The young mom says today is her husband's turn to preach. Together, they'll lead worship.

"We're in a rebuilding phase," says the older man.

That seems like a positive spin on a dire situation. I don't know what to say. I nod to show I'm listening and encourage him to continue.

"Our church is 35 years old. We've seen some highs and we've seen some lows." He pauses as if realizing just how low things are. "And this is a low time."

185

I nod, again. "Well," I search for the right words. "You have a positive attitude and a core group and a building and—"

"Another Assemblies of God church will help us turn things around."

"That's great!" I try to encourage. "In addition to a positive attitude, a core group, and a building, you've got another church to help out."

"We got a lot of work to do."

"I pray God will bless you, draw people who need a church home, and restore this church . . . " The Holy Spirit begins directing my words, "To restore this church to far beyond what it ever was, to boldly proclaim Jesus, to be a light to this community. May God use you to powerfully advance his kingdom."

As I run out of words, the young woman's husband, who is today's speaker, walks up and we repeat introductions. Then another woman arrives, increasing attendance to ten. With nine rows of padded pews, enough for 144 people, we all sit on the right side. For the first time, I focus on the building: The sanctuary's spartan décor contradicts the building's age and the congregation's history.

The only musical instruments are a keyboard and guitar. We sing five songs, ably led by today's assigned couple. We use neither the hymnals before us nor the projector overhead, instead referring to a two-page handout. One number is an old hymn, while the rest are contemporary tunes. Candy and I know three of the songs and easily pick up the other two.

Prayers of praise start the singing and occur between most songs. Although subdued, there's an occasional raised hand.

Another man arrives midway through, increasing the attendance to eleven. For the final song we sing "Shout to the Lord," while the kids take the offering. For the first four numbers we stand, but we sit for the offering. Ironically, this is when I feel compelled to rise.

For the sermon, a message of revival connects the 1900s Pentecostal movement with the early church in the book of Acts. I'm familiar with this topic and glad he celebrates the Holy Spirit's role in our lives and God's church. Yet, considering this church's denomination, the teaching strikes me as basic.

Though not gifted at public speaking or dynamic in delivery, our speaker's words resonate with me anyway. Once again, I remember that God doesn't need eloquent speech or polished oratory to connect with his people.

In Acts chapter one, the people wait and pray in anticipation of what is to come. This is part of their preparation. "The church," quips our teacher, "is a pencil sharpener." In Acts chapter two, the Holy Spirit shows up, just as Jesus promised. The church is born. Nineteen centuries later, the Holy Spirit again takes a lead role, exemplified in the Azusa Street revival of 1906. The Assemblies of God Church, he says, traces its roots to this event.

"The intensity of knowing Jesus could come back at any moment is lacking," our speaker says. "The church got complacent." At first, I assume he's referring to the global church, but then I wonder if he means this local assembly or perhaps their denomination. We need to "expect God to do miracles in our lives." He shares a miraculous healing he had, as well as supernatural acts by some of the pillars of the charismatic movement. He ends by quoting William Booth: "I don't pray for revival. I am revival."

After a concluding prayer, the service seems over, but our leader doesn't dismiss us. Instead, he invites us to give a personal testimony of God's work in our lives. Two people share, one at great length. Twenty minutes later, we stand to leave.

After the service, the people plan to decorate the sanctuary for Christmas. It feels awkward for us to stay to help, and they seem reluctant to start while we're there. I thank them for the opportunity to worship with them and affirm our speaker for his message. Though I sincerely mean what I say, I realize my words sound perfunctory. I doubt he receives my appreciation for his teaching.

We get in our car and head home. I'm preoccupied with this tiny church. From a human standpoint, their future is bleak, but with the Holy Spirit, anything can happen—just as it did in the second chapter of Acts.

Takeaway for Everyone: With God, all things are possible, but we should never attempt the impossible on our own.

Church #35:

❖

A Well-Kept Secret

Two weeks ago, on our way to Church #33 (A Shepherd Cares), we drove past this one. They're a well-kept secret, not coming up in our online search or in the local directory of churches. Once we know their name—only because we stumble upon their building—we find their Facebook page, confirming their location but nothing else. The locator section on their denomination's website lists service times, but it provides no contact information. If they have a phone, it's unlisted. Candy sends two messages through Facebook, our only means of contact, but after two weeks, there's no response. For the first time, we head off to church without having confirmed times or even if they're meeting. I wonder if they want visitors.

We arrive to a pleasant sight: cars in the parking lot. We ease into one of the last remaining spaces and walk toward the entrance. Only then can we read service times on their sign: "Sunday Divine Service" at 10:30 a.m. I'm not sure if "divine" is to make a theological point or if we're about to walk into something weird.

I take a deep breath and open the door for my wife. No one greets us. Everyone's sitting. The piano plays and people sing. Confused, I check the time: 10:23 a.m. *What the heck?* My impulse is retreat. I look at Candy. She offers no assurance. We slink in, slipping into an open spot in the last row. I nod at the man to my left and try to smile. He returns the courtesy but then looks away. The song ends — and nothing happens, absolutely nothing. For several minutes, we sit in awkward silence.

The sanctuary is compact, the smallest we've been in yet. With simple décor, a bit on the formal side, it contains no unusual elements. Only the deep-red carpet is dated. The five rows of padded pews will accommodate forty-two, and I count twenty-eight people. I'm grateful for seats in the back, as the only other space for two is in the front.

The pianist moves to the organ, looking as uncomfortable as I feel. He makes imperative facial gestures to a man in the front row. After a moment of confusion, the man walks behind the altar, retrieves communion utensils, and sets them out. It would have been easier for the organist to do this himself, yet he didn't.

A placard lists three hymns, and I look up the first. I'm not familiar with the song and notice it originates from the mid-1800s, as do the other two. Behind the altar is a wooden cross, not rugged, but finely finished. Smartly displayed in an artistic array, the cross is a pleasing focal point. A switch clicks, the cross illuminates, and everyone arises as the organist begins to play. Surely the real service is beginning. It must be 10:30.

Aside from being painfully slow, the odd timing of the song presents a challenge as we try without success to fit in the words. The entire congregation struggles, and I suspect the organist inserted a few wrong notes, though I'm not sure. The process is painful, but when we get to the second verse, a strong voice emerges to lead us. A man in a black suit behind the altar carries us through the remaining verses. Although no less challenging to sing along, his amplified voice nicely covers our indecision.

The song ends and the man in black reads from Zechariah, chapter two, verses 10 and 11. He prays and then grants us permission to sit. He shares an inspiring anecdote. I assume he's introducing the next song, but I soon realize he's begun the message.

He proclaims today as the first Sunday of Advent, something I didn't realize. He presents a series of thoughts, each one supported with a scripture verse and often a personal story or example, before looping back to the Zechariah text. His words are easy to hear and his presentation, given with ease. His slight accent is more endearing than distracting. He tells about emigrating from The Netherlands many years ago and pledging allegiance to the United States of America. "Will we pledge our allegiance to God?"

He punctuates the conclusion of his message with "Amen." The congregation repeats the word back to him with gusto. For an otherwise subdued group, this startles me.

As he prays, he folds his hands, interlaced fingers held close to his heart. Odd in appearance, I notice everyone has hands folded, some like him, across their chest, others at their waist. He concludes with "Amen." The congregation loudly echoes it back.

Holy Communion follows. All believers may partake. He blesses the elements and recites a bit of liturgy about the bread and wine. An usher releases us by row to go forward. "The body of Christ, broken for you," he says to each person, as he places the wafer in our cupped hands. The appropriate response is "Amen." I return to my seat, wondering how they will offer the cup. They don't. We only share the bread. Is this a point of doctrine or a practice of convenience? I feel cheated.

Some announcements follow before he dismisses us. Only then do people talk. Many introduce themselves, ask our names, and thank us for visiting. Up to this point, they'd been stoic, but now they're friendly. We talk at length with the minister and the organist, who also sports a black suit. We learn about their denomination, schedule, and plans for Advent.

I'm appreciative of worshiping with them today. I'm glad we went, despite a lack of communication and my urge to leave after our confusing arrival.

We worshiped God and proclaimed Jesus. It was good.

Takeaway for Everyone: When people walk into your church, are they embraced or ignored? Are they confused by what they find? Is their first impulse to leave?

Church #36:

❖

The Surprise

It takes longer to drive to church than we expect, arriving only four minutes early. With ten or so cars present, that's a good sign, but we walk inside to an empty lobby, hearing only an amplified speaker from another part of the building. With flashbacks to last week, I check the clock, confirming we're on time, a fact verified via email and their website.

We hang up our coats and head toward the sound. Down a hall is the sanctuary, with a smattering of people scattered throughout the large room. They sit, as a man behind the pulpit talks. Just like last week, we slink into a back row. Of the 162 padded chairs, they only use twenty. A young woman turns around, smiles broadly, and mouths "hello."

Sunday school must be running late, but if so, it's lasted ninety minutes. With no kids present, perhaps this is adult Sunday school. The speaker makes a few concluding remarks and asks everyone to stand. He acknowledges the presence of visitors and apologizes that there will be no church service today, just Sunday school. Their minister had an emergency, and they cancelled their service. He hopes we'll visit another time.

After a short prayer, the people leave. The young woman scoots up to introduce herself, a friend of our daughter from over a decade ago. Once she shares her name, I make the connection. She apologizes, profusely and repeatedly, for their cancelled service. With a starting time of 11:30, the latest of any so far, there's no chance to go elsewhere, so we linger to talk.

Our new friend shares her faith journey. God's work in her life is amazing. Her testimony encourages me. Perhaps we'll have church after all, unofficially so. She introduces her husband and mother-in-law, then later her brother-in-law and his wife. We learn about the church's history. Originally located twenty miles away, they moved to this building when it became available. Relocating such a distance wasn't an issue. None of their members lived near their old location. This new site is more centralized for their dispersed congregation and the building offers plenty of room for growth.

"Do you know what an apostolic church is?"

I hesitate. "We've been to several with that label, but they have little in common. It seems apostolic means different things to different people."

She nods.

Her husband speaks for the first time. "The basis for our church is Acts 2:28. Repent, be baptized in the name of Jesus, and you will receive the gift of the Holy Ghost."

I nod in agreement.

He pauses, and his wife continues. "As evidence of receiving the Holy Ghost, people will speak in tongues."

I sigh silently. At least I hope no one hears my inner groan. So far, we've visited three churches holding this position. This dismays me. I've read about this theology, once the dominant

Pentecostal view. Supposedly it's now largely replaced by a more inclusive understanding that being filled with the Holy Ghost may—but may not—result in speaking in tongues.

"If people don't speak in tongues," she continues, "then they haven't truly repented. They're holding something back."

Her words pain me. Though filled with the Holy Spirit, I lack the evidentiary gift of speaking in tongues. By her perspective, I'm unrepentant and not truly born again.

Even so, I'm ecstatic that she and her husband have Holy Spirit filling and am glad they have the spiritual gift of speaking in tongues. It's clear God's at work in their lives. At the same time, I'm sad they've turned their individual experiences into an exclusive theology. I nod to show I'm listening, but I no longer agree.

I keep quiet. Sharing my views would accomplish nothing and would show disrespect for their church. I'm a visitor. I have no right to come into their house and challenge their theology.

Having completed her discourse on doctrine, she shares the more tangible presence of God in her life, including working with youth—though we don't see any present, leading worship, performing clerical tasks, and preparing for next week's Christmas program. She smiles with joy as she speaks of her faith in action.

As we head for the door, she once again apologizes for there being no service and hopes a Sunday will open in our journey to return. I'm torn. I want to come back, but I know it would be at the expense of visiting another church on our list, not to mention all the rest that didn't make the cut.

Though a formal church service didn't occur, an informal fellowship did. We proclaimed Jesus, worshiped the Father, and celebrated the Holy Spirit—all without music or sermon. In this respect, today may be one of our best Sundays yet.

As we drive home, I ponder how today's surprise affects our plan to return to our home church on Easter, having visited fifty-two churches, not fifty-one.

"Every journey has surprises," my wise wife reminds me. "Today was one of them." She's so smart. Though we may return to visit them, it won't be part of this sojourn. "Although," she muses, with a smirk, "if they're so full of the Holy Spirit, you'd think he'd give one of them a message to share for their worship time."

"Yes, indeed."

Takeaway for Everyone: Do you need a minister to have church?

Church #37:

❖

Another Small Church

Having visited all the churches on our list to the west of where we live, the next five will be in the community to our southwest. For the first one, the church lacks curb appeal. The place looks abandoned. I sigh as I pull into their dirt parking lot. With only two other cars, today promises to be another tiny gathering.

The interior offers nothing to counter my gloomy assessment. A missing ceiling tile in the entryway reveals a giant cobweb moving at the whim of the wind that enters with us. Catching its motion in my periphery, I think something is falling, and I duck.

Going through a second door, we enter a small lobby. Before us is the sanctuary. French doors allow us to see a person at the pulpit speaking to a crowd of three. His amplified voice permeates the vestibule. Emanating from below is another amplified lecturer. From where we stand, they're equally loud, as if vying for our attention. I assume Sunday school is still in progress. Not knowing whether to enter or wait, we hang up our jackets with deliberate slowness. I'm tired of these awkward moments.

Another couple arrives. "What time is it?' Her question oozes irritation.

I don't need to check. I just did. "We're eight minutes early." My indirect response satisfies her. With an audible huff and barely breaking the stride of her determined shuffle, she pushes the glass doors open and plows inside, with her hubby in tow. We follow.

The room is nearly as wide as deep, but with its low ceiling I feel confined. Water-stained ceiling panels exemplify neglect. The padding on our pew is filthy, and despite wearing jeans, I'm hesitant to take a seat. Our bench shifts as we sit and even more so when we stand. Grabbing the pew in front of us isn't a wise idea either. Perhaps they're not bolted down, or maybe their moorings have decayed.

Up front is a piano and bass guitar. A rugged wooden cross, prominently centered, has a purple cloth draped over it and a white dove descending onto the crosspiece. The bird seems out of place until Candy reminds me we're at a charismatic church, so it must represent the Holy Spirit.

The speaker wraps up his words, with an instruction to "tell them we're about ready to start." Ten rows of pews accommodate 160 and eventually our numbers swell to twenty-one. There are fourteen adults—most older than us—and seven youngsters, ranging from early elementary to high school. During an informal greeting time, we shake many hands. All thank us for visiting, and a few invite us to return.

To begin the service, we stand, opening the hymnal to the announced page, but the words don't match what everyone else sings. We've never heard the song, so we can't participate. I'm frustrated, standing mute while others sing with abandon.

The accomplished pianist embellishes the music with more notes of her own to produce a fuller sound. Her peppy playing reminds me of ragtime. The bass player accentuates the rhythm. With enthusiasm, some clap, and it wouldn't surprise me to see someone slapping their thigh or stomping their foot. We've been transported to another time. Candy calls it a hoedown.

The minister announces a birthday, and we sing. It isn't the traditional birthday song but a different version. He doesn't need to ask who has a birthday. He already knows, just as you would for family. There's also an anniversary. We sing again, using the same tune with slightly different words.

The offering follows, and we sing again. They give no page number. Everyone knows the words—except us. Then members share prayer requests, and we stand as the pastor prays aloud—and several others do, too, all at the same time. Though Jesus can sort out their words, I can't, comprehending little of what anyone says.

We discover they have two hymnals, and we both grabbed the wrong one for the first number. When the pianist announces the next song, we know which book to use. For the rest of the songs they use an overhead projector to display the words—something I've not seen in years. One of the teens switches out the transparencies, a role he takes seriously. The congregation sings with fervor. Even the kids participate fully—with a few belting out parts of choruses, out of tune but full of gusto. This congregation likes to sing, and their pianist makes it fun.

With the singing over, we stand while the minister reads today's text, John 1:1. He launches into his message, reeling off various verses relating to Jesus and the salvation message. He uses the KJV. Today I'm struggling with this version more than usual. The words jumble. I'm confused. It might be how he's reading it, but more likely it's me. I'm having an off day.

The preacher's over-amplified speech reverberates through the sanctuary, especially when he raises his voice, making the emphasized portions of his message more akin to yelling. A buzz builds in my brain. Though headaches are rare, I sense one coming.

He shares two stories from his childhood and references a book, popular some four decades ago. His older audience follows intently but not the younger crowd. Many, especially the little ones, bound from seat to seat and occasionally leave, perhaps to get a drink or use the restroom.

He concludes with an altar call for "rededication" or to "receive Jesus." Three people come forward. The preacher goes over to each, placing his hand on their heads, perhaps offering a blessing or a prayer. As he attends to them, we sing a final song. A woman behind us praises God out loud. Though some words are English, others are not.

Afterward we learn the pianist — who is self-taught and plays by ear — is the pastor's wife. Six of their ten grandchildren are present, making up all but one of the younger crowd. We talk with two people I've served at the food pantry. A couple of others share their stories of coming to this church and how much it means to them.

This church is a close, spiritual family.

Takeaway for Everyone: Look at your building with a critical eye. Fix it, clean it, and update it as needed. Make the church building inviting, not repelling.

Church #38:

❖

A Refreshing Time

Today's the fourth Sunday of Advent, two days before Christmas. Candy complains that for the last three Sundays we sang not a single Christmas song and heard only brief mentions of Jesus's birth. Today we expect different. Today we anticipate a reminder about the *why* of Christmas.

We originally planned this church for next week. Then we learned the pastor would be on vacation. We swapped the next two churches, so we could hear him today. I'm glad we did.

We visited them once before, shortly after their launch, about five years ago. Their worship leader used to attend our current church, and their pastor was from our prior one. He and I meet periodically to hang out and talk about what it means to follow Jesus. Because of these connections, I consider skipping this church, but it seems important not to.

They meet in the all-purpose room of the local middle school, the third church we've visited to do so. Large portable church signs sit at the entrance to the campus and another one guides us to the appropriate parking lot. Once inside we meet my two friends, both passionate Jesus-loving guys.

People mill about: talking, sipping coffee, or munching snacks. Only a few sit. Someone realizes they need more chairs, which they set up as we enter. The people represent all age groups, with many kids. The common garb is jeans. I fit in, but with my button-down shirt, many wear more casual attire. This is a first.

A team of four—guitar, bass, drums, and vocals—leads us in worship. The audio is optimally adjusted. The ideal sound tech is the one you're unaware of—it's only because of mistakes that anyone notices. This one is good. I used to be a sound guy and appreciate excellent work. When I turn to check, I see another friend at the controls.

As a special treat, three ladies from a local ballet company worship with us in dance. Ballet and guitars strike me as an odd pairing, but the result is a worshipful encounter. Without prompting, a few young girls come forward to join them. Although the dancers must now move with extra care, it warms me to see the prepared professionals and the inspired laity worshiping God together through movement. I can't give them full attention and sing, too, so I worship God by admiring the beauty of their movement instead of through the movement of my mouth. I think I chose right. Though many would disagree, dance belongs in church. It adds depth to our praise of God.

A brief pre-message by one of the members covers the Christmas story from Luke 2. Then we sing "Silent Night," and the kids leave for their own activities. Their exodus cuts our numbers in half, with about fifty people remaining.

For the past several weeks, we've seen traditionally-dressed ministers give traditional-sounding sermons. I desire something fresh. Today's pastor and his message provide a much-appreciated alternative. He doesn't stand on the stage or behind a pulpit, but remains on our level, using a simple music stand. His style, accessible and calm, seems more suited for a hip, suburban church than a rural assembly.

"Isn't the story of Jesus's birth absurd?" This isn't a rhetorical device or a rational denial, but a challenge to deeply consider all the Bible offers and the ramifications of its narrative. Instead of focusing on the familiar and skipping the confusing, he digs into the Bible's perplexing passages—and encourages us to do the same. He says that when a segment of scripture doesn't make sense, it signals he's using the wrong perspective. His goal is to adjust his viewpoint until clarity emerges.

As he speaks, he occasionally pauses to control the passion that creeps into his voice and threatens to flow from his eyes. God's immense love overcomes him, forcing him to pause before he can resume. This man adores the Almighty.

At the touch of his iPad, he displays the verses on the screen stationed to his right. Most in attendance expect this and don't have their Bibles. Only visitors brought theirs. Today he reminds us of the Christmas story, not in the traditional way but in the manner our hearts craved. The kingdom of God starts now, today. He encourages us to ask tough questions about the Bible and God, inviting us to journey together toward Jesus.

The worship team returns for the closing number. It's a joyous time, with our leader giving us the freedom to dance—and the freedom not to. I don't have a danceable bone in my body, so I appreciate the permission to stay still, yet I'm disappointed when only a couple of people accept his offer. This time I know the song well, so I can sing along *and* watch the celebration unfold as we sing "Go tell it on the Mountain."

Afterward we stay to talk, as do most people. In addition to friends who go to this church, we know several visitors as well. We reconnect with them all, talking about family and faith.

God provided what I desired today. He refreshed my soul.

Takeaway for Everyone: Embrace physical forms of worship, allowing people to participate or just watch.

Church #39:

A Great Way to End the Year

Today we'll attend our final church service of the year. With it falling between Christmas and New Year's Day, I expect a light attendance due to folks traveling or just taking the day off. It's another Baptist church and I need to guard against a been-there-done-that complacency. Our pre-departure prayer reflects that.

With a mild winter, today's trek to church is the first of the season where the roads aren't clear. I didn't anticipate that. While conditions don't pose a problem, I drive with care, wishing I'd allowed more time. We pass Church #37 ("Another Small Church"), turn the corner, and drive a few more blocks. We find the building easily, stationed at the intersection of two of this small village's better-known streets. The corner parking lot is half-full, with enough cars to confirm a healthy attendance. Most have fresh snow on them, so I suspect their drivers came an hour ago for Sunday school.

Inside, friendly faces and hearty handshakes greet us. Even after visiting thirty-eight churches, I still feel a foreboding each week, with sweating palms, a racing heart, and a grumbling gut. Today my apprehension subsides quickly. People receive us as first-timers, acknowledging that fact but without fawning over us.

We ascend a short flight of stairs and enter the sanctuary. I'm awestruck. Candy is likewise impressed. The edifice, though neither new nor grand, possesses a simple elegance. It feels right. The building must be sixty years old, but the floor plan belies its age. The sanctuary is square, about forty-five by forty-five feet. The focal point is the opposite corner, with a typical pulpit centered on a platform. Three stained-glass windows serve as a backdrop, with a cross hoisted overhead. The walls on either side each boast four larger stained-glass windows. Although the morning sun shines on the opposite side of the building, ample light makes its way inside to produce a warm feel.

The pew arrangement further belies its age. Stationed in four sections, each one is angled toward the front. This gives everyone a straight-ahead view. Though this isn't unique for contemporary designs, I suspect it was quite progressive for a church built in the mid-nineteen hundreds.

We slide into the fifth row, which is also the back row. Though I applaud the design of the building, I'm dismayed over the pews' lack of comfort. Padded cushions strewn on the seats offer a welcome solace, but they lack the reinforcement my back craves. I consider sliding a hymnal behind the small of my back for some lumbar support.

The sanctuary seats about ninety, with two balconies, one seating perhaps twenty more and the other closed off, repurposed for a different function. I count fifty-five people, but with a few late arrivals, our numbers eventually surpass sixty.

A piano flanks the left of the stage, with an organ to the right. Today we use the piano and sing from the hymnal. After the first song, the minister gives an opening prayer, reads Mark 12:28–34, and shares announcements. Two families are away for the holidays and several members are absent due to the flu, with a few hospitalized. Had everyone showed up, it'd be packed. In case the facility contributed to spreading the sickness, volunteers disinfected it during the week and set out hand sanitizers.

In a first for us, the congregation recites their "memory verse" in unison, Romans 5:8 as rendered in the KJV. The pastor then challenges them to recall their prior memory verse, which he leads them in saying.

We launch into the next song. After two verses, we pause to greet one another. The minister grants us permission to avoid shaking hands, but everyone does anyway. During this extended time, we meet most of the adults. As the greeting winds down, the aroma of hand sanitizer fills the room. We conclude the greeting time by singing the last two verses of the song. Next is a prayer and offering, followed by another song, when the children leave for junior church.

Teaching from Matthew 9:14–17, the pastor pulls out a series of insights from the four verses, but he frequently returns to his theme of loving God more in the coming year. Presented with simple clarity, I'm struck by its profound meaning. Being intent on loving God more next year surpasses every New Year's resolution and trumps any annual goal. I appreciate his future-focused thinking. What a fitting way to transition into the next year. He concludes by challenging us to make a pledge: "God, I will love you more in the new year." *May I do so.*

After a closing prayer and final song, the service ends. Many people again thank us for visiting and invite us back. There's talk of going to a restaurant afterward. One man asks us to fill out a visitor card, which I hand to Candy. When she returns it, he gives us a personal invite to join them at Arby's. He carries a folder stuffed with coupons and tries enticing us with the deals.

I desire to head home, but my wife wants to go. Though I don't need much of a nudge, I do need her encouragement to join them. As we drive to the restaurant, I consider our impact on the staff there, with a bunch of "churchgoing folk," arriving en masse, possessing a conspired coupon strategy to get the most food for the least money. Candy fails to comprehend my concern, so I drop it.

About twenty-five of us show up. We'll sit together as a group. Candy and I are among the first, selecting a booth, but no one joins us. There's some general discussion between tables, and our host — the coupon guy — interacts with us a bit, but we feel alone within the crowd. It would have been an awkward affair, if not for one of the ladies sliding into our booth midway through the meal. Her interaction with us turns an uncomfortable situation into an enjoyable time.

It only takes one person to make the difference between a visitor feeling accepted or ignored. When we return to our home church, may I be that person.

Takeaway for Everyone: It should be everyone's job to embrace visitors, helping them feel welcomed and accepted. Don't expect someone else to do this important job.

Church #40:

❖

No Time to Return

Our destination is a church we've heard of often but know little about, a local Mennonite congregation, part of the Fellowship of Evangelical Churches. Our impressions are favorable, suggesting a thriving, dynamic congregation. On our drive we pass our destinations of the past two Sundays, recalling fond memories.

We find the location easily. It's a striking structure. With a small parking lot in front and another in back, we choose the closer one. Only after getting out of our car do I see the "offices" sign by the lone visible entrance. Another sign marked "sanctuary" points around the building. With no sidewalk to guide the way and an icy parking lot, I decide it's better to wander around inside than out.

I ask a young couple if the office entrance will get us to the sanctuary. They assure us it will. Then Candy recognizes the young man—and he, her. He went to school with our kids, and she greets him by name.

The office entrance is only a few feet from the back of the sanctuary. Along the way, the young man introduces us to his wife, and they invite us to sit with them. Only once before has someone offered this kind gesture. Though we prefer to sit by ourselves—it's easier to meet new people that way—we gladly accept his visitor-friendly outreach.

The contemporary room is impressive in size and most inviting. It likely seats three or four hundred, and I estimate two hundred people present. A quiet buzz of pre-church conversation heightens my anticipation. The praise team makes their way forward. There are two on guitar, a bassist, drummer, pianist, and flutist. Two vocalists round out the ensemble of eight. With a light pop sound, we sing three contemporary choruses to begin the service. A sign language interpreter signs throughout the morning. During a lengthy set of announcements, I peruse the bulletin, noticing events scheduled every weekday.

Skipping the sometimes awkward, sometimes engaging, greeting time, they pass a friendship pad for everyone to sign. It contains a visitor card, which Candy completes, but she doesn't know what to do with it. One common option is dropping it in the offering plate, but Candy slides it back in the friendship pad. After the collection, the minister offers "the right hand of fellowship"[134] to six new members. Following another song set, the children leave for their own activities.

The message is on *vision*. Foremost in their church vision is prayer. "There is power in prayer," states the preacher. "Prayer should be our default inclination." This is the start of a new series, which matches the start of a new year. We'll look at the book of Acts to see how the early church functioned. The minister says prayer occurs more in the book of Acts than any other book in the Bible. I make a note to investigate this further.[135]

He presents a three-point sermon, a format I'm familiar with

---

134 See Galatians 2:9.

135 In the NIV, Psalms and Acts both mention "pray" 34 times, to lead all other books. Psalms mentions "prayer" 29 times to lead the Bible. 2 Chronicles is second at thirteen, with Acts coming in at eleven.

but which we've not seen much during our sojourn. Although predictable to the point of tedium, three-point sermons are easy to follow and great for notetaking. Plus, in the event of distraction, they're easier to plug back into. I wonder if three-point sermons are old school, giving way to a narrative style. If so, I might be a bit old school and don't like the implication.

"The secret of the early church," he notes, "is their prayer meetings." They utterly depended on God, and we don't often pray as they did. He reels off a list of contrasts, showing what prayer often looks like, compared to what it could be. The difference is convicting.

The service concludes with a final song. Several people come up to talk. I get brave and ask one man a question I've pondered most of the service. "Is this a typical Mennonite congregation?" It certainly wasn't what I expected.

Surprised, he considers his answer. "You know, I'm not really sure." He shrugs, pauses some more, and then explains. "This is the only one I've ever been to."

I nod but am no closer to my answer.

"It kind of feels like a Baptist church," he adds with a smile, giving a hopeful look that he provided useful information.

"Yeah, I think you're right." We've now put an effective label on this church, but I'm no closer to knowing if we had a typical Mennonite church experience today.

Our seatmates offer us a tour of the facility. We first visit the welcome area. Had we parked in back, this would have been our entry point. Next is the library and then the gym, flanked with classrooms. We turn the corner to more classrooms, making our way to the original sanctuary. Tiny in comparison, this room is now the domain of the youth, who put their unique stamp on it. Last is a corridor with the church offices, which leads us back to the sanctuary.

Along the way, we run into people who want to talk, delaying our tour. At different points, three people ask us if we go to church there. The congregation is big enough for them to not know who's a visitor. We end by chatting briefly with the pastor. I want to compliment him on his message, but I fear my genuine effort would come across as requisite small talk, void of sincerity.

We thank our tour guides for their kindness. Another friend, an elder, invites us back. Part of me wants to accept. This church would be comfortable to slip into. I subtly shake my head, sharing about our journey, with the intention to return to our home church at its conclusion. Our schedule doesn't allow us to come back next week.

Two hours after we arrive, we head to our car, thankful for the new acquaintances we made, the past friends we reconnected with, an engaging time, and a message to contemplate. Though I doubt we witnessed a typical Mennonite church service, it was a good one.

Takeaway for Everyone: Offering visitors a tour of the facility is a smart way to help them feel comfortable and accepted.

Church #41:

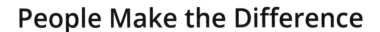

People Make the Difference

"Hi, are you the DeHaans?" The usher's question surprises me.

"Yes, we are." I nod, likely with confusion showing on my face. But I appreciate his directness. It's nice to be known.

"I'm Greg." He looks at Candy. "I answered your email."

I nod again, this time with a smile. "Thank you so much, Greg. It's nice to meet you." Either he took time to Google Candy's picture or he assumed the new people matched the name in the email. Regardless, the extra effort honors us. He starts to hand us each a bulletin, but we already have them, courtesy of the greeter by the front door. We exchange quick pleasantries and then head into the sanctuary. With few people milling about and most sitting, we do the same.

Today we're at the last of the five churches in this small community southwest of our home. They're on the main road connecting this village with the one to its north.

The building is newer and doesn't look like a typical church. The sanctuary is elegant in an understated way, possessing elements of grandeur without being ostentatious. It's open and inviting, with a comfortable feel. We sit in padded chairs, not pews. Able to accommodate about 135, the attendance approaches two-thirds of that number. Though there are a few young families, the crowd is older and heavily skewed toward women. I see only two teens and count about a dozen small kids who come up for the children's message. Most came with their grandparents.

The minister has a pleasant countenance; his smile, inviting. During the message we learn he retired after forty-five years of ministry—and has been at this church eighteen months. I wonder if he unretired, works part-time, or volunteers. Their size and giving suggests being able to support a full-time minister, so I'm perplexed.

The flu season is in full swing, and we're officially in an epidemic. Mindful of this, I wish to minimize physical contact. Before the greeting time, the minister gives us permission to avoid hugs and handshakes. Instead, he suggests an "elbow bump." I test this on my wife. She's not amused and makes a snide remark. Though a few people follow our leader's suggestion, most opt for a handshake, with some hugging, a few despite protests from the recipients.

The service leans toward formality but in a casual way. We sing hymns with organ accompaniment. They have two hymnals, which most people use, but they also display words on a screen, which Candy and I use. Brief bits of liturgy occur throughout the service. The words, printed in their oversized bulletins, also appear overhead.

A choir of ten sings an upbeat song to spirited piano music. At eighty percent female, the ladies take the lead, but the two guys hold their own when it's their turn on the second verse. The words lack spiritual significance, but the congregation applauds with gusto. Since the words lack a godly tone, I assume the applause is for the performers and not their creator.

The sermon, "The Chosen One," uses the text in Luke 3:15–17, 21–22.[136] The minister talks about Jesus's baptism, which God used to confirm his Son's ministry, as well as the call of others into their ministry, including his own. To punctuate his message, he shares a couple of memorable anecdotes. He concludes with a blessing.

We head to the fellowship hall for refreshments. Though no one invites us to join them, the bulletin does. We pick up a beverage and some treats. Then we look for a place to sit. Many of the tables are full, with the rest hosting people engaged in intense conversations. Rather than interrupt, I pick an empty table. I'm curious if anyone will join us.

Candy and I talk quietly as we munch our snacks and people watch. Amused, she points out I picked the only table with a red tablecloth, whereas all the others have red and white checkered coverings. Did I inadvertently sit at one reserved for some special function? Given its position, had this been a banquet, we could be at the head table. If I've committed some faux pas in our seat selection, there's no point in calling further attention to ourselves by moving, so we remain seated.

After a few minutes, a woman asks if she can join us. We gladly accept, enjoying an exciting conversation as we share our faith journeys. Our talk warms my heart. She readily understands our sojourn, and we discuss the vast variations we've seen on our trek.

Just as with our after-church fellowship experience two weeks ago, one person made the difference between us feeling

---

136 This is one of the texts from the Revised Common Lectionary for this Sunday.

welcomed and ignored. Today marks another memorable morning at church.

Takeaway for Everyone: A church community should be about people connecting with people.

Church #42:

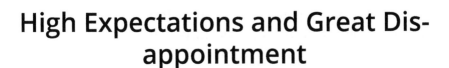

High Expectations and Great Dis-appointment

For this Sunday and the next two, we'll visit the remaining churches located in our local school district. Today's destination is on the east edge of the school system's large territory. The church has two services and we head to the second. A winter storm swept in overnight. Though the roads aren't hazardous, they could be slippery, so we allow for extra travel time.

The drive goes quicker than I anticipate. We arrive fourteen minutes early and take our time heading inside. Sunday school is wrapping up, and people migrate to the sanctuary. Despite being in a throng, no one acknowledges our presence. We're invisible. Do they even care about visitors, or are they too big to notice? Aside from a greeter by the front door who hands us a bulletin and an usher who gives us sermon notes, no one else talks to us, so we sit down and wait in silence.

I've wanted to visit this church for a long time. I've heard a great deal about the minister. He's been here thirty years and is on the radio. When the church of my youth went through a difficult stretch, some in our congregation started attending this one and others visited on occasion. All spoke highly of it. Even though that was decades ago, I expect to see people today who I knew then, but I don't.

The sanctuary, utilitarian and simple in design, seats about 250 and is slightly over half-full. Some of the older men wear suits, but the majority dress casually. Most people are our age or older—which may account for the eleven handicapped spots in the parking lot. There are a few younger families, only a couple of youth, and no kids. I wonder if their first service matches this demographic or if it's a younger crowd.

The service begins with a greeting from the pulpit and then singing a hymn to organ accompaniment. The song leader keeps time with the cadenced movement of his arms. The old English words distract me. Have I overlooked them in the past when we've sung hymns, or are today's selections more laden with antiquated lyrics?

The service proceeds with an awkward rhythm, with a song— or even a couple verses—interspersed with other activities: announcements, greeting time, offering, prayer, and special music. The transitions occur abruptly, as if they're behind schedule and racing to catch up.

Though I can't identify it, something's disconcerting. Candy easily puts words to it. "It's as though we've gone back in time, back into our own past." She's right. The service is a copy of a church we attended thirty-five years ago. Then it was exciting. Now it's tired. For all my anticipation, I'm painfully disappointed.

The message is part of a continuing series. Today's text is 2 Corinthians 9:6–15, about giving. The minister's delivery is smooth, albeit quick. After a few minutes, I hear the synchronized turning of pages. Everyone is following along in the notes we received when we arrived. Numbered pages 140 to 146, with three holes punched on the left, I suspect they can go into a binder to produce a book-length treatise on Paul's second letter to the Corinthians. The minister is indeed reading his message, periodically inserting anecdotes and illustrations into his written text.

I begin following along. It's disconcerting to watch him. Each time he glances up, he looks to his left, gazing above the people. Then he moves his head to his right—and upward. I become so convinced he's looking at something above me that I'm compelled to turn around to look—twice. Of course, there's nothing there. Then he returns to his notes. I don't think he ever looks directly at us.

Doctrine is important to them, perhaps ultimately so. We learn this from the opening prayer, and the message confirms it. From the lens of a traditional church perspective, the teaching is grounded in scripture, but he makes assumptions that aren't in the text. Delivered with dogmatic passion, at times I feel he's yelling at us.

His teaching veers close to a prosperity gospel, though he assures us it's not. He draws faint lines of demarcation between that theology and his own. Multiple times, he decries "heretical charismatic ministers." Though he might be referring to specific charismatic ministers who teach heresy, from his tone and context I infer he thinks all charismatic ministers are heretics. It's human nature to vilify what we don't understand.

Toward the end of his message he says, "There's a connection between giving and redemption." I write it down. I'll contemplate it later. Perhaps this is my take home thought.

He concludes with instructions of what to pray to receive Jesus, though he gives no altar call. We sing a final song, and the service ends. One couple introduces themselves, the only ones to do so. It's hard to feel welcomed and make connections at larger churches. There's no social time afterward — it occurred between services.

We shake hands with the minister. I wish him a great vacation, something he mentioned from the pulpit. He's pleased at my thoughtfulness. As we exit, I notice building plans on the wall. I'm not sure if it's for an addition or a new facility, but regardless, they have a vision for expansion.

When we pull out of the parking lot, I notice the couple who took time to introduce themselves. We wave at each other and smile. What a nice parting memory.

Takeaway for Everyone: What once was successful may now hold a church back. Continually tweak what you do to remain relevant.

Church #43:

❖

A Welcoming Church with Much to Offer

"Hi, I'm Jim. You don't have nametags." He isn't being critical, just desiring to help. "Didn't they give you nametags, or do you want to remain anonymous?" He smiles, allowing us to accept or decline his offer.

"Hi, Jim. I'm Peter, and this is my wife Candy." We shake hands, and Jim glances behind him at a bulletin board holding nametags of the regulars. Nearby are two greeters. "Sure, nametags would be fine."

Jim grins. "They must've been shirking their duty."

"We talked with them when we came in. I guess they just missed the nametag part."

Jim reintroduces us to the greeters. Embarrassed at their oversight, they quickly make our nametags as they welcome us again. With excitement, Jim tells us that in a couple of weeks their new minister—a twenty-something, recent seminary grad—will join them for her first service as their new shepherd. Jim's not the only one to share this news—before we leave, several more will too. There's a collective anticipation over her arrival and the fresh energy her youthfulness will pump into this older, yet energetic, congregation.

Located in a building with shared tenant space, they're just down the street from last week's church. It's an inviting location, easily accessible with nearby parking. The cramped entryway, with office space on our right and a kitchenette to the left, gives way to an open sanctuary. The thirty-six by thirty-foot room, simple in its décor, possesses a tasteful elegance, with two-tone walls and an open feel. About a hundred padded chairs—we'll use half of them today—fan out in concentric semi-circles, facing the communion table centered along one wall. The speaker's podium stands to the right. Next to the podium is an electronic keyboard, around which the eight-member choir will gather. Behind the communion table are four contemporary art canvases, sized and positioned so their shared borders reveal a cross. On the adjacent wall hang a couple dozen crosses of various sizes and designs, ranging from simple to ornate.

With not much room to mingle, we sit down, as do most people. But rather than let us sit in awkward silence, several people come over to greet us. This is not a rote welcome, as we too often witness, but a genuine expression of appreciation for visiting and a sincere invitation to come back.

By now in our sojourn, we've identified two key elements that make us feel truly welcomed at the churches we visit. The first is sharing names: people offering theirs and asking ours. Even when people forget names, as is often the case, we appreciate the gesture. It adds a meaningful touch to our interaction. The second element is the effort to make a connection. Any query or comment works, provided it doesn't become an interrogation. Another requirement is a graceful exit before an uncomfortable silence descends. Most people who try to connect with us today, do so well.

At some churches people don't even make eye contact when they shake hands because they're already seeking their next target. This pattern tends to exist on a church-wide basis, with most members either sharing names and taking time to connect or alternately offering mechanical welcomes in rapid succession.

This church welcomes us well: before the service, after the service, and during the official greeting time within the service. They excel at this and are among the best we've seen.

As we expect, the service is liturgical, with much of the needed information printed in their multipage bulletin. Right from the start, I get my pages out of order, fumbling to find my place at each transition. After the service, I joke about my liturgical ineptitude with an elderly man. His response is serious, "We really *have* to get a projector and display the words on the screen. I've wanted this for years." The man must be in his late seventies and his progressive, forward thinking inspires me.

Except for the prayer and message, the members handle the service. I appreciate that. For the minister's part, her peaceful demeanor draws me in. She exudes calm while avoiding any hint of that disingenuous sugary sweetness of someone trying too hard to be nice. I see Jesus in her.

Concepts from her concise teaching resonate with me: priesthood of believers, called to a covenant community, healing connected with forgiveness, and Jesus's request to "follow me" as an invitation into community. She says the typical American consumer mentality toward church prohibits community from occurring. Her insight embraces me. After the service, another person expands on this theme.

A couple of people invite us to stay for coffee and cookies. We accept, but we end up talking to so many people for so long, that they're cleaning up by the time we leave the sanctuary. That's okay. Conversation is more important. We didn't need food to facilitate interaction.

Lastly, we talk to the minister. Her public conduct matches her personal character. She possesses no pretense. Though not my intention, we talk at length. Her passions for church and community and God match my own. My soul connects with hers. When I reveal our journey, she readily comprehends, offering encouragement. She and her husband co-pastor a nearby church of the same denomination. Perhaps we might want to include them in our schedule. She also invites us back to this church in a few weeks to meet their new minister. Though our schedule to visit fifty-two churches won't allow us to consider either, in the future I hope to do both.

Takeaway for Everyone: There are three opportunities to interact with visitors: before the service, during the service, and after the service. Pursue all three with diligence.

Church #44:

❖

A Familiar Place

We discuss whether we should visit today's church. We used to attend there, some fifteen years ago. Although they have a different pastor now, we know several people, some from our prior involvement and others we met at school or the food pantry. They're also from the same denomination as our home church, and I expect a service that's not too different from ours. This won't be a visit as much as a reunion.

We delay our arrival a couple of weeks, as their pastor was out of the country, serving as a military chaplain. Today is his first Sunday back after a three-month deployment.

With snow-covered roads, our trek takes longer than expected, and though we still arrive in plenty of time, it's not as early as I wish. This building is twenty-five years old and maintained nicely. People mill about. Friends notice us, and we chat. Others, surprised at our presence, do a double take, saying "Hi" or waving as they walk by. A surge of music from the sanctuary alerts us to sit down. By then, most already have. We abruptly end our conversation and scurry to find seats. As the last to do so, our entrance is more visible than I prefer.

Seating about 250, the sanctuary is slightly over half-full. Padded chairs, new and comfortable, reside in three sections, with the outer two angled toward the front. A worship team of nine leads us: their leader on keyboard, a drummer, lead guitar, bass guitar, and baritone sax. Four vocalists, two men and two women, round out the group. They have a full sound, upbeat and energetic, yet most of the congregation stands stoic. Occasionally, an arm rises in praise, but such movements are rare.

With a utilitarian design and smartly furnished, they make wise use of their space. An array of three crosses serve as a backdrop to the stage, with a screen to the right displaying lyrics and, later, scripture verses.

Inserted into the five-song opening set are announcements and a greeting time. Since we slid in as the service began, we've not interacted with anyone around us. Now is our chance. We know no one in our vicinity, and no one knows us. For the greeting time, they see us as unknown visitors. All smile and are friendly as we shake hands, but no one shares their name or asks ours, a gesture I've realized is important—at least for me. Music resumes, ending our interaction. We sing some more and then move into the message.

Today begins a series on the Apostles' Creed, a concise statement of Christian belief, emanating from the fourth or fifth century. I'm quite familiar with this creed, having recited it often in church over the years. But I wonder when I've *last* recited it. Has it been in the past forty-four weeks? I'm not sure.[137] We've said the Nicene Creed twice (Churches #17 and 18). It's a longer faith statement that is as unfamiliar to me as the Apostles' Creed is familiar. To introduce the topic, they play a recording of "Creed" by Rich Mullins. Then they display the lyrics and encourage us to sing along.

---

137 According to my notes, we recited the Apostles' Creed at Church #5 (Catholics are Christians Too), though I may have failed to note more recent occurrences.

Afterward, the pastor steps forward. Without a pulpit, he uses a tall table with two chairs, giving a coffee shop vibe. I didn't notice this before, instead looking past it at the worship team. But now it becomes the focal point on the platform. Walking up with a cup of tea, the minister sits in one of the chairs to begin his message. He introduces today's topic and then gives a dramatic pause while taking a sip of tea.

The table only serves as a temporary resting spot, as he leisurely moves about the platform, engaging in casual conversation with the congregation. He talks about belief, quoting from a diverse group: Audrey Hepburn, Martin Luther King, Anne Frank, John Lennon, and Billy Sunday. Next, he relates what the Bible says about the subject. Then he asks two key questions: "What do you believe?" (The easier part.) And, "How are you living it out?" (The harder part.)

Midway through the sermon, I catch a whiff of popcorn. I whisper this to Candy, who starts to give me a "you're crazy" look, but then she smells it too. As a huge fan of this mouth-watering treat, the scent preoccupies me.

We end the message by reciting the Apostles' Creed in unison and then the worship team concludes the service, leading us in a final song. A message on the screen invites us to stay for coffee and cookies.

Stationed at one of the two doors between the sanctuary and the narthex, the minister shakes hands with each person and talks with them at length. He's good at this, but the line moves slowly, perhaps more so today, since this is his first Sunday here in three months.

He's aware of our journey, and after discussing it a bit, we make our way toward the cookie table. Our neighbor made today's goodies. I've enjoyed her cookies many times and anticipate another taste today. My taste buds tingle in expectation. Alas, we never make it to the cookies, as past friends come up to reconnect. Though they keep us quite occupied, I'm still able to meet a few new people. As the crowd dwindles, we continue in conversation, being among the last to leave — but not before snagging some leftover popcorn.

Today, we returned to a familiar place, enjoyed the company of long-ago friends, and heard a message worthy of contemplation.

Takeaway for Members: The goal in greeting people is not the quantity of interactions, but the quality: smile, make eye contact, and share your name. Then be open for conversation.

---❖---

Part Three Perspective

The churches are starting to blur. Every week seems the same, offering only slight variations on a theme. I'm growing weary of our journey. I've realized this for a few weeks but didn't want to admit it. Yes, I still notice kindnesses offered and innovations presented at the various branches of Jesus's church. But I worry that I notice more the actions that discourage me and disparage the reputation of my savior. Have I become cynical? Am I truly able to see what God wants me to see? My prayers before we leave for church lack freshness. Have they become vain repetition?[138] My anticipation for the service is no longer as expectant, yet God prevails and teaches me anyway.

For the first half of our journey, I picked our destinations solely by the driving distance from our home. But heading in different directions each Sunday became disconcerting, making it challenging to synthesize an understanding of congregations within communities. In retrospect, I should have divided our fifty-two churches into four groups: those within our local school district, those in the village to our west, those in the village to the southwest of us, and those on the western edge of the city to our east.

---

138 Matthew 6:7 in the KJV says, "But when ye pray, use not vain repetitions, as the heathen do: for they think that they shall be heard for their much speaking."

For the third part of our adventure we focused on the first three of these geographic areas, while remaining within ten miles of our house. This allowed us to better comprehend the churches within their local context.

The village to our west has twenty-one churches. We visited twelve in the first half of our journey, calling on the remaining nine for this phase (Churches #27–36). Together they comprise a wide-ranging group, offering an array of options.

Next, we turned our attention to the village to our southwest, with its five churches (#37–41). Although one was struggling, the other four weren't. They were vibrant and growing, each with its unique appeal and offering a different approach to worshiping God.

To conclude this phase of our sojourn, we visited the remaining three churches in our local school district (Churches #42–44). They're all on the district's eastern side. Churches #1 through 6 are in the school district and Church #7 ("The New Church") relocated here since we visited them.[139] This puts the total at ten.

These ten churches are noteworthy because our local food pantry serves people living in the school district. Sometimes pantry clients ask me about area churches. Now that I've visited all ten, I can share firsthand information, directing people to the one that best meets their needs and preferences.

Some of our clients attend church outside of the area, and I've seen them at several of the gatherings we've visited. I have

---

139 Our local school district covers our local village, so Churches #1 through 5, along with 7, are in the village and in the school district. Churches #6, 42, 43, and 44 are inside the school district but outside the village.

mixed feelings about this. Part of me wishes each congregation would care for the needs of their own, while the other part of me would decry each church replicating the same program. Having an area food pantry is not only practical, but it's also a great community service, with five of the district's ten churches involved in a truly ecumenical outreach.

* * *

At the halfway point in our journey, I noted the importance of community, with some churches excelling at it, a few failing, and most falling somewhere in between. The prelude to community is greeting. Churches that greet well, embrace visitors and foster connections.

Liturgical churches, I observed, struggle with greeting and fail at community. Fortunately, this isn't an absolute principle, merely a tendency. Church #43 ("A Welcoming Church with Much to Offer) and Church #32 ("Commitment Sunday and Celebration") proved liturgical churches can greet well and foster meaningful community. Church #43 excelled at this, perhaps even more so than the non-liturgical Church #22 ("A Caring Community"). Two other non-liturgical churches that greeted well were Church #38 ("A Refreshing Time") and Church #41 ("People Make the Difference").

I'd like to revisit them all, simply because of the amazing way they greeted, welcoming us into their community. We made connections. We had relevant conversations. We shared a spiritual camaraderie.

There are three opportunities to greet visitors: before, during, and after the service. Churches need to master all three. Few do, but Church #43 (A Welcoming Church with Much to Offer) did.

Two churches ignored us beforehand and had no greeting time during the service, but they did embrace us afterward: Church #28 ("Intriguing and Liturgical") and Church #35 ("A Well-Kept Secret"). But it's hard to overcome a bad first impression. While Church #28 did, enough so that I want to return, Church #35 didn't.

The opposite error is not ending well. Church #27 ("A Charismatic Experience") ignored us afterward. With no one who approached us and no one available for us to approach, we had two choices: stand there and look pathetic or leave. We left.

Then, one church, a non-liturgical one, failed at all three opportunities: they ignored us. This was Church #31 ("A Day of Contrasts"). It was as if we were invisible. Though their service was most impressive, their cold demeanor isolated us, effectively pushing us out the door as soon as the service ended. Yes, they did have two assigned greeters at the front door, but the personable pair couldn't overcome the 150 indifferent people inside.

Yes, greeting well is important. Without it, visitors cannot hope to find community. So why would they want to come back?

* * *

Overall, our time at charismatic gatherings continue to disappoint. While Church #27 ("A Charismatic Experience") came close to providing a true charismatic encounter — or at least my perception of one — they also had some disconcerting shortcomings, including a rambling message and not being friendly.

The narrow doctrine at Church #34 ("Acts Chapter Two") and Church #36 ("The Surprise") especially dismayed me.

Like Church #14 ("The Pentecostal Perspective"), they placed an unbiblical emphasis on speaking in tongues, viewing it as a requirement to signify true salvation.

Church #42 ("High Expectations and Great Disappointment") went to the opposite extreme, dismissing charismatic followers of Jesus as heretics and doing so with a most dogmatic fervor. The way these otherwise well-meaning clergy divide Jesus's church grieves me. This error, of rejecting other Christians because they fail to meet some personally held opinion, is perhaps the biggest shortcoming we've seen at any of the churches. I wonder if they've lost their first love,[140] if they truly comprehend what it means to follow Jesus. Seriously, I do.

Conversely, Church #29 ("Led by Laity") greatly encouraged me; they conducted their entire service without any clergy. I wish more churches would follow their example. I beg churches to do so. Through Jesus we are all priests. We shouldn't need ministers to do for us what we're supposed to do ourselves.[141]

As I consider Church #37 ("Another Small Church"), sometimes a church just needs to close. This church has more people on the outside trying to save it, than there are local people who attend. Yes, God can do the impossible, but without a clear instruction from him to persevere, the wise action, the prudent option, is to simply shut down and stop wasting resources on an unpromising situation. Interestingly, there was once local interest for this church to merge with another, but their respective denominations wouldn't permit it. Their de-

---

140 Consider John's stinging rebuke in Revelation 2:4-5 against the Church in Ephesus: "Yet I hold this against you: You have forsaken the love you had at first. Consider how far you have fallen! Repent and do the things you did at first" (NIV).

141 See 1 Peter 2:5, 9 as a starting point.

cision was self-serving and not kingdom-focused.

Lastly, some churches, despite many good traits and positive elements, showed us some bizarre practices:

- Greeting strangers with a holy kiss was creepy, Church #28 ("Intriguing and Liturgical").

- Church #30 ("Misdirected and Frustrated") duped us into attending Sunday school and angered me.

- Avoiding all forms of promotion made them hard to find, Church #35 ("A Well-Kept Secret"). We stumbled upon them by accident.

- Cancelling services, because the minister was called away, disappointed us, Church #36 ("The Surprise"). Hold services anyway. Church #29 ("Led by Laity") did.

- Having a dirty sanctuary made me reluctant to sit down, Church #37 ("Another Small Church"). The overall neglected condition of their facility didn't help.

- Heading to a restaurant after the service was interesting but unusual. Although arming us all with coupons may not have left the best impression on the restaurant staff, Church #39 ("A Great Way to End the Year").

Takeaway for Everyone: Set divisive theology aside and celebrate commonality in Jesus. Seek ways to work with other churches, not oppose them.

Part 4:

The Home Stretch

We've just completed a stint of visiting churches in three specific geographic areas. Now our focus shifts to churches east of us. We've already visited eight of them (Churches #9, 11, 13, 15, 20, 24, 25, and 26) with scores more remaining, but we only have seven weeks to squeeze them in. We strategically select which ones we'll visit, skipping the rest—at least for now.

Our journey is winding down. I have mixed feelings. Visiting a different church each Sunday has been fun, enlightening, and educational. Already, I'm lamenting that our adventure will soon end. We must skip many churches, with dozens more that, although further away than ten miles, would be illuminating to visit.

But I'm anxious to return home, to revisit the familiar and reconnect with friends. The pull of reunion is powerful. Our journey has worn on us. Every week we must plan where to go, confirm service times, and verify their location. Each Saturday night we go to bed, asking, "What time is church tomorrow?" Our schedule for the entire day hinges on the answer. We hope we'll remember the right time and not be late. And even though you'd think I'd find visiting churches easy by now, I'm still anxious every Sunday morning.

Takeaway for Everyone: Remember that visiting a church is hard. Do everything you can to embrace visitors.

Church #45:

❖

Another Doubleheader

Several years ago, Candy visited this church, but today is my first time. The sprawling facility is impressive. The front parking lot is full, so I drive around the building, eventually finding a spot in the back. Today we'll enjoy another doubleheader: a traditional service followed by a contemporary one.

Another couple goes in an unmarked side door. Unsure of where it leads, we don't follow. Instead, we make our way around the building to the front. Someone sees us approaching, opens the door, and greets us warmly. As we wander inside, several people acknowledge our presence, thanking us for visiting. But beyond that no one says anything more, so we meander into the sanctuary. The worship area is a gymnasium, though I wonder how often someone goes to the trouble of moving the chairs to use it.

The room capacity is over five hundred and with about 190 chairs, there's plenty of room for growth. Along the side of the tastefully painted and nicely maintained space sits a huge stage. If not for the tile floor and retractable basketball hoops, we could easily forget we're in a gym.

Everything gives off a progressive vibe: informal space, padded chairs, round tables in the back, a large screen up front, and an array of musical instruments on the stage. Aside from a decidedly older crowd, there's little to suggest a traditional service is about to unfold.

A clock on the screen counts down the seconds until the service starts—hardly a traditional church practice. From stage, the assistant pastor greets us with a reminder of a psalm: "Lift up your hands in the sanctuary and praise the Lord."[142] He asks us to prepare to do just that for the opening song. Though I've been to many traditional services over the years, never once did I see attendees raise their hands en masse, but that's exactly what we do today.

For instrumentation, we have a piano, keyboard, and trumpet. The organ sits unused in the corner. Our worship leader stands behind the pulpit, keeping time with his right arm. We sing old-time hymns and choruses with the words displayed in front of us. There are no hymnals. Interspersed among the songs are announcements, a prayer, an offering, and a testimony via recorded video, foreshadowing the sermon.

At one point, the minister invites people to come forward to the altar. Doing this in the middle of the service is unusual, and I don't catch the purpose. One person ambles forward and then another. Eventually a half dozen participate, lowering themselves onto long kneeling benches. They bow in contemplation or prayer, but once the music stops, they scamper back to their seats. Wrapping up the first half of the service is a special music number, which garners applause.

Though he previewed it last week, today the minister starts a new series: "212°—The Extra Degree." He says that at 211° F water is just water, but raising it one degree causes it to boil, turning it to steam. Then it can do powerful things, such as move a train.

---

142 Psalm 134:2, NIV.

Today's sermon is "The Missing Degree: A Relationship Based on Passionate Spirituality." In Revelation 2 and 3, John addresses seven churches. The church in Ephesus has lost its first love, whereas the church in Laodicea is lukewarm in their faith. We need to trade stale religious obligation for passionate spirituality. "Religion can't save you," he says, but "Jesus can save you from religion."

We follow along using the outline in our bulletin. He's a good teacher, but I struggle to stay awake. This isn't his fault. It's mine. A powerful urge to close my eyes—just for a few seconds—overcomes me. The minutes tick off with infuriating slowness. *Will the message ever end?*

Eventually it does but not before he instructs us to close our eyes to contemplate if we're as passionate for God now as we once were. It's a great question, but never tell a man who's fighting off sleep to close his eyes. I rest my chin on my hand. It's good that I do, because I nod off—twice. During our silent introspection, the piano plays softly, giving way to a final song to wrap up the message and the service.

Between services is a pastor's breakfast for guests. We knew about this beforehand, read it in the bulletin, and several people invite us, as well. At first, they merely say it's in the library but fail to explain how to get there. Eventually someone shares this critical information.

We arrive to the smell of sausage and Belgium waffles. Rounding out the meal is fruit, coffee, and juice. In addition to us, there's another couple, the pastor and his wife, and two members, serving as our hosts. After getting to know us and sharing the church's vision, the pastor excuses himself for the next service. I'd like to talk more with the other visitors, but we can't if we're to make the second part of our doubleheader.

By the time we return to the gym, the contemporary service has begun. We slide into the back row in case we decide to skip the sermon. High school students make up the worship team: two on guitar, electric bass, drums, keyboard—now moved to the front of the stage, and piano. Two musicians, plus a third vocalist, take turns leading us. Their song selection is contemporary, matching their music.

Although the songs are different, the order of worship is the same, minus the special music number. This time no one encourages us to raise our hands and though some people do, the crowd is lethargic. Candy quips, "It's as though they just crawled out of bed and rolled into church"—and many roll in late.

Aside from music selection and instruments, there are other contrasts between the two services. The rearranged stage no longer has a pulpit. With direct lighting for the first service, this one relies on indirect and natural illumination. An hour ago, everyone was our age or older. Now we're among the eldest. We see families and young kids, but aside from the worship team there are few teens. Many attendees at the first service greeted us, but this time they're not as outgoing. Only a few people talk with us.

By the time the sermon begins, my fatigue is gone. The minister's words flow smoothly, and time passes quickly. I pick up a few new thoughts. Maybe I caught more of the first service than I realized. Though he follows the same outline, he uses different phrasing. I wonder if it's on purpose to match the audience or if the Holy Spirit directs him to change what he says. This time there's no closing number, and the pastor concludes the service.

Today we witnessed a traditional service that wasn't as reserved as we expected and a contemporary one that wasn't as exciting as we hoped. Despite that we worshipped God with an array of music and songs. We made new friends and heard a convicting message. It was a good morning.

Takeaway for Everyone: Labels of "traditional" and "contemporary" mean different things to different people. They may be more likely to confuse than clarify what visitors can expect.

Church #46:

❖

False Assumptions

The sprawling facility provides an impressive view. It's one of the biggest churches we've visited so far. Their large, new building suggests a thriving, dynamic community. I'm excited for what we'll find.

With no one responding to Candy's phone messages or emails, she can't confirm the service time, but we proceed based on what their website and phone message says. But as we pull up, doubt forms. Only a few cars sit in the large parking lot. My typical pre-church disquiet only heightens.

A man walks toward the building. It's unseasonably cold, a mere four degrees at dawn, though in the mid-teens now. He wears only a light jacket. I ask if he's staying warm. He smiles, "I was a mailman for thirty-three years. Cold doesn't bother me."

He pegs us as visitors, which seems strange. Large churches seldom know who the visitors are. He offers to take us in a side door, and we follow. After walking a dark corridor, we emerge into a huge sanctuary. Without a word, he disappears, and we stand alone, waiting for our eyes to adjust and wondering what to do next.

A woman approaches, smiling. She extends her hand and shares her name. She, too, knows we're visiting, "There's coffee in the lobby." We leave the sanctuary and find a small coat rack tucked off the lobby. Though it's the only one I see, there are few coats on it. We return to the sanctuary, without any coffee.

A greeter at the door also recognizes us as visitors and thanks us for coming, though she doesn't know what to say next. She holds a stack of brochures, but she doesn't offer us one. Finally Candy asks, "Are there any bulletins?" Embarrassed, the greeter gives us one. There aren't many people present, and no one seems available for conversation, so we wander in and select our seats. Though void of people, strategically placed Bibles and purses lay claim to the back rows.

The impressive sanctuary must accommodate over 500. With a sloped floor—the first we've seen—the pews sit in six sections, with the outer two roped off. The stage is large but it's not as spacious as last week. It's stocked with an abundance of artificial bushes and plants. There's a striking, almost ostentatious, baptistry behind the stage, with a backlit cross above it. They've tried hard to impress, but they miss—by about twenty years.

I attempt to interact with an older woman behind us, but she does little more than acknowledge our presence. In the row ahead is a younger woman with a busy toddler. As the child scoots down the pew, an exasperated mom gives chase.

"He sure is a busy guy," I say, trying in vain to spark interaction.

"Yes, *she* is." I hit a nerve with mom, but I don't feel too bad. If your child has short hair and wears black, don't get upset when people assume she's a boy. I suspect she's wearing hand-me-downs and consider asking if there's an older brother (it turns out there is), but I keep my mouth shut to avoid causing further offense.

With no one else to talk to, I alternate my attention between the bulletin and announcements projected on dual screens. One of the messages displayed overhead offers large print song lyrics for people who have difficulty reading the screen. Am I the only one who finds this ironic?

The congregation leads the service, and their involvement heartens me. They open with a medley of older choruses. Four vocalists lead us, with heavily orchestrated background tracks booming over the speakers. The sound feels overproduced for a church service. An organ and piano sit unused in opposite corners of the stage and the only live musician is a man on a twelve-string guitar. I'm convinced I can occasionally pick out his playing, but Candy disagrees. She's probably right.

With two-thirds of the seating in front of us, we see only a smattering of people. Most sit behind us. I remember a quip from our past: "back row Baptists." Even so, there are only about 110 people present, a crowd further dwarfed by the large sanctuary.

I zone out during a lengthy set of announcements, but the congregation comes to life and begins circulating during "greeting" time, as they shake as many hands as possible. Then the choir sings a song, earning enthusiastic applause, though I'm not sure why: their vocals pale in comparison to the grandeur of the recorded orchestral arrangement that overpowers them.

The pastor asks first-time visitors to raise their hands for a visitor brochure. This amused me at Church #1 ("A Friendly Place with a Homey Feel") but not this time: it was novel then, now it's trite. I make a half-hearted effort to comply, turning around to see if anyone notices my raised arm, while not caring if they do. Soon someone offers a visitor brochure to Candy. She fills out the information card.

We sing some more. I can't push past my annoyance over the background tracks. The music overwhelms, distracting me from the words. On our sojourn we've heard all manner of music, from professional to amateur, from pipe organ to rock band, boombox, and even a cappella, but this is the first time the music so fully blocks my worship.

Now is the minister's turn. An affable man, with slicked-back hair, he wears a gray vest (sans suit coat) and maroon shirt, open at the neck. I've been fighting negativity since I arrived, and his appearance doesn't change my opinion. He tells the congregation to open their Bibles and follow along as he reads from 1 Corinthians 5. The verses don't appear on the screens. With our version not matching his, it's disconcerting. There's a fill-in-the-blank outline in the bulletin, and I follow along. During the sermon, "Discipline (Not Punishment)," the outline does appear on the screen with the missing words inserted.

The minister's a gifted communicator—and entertaining. I appreciate his teaching about church discipline. He soon wins me over. His instruction is practical, laced in love and void of the dogmatic proclamations that often exude from fundamental preachers. I note the scripture verses he mentions, planning to study them further, all the while wondering if I will. He shares personal anecdotes of church discipline gone awry, contrasted with the practice done right. He concludes by saying, "We cannot judge the lost, but we do need to judge ourselves."

A video of a comedy sketch illustrates his point. "Sin in the church, like leaven [yeast], affects everyone." Churches must deal with the sin of their members and not ignore it. He ends his message by offering a "judgment-free time" for people to come forward to kneel on the steps of the stage and privately deal with any confession or conviction they have. He and his wife make themselves available for those who desire prayer or want to "receive Jesus." Nearly twenty come forward and kneel. The Holy Spirit is at work. I wish more churches provided opportunities for prayer and confession.

Afterward he dismisses us, only to suddenly remember he forgot something: "Members," he calls out, "I'll entertain a motion to reschedule our business meeting." Several wave dismissively and voice their consent as they walk toward the exits. I don't hear anyone second the motion, but the pastor conducts a quick voice vote before the people scatter. There's a murmur of agreement and no dissent.

A couple of people thank us for visiting and invite us back, but no one — except for the lady when we first arrived — bothers to ask our names. Candy spots a long-ago friend, and they catch up. Another acquaintance greets us too.

After that, we turn to leave. No one notices or seems to care. I made some false assumptions about how grand this church was and set myself up for grave disappointment.

Takeaway for Everyone: If you're doing the same thing you did twenty years ago, you're probably doing the wrong thing now.

Church #47:

Significant Interactions

When Candy confirmed the time for this church, they invited us to arrive early for coffee. Had they asked us to stay afterward, I'd certainly say, "Yes," but to come early is more awkward than I'm willing to endure. I should be brave, confront my fear, and accept their offer. I don't. Our journey is wearing me down. Even my pre-church prayer seems mired in the rut of routine. So it is when we pray this morning and head out.

We roll in ten minutes early. There's a side door that others head to, avoiding the double doors at the main entrance. We follow. As we head in, we see others, but they don't see us. Once again I feel invisible, a theme that recurs too often. After following the flow of people, we find ourselves in the narthex. To our right is the sanctuary and to the left, coffee time is wrapping up. For a moment we stand, immobile. People walk by, but no one approaches. Not wanting to appear lost and pathetic—even though we are—we meander into the sanctuary and sit down.

Though not dim, the worship space certainly isn't bright either. We sit, not in pews or chairs but "pew-chairs," interconnected benches that look like long chairs and resemble pews. After a while, my eyes grow used to the lighting.

Just as I resign myself to another Sunday with minimal interaction, a woman approaches. With a wide smile, she extends her hand and shares her name. "Let me tell you what to expect in our service." She explains their worship style and adds, "We really like to sing, and there will be lots of clapping."

I smile and nod. I start to mumble my thanks when she continues.

"We take communion every week. It's open communion."

I nod again. I ponder this question at each church when they serve communion—and the answer is seldom clear. "Thank you so much for letting us know."

"You may partake whenever you want. We don't do it all together."

I nod again, assuming about what she means. No one in the past forty-six churches has told us what to expect during a service. Her thoughtfulness makes so much sense. This lady certainly helps us feel welcomed; it's a gift. But she's not done. Before the service starts, she introduces us to three more people. All warmly greet us.

Though my initial impression of this church wasn't favorable, she reverses my perception. Other people also walk up and introduce themselves. This would have continued, but the service begins, ending all conversations.

A worship team of six leads us: two guitars—one acoustic and one electric, bass, drums, and two who alternate on lead vocals. Their style is a safe sound with a subtle beat. The congregation sings along but isn't as engaged as our friend represented. The songs are contemporary choruses, some with thoughtful words, but the subdued playing of the worship team detracts from their otherwise powerful impact. Though she predicted clapping, none occurs, and the only movement is an occasional raised hand.

After four songs is a message previewing communion. For a time, I wonder if it's the sermon, but the speaker concludes his remarks after a few minutes, and the ushers serve the elements. They pass plates with the bread—in this case, tiny communion crackers—immediately followed by the juice, in small plastic cups. Now our host's instructions to "partake whenever you want" become clear. Not needing to watch others to determine what to do and when to do it, I bow my head and thank Jesus.

I've lost track of how many times we've taken communion on our journey, but today is the first where I'm free to focus on the moment and not worry about the method. When format overshadows substance, we lose meaning. Today, courtesy of our new friend, I truly celebrate the Lord's Supper for the first time in a year.

The minister is starting a new series about "big church words." Before he begins, he turns his back to us to face the cross and pray. I love the symbolism. His prayer isn't a performance for us but a conversation with Jesus.

The big church word today is *justification*. I jot down some good one-liners about this word and am glad to receive them. Though had I not known what justification was beforehand, I'd be no closer to understanding it now. I also realize the fault may not be the preacher but me. Perhaps the whirl of observing variations in forty-six churches has left me unable to focus on the teaching. He wraps up his message with a salvation invitation and an altar call. Then we end the service singing a song.

Afterward we meet many more people, enjoying meaningful conversations. A man greets us. After exchanging names, I share our journey. He asks, "How can I pray for you?"

Though nothing comes to mind, I applaud his question. "You know . . . " I pause to make sure I'm not misspeaking, "We've visited forty-six churches, and this is the first time someone's asked us this—I really appreciate it."

"And this is the first time I've asked!"

We simultaneously acknowledge this is the work of the Holy Spirit.

"And I'm going to do it more often." He thanks me for the encouragement, and then Candy shares a need with him. Though he doesn't pray for us then, he jots it down, and I know he'll pray later—perhaps even as we head to our car.

Takeaway for Everyone: Offering to pray for people at church should be the norm, not the exception.

Church #48:

❖

Small, Simple, and Satisfying

We repeat our path from last Sunday, even turning into the same driveway. But instead of going straight, we take a right into a different parking lot. These churches are next door to each other, with a shared drive. Last week their signs confused me, and I would have gone to the wrong place, if not for Candy. Since their starting times are different, that would have been an awkward mistake.

There aren't many cars in the parking lot, so we expect a sparse attendance. Several people greet us inside. One asks us to sign their guest book but then scrambles to find a pen. We've been to a few churches that use guest books. I suspect it was once common, but it now seems archaic.

The greeters wear buttons with their names. I talk to them as Candy fills out the registry. Music starts. I worry that the service is beginning without us. We didn't arrive as early as hoped. Though our greeters aren't anxious, we hustle off toward the sound.

Candy spots a friend standing just outside the sanctuary and exchanges a quick greeting as I head inside. I select our seat, second row from the back — or sixth row from the front, depending on perspective — but before we sit, Candy's friend invites us to join her and her husband. We move up a row

251

to sit with them. This is the third time we've enjoyed this visitor-friendly gesture.

The music was just a prelude, so we have a few minutes to settle in and read the bulletin, but I'm more interested in the sanctuary. The room holds eighty-four padded chairs, with twenty people present. Most are older and more formally attired. A self-supporting cross stands in the aisle. I wonder if this is a regular fixture or something added for Lent. Regardless, I appreciate the symbolism of a cross being at the center of the space, serving as a focal point for all who enter.

The room is pleasant, with a comfortable feel. A raised stage in the front has a podium on each side and an altar toward the back. A man lights a solitary candle to start the service.[143] We sing an old-time hymn with piano accompaniment, though they use the organ for the rest of the service. Our friend points to their three hymnals. Without knowing this, I'd have grabbed the wrong one for the second number.

Their pastor is out of town, and the laity leads the entire service, just as with our time at Church #29 ("Led by Laity"). I applaud their ability to fully conduct the service on their own. The result is a subtle, comfortable feel, lacking any hint of pretense or performance.

Our leader gives some announcements and then asks for more. Several people stand in turn to share, ranging from personal news to congregational updates. Then Candy's friend stands and introduces us to the crowd. It's a nice gesture, and many murmur their welcome.

---

143 Of all the churches that lit candles to start their service, I think this is the only time there was just one. Another time there were three, but for most churches it was two.

Next is the official greeting time, where we stand to address one another with the phrase "passing the peace of Christ." I don't know why, but I have trouble repeating a prescribed phrase. I always have, with the words escaping me and leaving me tongue-tied. At best, I mumble "peace to you," but for most people I just smile and nod.

There's a liturgical call to worship, delivered with vigor—just as with the singing—belying our small number, even though we've now grown to about thirty-five.

Today's scripture reading, Luke 13:1-9, follows the Revised Common Lectionary for the third Sunday in Lent. A children's message, given to four kids, corresponds to the text about the fig tree. The kids' treat is Fig Newtons.

After another song, they offer "prayers for the people." Our speaker for the day starts the prayer time and then pauses. After a bit of silence, someone behind us prays and a few more follow. Some churches share needs first and then pray, while other congregations share needs and then agree, but I like their approach to simply pray, effectively sharing with each other as they talk to God.

We sing another song in preparation for the message, which the bulletin calls "reflections." Our speaker gives a poised delivery. I later learn she's a retired minister. This congregation apparently has several trained clergy among their attendees. She reads her message, delivering her words in an effortless manner that's easy to hear. Referring to the fig tree in Jesus's parable, she notes "Christianity is a religion of second chances." As she mentioned earlier to the kids, we don't know what happened to the fig tree. Did it eventually produce fruit or did the gardener uproot it? "The outcome is ours to choose"—both for the story and for us.

After more singing and the offering, the service ends sixty minutes after it started. We stay for coffee and cookies, meeting more people and learning about their congregation. We talk for another forty-five minutes before heading home, happy for our time at church today.

Takeaway for Members: If you know visitors, invite them to sit with you. Perhaps even ask someone you don't know.

Church #49:

Large and Anonymous

Last night we moved our clocks ahead one hour in our annual "spring forward" to daylight saving time. Not only must we deal with our weekly question of "What time is church tomorrow?" but we must also factor in a six-ty-minute time shift into our morning schedule. The church has two services. With us going to the second one, at least we'll have a bit more time to deal with losing an hour of sleep.

After cutting things a bit too close last Sunday, I overcompensate this week. We arrive seventeen minutes early. It's a huge church, our largest so far—though I expect next Sunday's will be even larger. The packed parking lot holds hundreds of cars, and I wonder if I'll even find a space. I fight off a panic to flee. I spot plenty of spaces in the far back of the church, a good hike from the building, but as I drive toward them, I discover a few that are much closer.

To kill some time, we decide to reset our car's clock, a multi-step procedure that is not intuitive and requires the manual and great patience. After several failed attempts, the time is once again correct. This took us five minutes. Now we head to the door.

With hundreds of people milling about, it's a packed place. Just inside, a man comes up to us. "Have I met you before?" We assure him he hasn't, but he thinks he should know us.

He's wearing an ear mic. I wonder if he's the pastor, but if he is, he doesn't say so, merely saying, "Hi, I'm John." We shake hands. Most ministers have a need to share their title during introductions. John possesses neither the ego nor the insecurity to do so. I immediately like him.

"Hi, John. I'm Peter and this is my wife, Candy." He honors us as he repeats our names slowly, implanting this information in his mind with care.

"What brought you here today?"

His question is sincere, so I resist a smart-aleck urge to answer literally by saying "our car." Instead, I say, "My wife and I are taking a year to visit a different Christian church every Sunday." I've said this too many times, and I'm bored with repeating it. "And this week it's your turn!" I intended my ad-lib to sound fresh but fear I came across as snarky. If so, John ignores it.

"Well, thank you for visiting. I hope you have a wonderful time here."

I thank him, shake his hand again, and we move forward to navigate the masses. Candy spots a coat rack and we head toward it. It's full and so is the next one. The third one has room. We hang up our coats and meander toward the sanctuary, skipping a side entrance to use the main one.

A sloped floor gives way to a huge stage, artfully accessorized with a tree motif. Pews, arranged in six sections, offer a 150-degree view of the front. There will be no counting people today or even estimating capacity. I guess it accommodates a thousand and will be over half-full. (Their website says the average attendance for the two services is 1,300.)

A bell choir starts the service. I think something is seriously wrong with their playing, though Candy says it's because the song is unfamiliar. They garner a tepid applause. A lengthy set of announcements follows, and I soon tune them out. Next is a prayer, formal and jargon-filled, sounding nice but with little meaning.

Following this is the middle school choir. I'm surprised to see a nice gender balance. Talented and well-rehearsed, they perform with excellence, singing in parts and earning a deserved ovation. They enjoy singing.

For the worship music, a team of nine leads us: with four vocalists, two guitars, a bass guitar, cello, baby grand piano, and electric drum set. The worship leader both sings and plays guitar. The instruments feel out of place for the more formal vibe of the church, but these contemporary tools still produce a traditional sound.

For the offering, the bell choir returns. This time I enjoy their playing and others must have as well, given the enthusiastic applause afterward. The men taking the collection all wear medium blue button-down shirts, with the church's logo on the left side. *Uniforms? Really?* We sing another song, and it's time for the message.

I'm not surprised when John walks up to the podium. He doesn't preach a sermon as much as he teaches a lesson. He's good, really good, the best we've heard. Though a couple of preachers have been more dynamic, he's the most effective communicator. This makes sense when we learn he's a former seminary professor with a Ph.D. in biblical history.

His text is Revelation 3:14–21, the letter to the church at Laodicea. We stand as he reads from the NKJV. When we sit, he teaches that the seven churches mentioned in the second and third chapters of Revelation follow a geographic path, while the theme of their letters follows a progression of church history. Oh, how I want to hear more.

Today's focus is on the Laodicean's materialism. I've studied this passage in depth, but as John mines its words for meaning, he unveils deeper truths I never considered. "Jesus was nauseated by their materialism,"[144] he says. "It was the only thing that ever made him sick." This church "didn't need a thing"[145]—not even God. However, "we are not to be independent," but dependent on him.

John then segues into seven key lessons from Jesus about money. Our teacher presents these truths directly, without guilt-producing manipulation or nary a hint that we must give more. He's content to allow the Holy Spirit to provide the application and offer any needed conviction. After a brief concluding prayer, the service ends with no fanfare.

We stand, gathering our things to leave. At one point in his message, John instructed members to look around for visitors to greet. Though he modeled this before the service when he met us, no one else makes any effort, not even the man sitting in front of us who wears a deacon nametag. He looks right through us.

We know many people who attend this church but see none of them. Only one couple approaches us. They look vaguely familiar. The wife recognizes Candy. We attended the same church over a quarter century ago. Aside from them and John, several hundred other people ignore us, perhaps not caring or maybe assuming someone else will offer a greeting.

---

144 See Revelation 3:16.

145 Revelation 3:17.

If you want to go to church and remain anonymous, a big church is where it can happen. And at this church, it was painfully easy.

Takeaway for Everyone: The larger the church, the easier it is for people to be lost in the crowd and the harder it is to embrace visitors.

Church #50:

❖

Saturday Mass

A few months ago we went to church on Saturday morning, a Seventh Day Adventist assembly (Church #31, Misdirected and Frustrated). Today we head off for a Saturday evening mass, our third Roman Catholic visit. Though we could justify skipping this as a repeat of our two prior encounters with Catholicism, I don't. First, a Saturday evening service will be new to us. Second, the Roman Catholic service still eludes me. I need more exposure if I'm to embrace it. Third, this is a campus parish, so I expect a younger crowd and hope for a more accessible service.

The service starts at 6 p.m., which is an awkward time for us. Eating before is too early, while waiting until after is too late. We decide to eat first.

Though located on an obscure side street, it's easy enough to find. People park on the street, so either they don't have a parking lot or it's already full. We park a couple blocks away and hike to where we hope the entrance is. Along the way, we talk with a woman and seem to make a good connection. Recalling the other two Roman Catholic services, I consider asking if we may sit with her and follow her lead during the service. But it doesn't matter. Once we reach the door, she breezes inside and scurries away. Left alone, we sit by ourselves—so much for making a connection.

The facility is stylish and contemporary: open and airy. The altar is in the center, with chairs—not pews and no kneeling rails—positioned around it. I estimate it seats over four hundred, and there are about 240 present, most are middle age and older. I only see a few who are younger and don't see many college students.

The worship team contrasts from the first two Roman Catholic parishes we visited (Churches #5 and 18). Today it consists of a guitar, bass guitar, drum set, and piano. Along with four vocalists, three of the instrumentalists also have mics. Their songs are likewise more contemporary, though none are familiar.

The worship leader announces the page number for the liturgy, but I still can't locate it. You'd think "page one in the white book" would be easy enough to find, but not so, though I do locate most of the songs. As the service progresses, we read from Ezekiel, Romans, and John.[146] The leader only gives the names of the books, not the chapters and verses. This makes it impossible to follow along. For the text from John, the priest instructs us to close our eyes and imagine the words as he reads. The story is about Lazarus. After the reading, I locate the Lazarus account in John 12.

We also recite an unnamed creed. It's not the Apostles' Creed, which I know well. I suspect it may be the Nicene Creed, which I'm not familiar with. We say Jesus is "consubstantial" to the Father. I jot down the word, so I can look it up later.[147]

---

146 I suspected these to be from the Revised Common Lectionary, but they weren't.

147 In general, consubstantial means "of the same substance, nature, or essence." Specifically, consubstantial relates to the three persons of the Trinity.

The priest gives the message, focused on Lazarus and drawing parallels between him and Jesus, although being careful to stress that for Lazarus it was "a resuscitation," whereas for Jesus, it was "a resurrection." I'm not sure if this is semantics or a theological distinction. Though my impulse is to disagree, this provides something to contemplate.

The Eucharist is next. The priest says nothing about visitors, though I know the official church stance is that we may not participate. I've already considered this, realizing I can still have the spiritual encounter of Holy Communion without physically taking part. Even so, their process distracts me, and I miss connecting with God during the ceremony.

The tradition of sharing the chalice still disgusts Candy and me. Most participants receive the wafer but bypass the cup. I suppose for some, they must avoid alcohol, while for the rest I assume it's a sanitary concern. The process is quick and orderly. Then we have a time for silent reflection.

A lengthy series of announcements follows. This is a busy parish, and with Easter only two weeks away, there are even more items to share about Holy Week events. Exams are next week at the local university, and the church has care packages for the students. Given the number of packages sitting out and the few takers present, I assume most of the students will attend mass tomorrow — at least I hope they will.

In a time of testimony, a girl shares that she just earned her "I love my faith" pin from the Girl Scouts. It's also a member's birthday, so we sing "Happy Birthday." The congregation celebrates him in song, ironically with more energy than in their singing to God.

The service ends, and I spot a friend across the room. After a nice reunion, Candy and I also chat briefly with the priest. He knows we're visitors but doesn't ask our names. This might be because he's distracted by a member hovering about, anxious to talk to him. We stroll to our car, leaving exactly one hour after the service started.

On the drive home, we discuss what happened. I still find Catholic services inaccessible, though this doesn't bother me as much anymore. Perhaps this is because I now have a better idea of what to expect. Another thought is I felt at home because the service was less formal. But most likely, it's a result of me simply being less uncomfortable over not knowing what to say or do during a service.

Given time, I suspect I could find a comfortable rhythm with Catholic practices. Despite this parish being friendlier than the other two, making personal connections at Catholic churches is challenging. This troubles me. The community aspect of church is what matters most—at least to me.

Takeaway for Members: Members need to give leaders the time and space to interact with visitors.

Church #51:

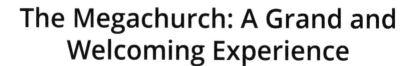

The Megachurch: A Grand and Welcoming Experience

I'm both excited and apprehensive.

My excitement comes from visiting a church we've heard much about, all positive. It's the largest church in the area—our local megachurch, if you will—so that's noteworthy in itself. Dynamic, growing, fresh, and spirit-led are all words I associate with this congregation.

I'm also apprehensive. The last two churches I had lofty expectations for (Churches #42 and 46) left me gravely disappointed. I fear I may again be setting myself up for a letdown. I'd rather be pleasantly surprised than unpleasantly disillusioned. So it is today. I expect much but fear disenchantment.

* * *

When a church we visit has two Sunday services, we've always attended the later one, assuming they're both the same style. This church has two,[148] but Candy lobbies we attend the first one, a 9:30 a.m. gathering, instead of their second one,

---

148 It turns out they have three services. The two we are aware of both have the same format. We later learn about the third service, with a different format. It will be worth checking out in the future. (To further confuse things, they have a fourth service at a second location in a nearby city.)

scheduled for 11:30. I agree that going to church that late in the morning cuts into our day too much. Plus, she's been a good sport about this whole adventure, and there's no point in adding needless frustration, so we head off to their first gathering.

At 9.9 miles away, requiring a side street or two to keep it under our ten-mile criteria, this shortest path, however, isn't the quickest. I jump on the highway, adding a few miles to our journey, but shaving off several minutes. Although in the opposite direction, the same situation occurred with Church #36 ("The Surprise"), where we also tweaked our theoretical route to keep it under ten miles.

I wish I allowed a bit more time. Once I exit the highway, the reality of the situation hits me. There's traffic, lots of traffic — not traffic jam congestion, but enough to require extra time and demand more patience. A police officer stands at the intersection, ensuring a smooth flow of cars. Had he not been there, gridlock would have resulted.

Once on the side street, a sign directs us to their entrance. Everyone turns. No one drives past. A second sign tells first-time visitors to turn on their four-way flashers — because we are their VIP, and they want to give us VIP treatment. I don't bother with my flashers. Instead, I follow the flow of cars. Several visible parking lot attendants, with matching reflective vests, efficiently guide us to the next available space. It's reminiscent of a large amusement park, except this crew does their job better — and is happier doing it.

The facility consists of two buildings — and we see people head for both. The original building, a present-day cathedral, courtesy of the prior owners, is further away. The new building, dwarfing the first one, is closer and attracts most of the people. We head to its nearest door. A smiling man, clad in a bright T-shirt that identifies him as part of the welcome team, stands by the door. Before the day is over, we will see scores, if not a hundred more, of similarly-outfitted volunteers.

In a most gracious gesture, he opens the door wide for us long before we reach it. It's below freezing, and as I breeze by I tell him the obvious: "You need a coat."

"I wasn't planning on doing this today," he says with an amused smile. He handles his impromptu assignment well, glad to help despite being unprepared. Then he adds some curious information, "It's nametag Sunday."

I nod to let him know I heard—even though I don't understand what he means.

Once inside, we meet more greeters, sporting the same smartly decorated T-shirts. "It's nametag Sunday!" they say again. Then they gesture behind them and add "by the sanctuary." Had we been regulars, I'm sure this would have all made sense, but to us it's confusing. Of course, the size of the building, the bustle of activity, and too much sensory information overwhelms me. *Where is the sanctuary anyway?* We haven't a clue. Perhaps I should've taken the VIP route after all.

We surge forward with the masses, bypassing a prominent and well-staffed information station. We walk by a bookstore and coffeehouse. Candy's intrigued, even though she sipped her own brew on the drive here. We still wonder where the sanctuary is and where to get nametags for "nametag Sunday." I consider settling for merely finding the sanctuary before the service starts.

That's when we both realize the sanctuary is to our right. But as we head in that direction, I spy a line by a table that might have nametags. We divert our path and soon make our own hastily scrawled labels. We peel off the adhesive backing and stick them to our clothes. Then we wheel around to head inside.

Greeters by the door cheerfully hand us two items. One is a four-color glossy brochure highlighting the events of the day and the church's programs. The other is a four-page teaching handout. We step inside a darkened room, completely overwhelmed. The sanctuary is an auditorium, a sunken arena with stadium seating. On the floor level below are a couple dozen square tables, each with four chairs. I wonder if that's the VIP seating.

Innovative in every way, one item stands out: a shiny black SUV parked on stage. That's an extravagant prop. I stand, not moving. "There are plenty of seats." The usher smiles broadly as he makes a grand panoramic gesture. He's right. But I stand frozen. "Or would you like me to help you find a seat?"

I shake my head and shuffle in, almost in a stupor. I spot a dozen open seats in the fourth row from the back, but a couple sitting next to the aisle blocks our access. I ask if we can scoot by. With a smile they grant us passage. I take off my coat and sit down. A huge display presents a countdown timer: 3:07 until the service begins. To each side are two slightly smaller, but still large, ancillary displays, telling us the same information. A few months ago, Church #31 ("A Day of Contrasts") used the most technology in their service of any church up to that point. This church far surpasses them, impressive and first-class in every respect. I try to estimate the capacity, but eventually give up. A thousand to twelve hundred is a reasonable guess, but it could be more. It will end up being about 80 percent full.

The worship team is already up front. Five people stand in an arc on a mini-stage in front of the main platform. In the center is the worship leader, with a guitar player to his left and bass guitar on his right, both with mics. Next to each of them stand two backup vocalists. Centered on the main stage is another guitar player. Given the array of electronics at his feet, he must be lead guitar. To his left is a keyboard player, with two instruments to choose from. To his right is the drummer, encased in a Plexiglas sound enclosure.

The countdown timer hits 0:00 and the worship leader steps forward to welcome us. He opens the service with a passionate prayer from his heart and then teaches us a new song. Each of the three displays shows video of the worship team, with words to the song underneath. The technology preoccupies me, and I soon give up trying to learn the song. I eventually locate five cameras: three stationary, one handheld, and one on a boom. There are three people in the sound booth below us, with a couple more in the video control room, high and to our left. I'm just beginning to grasp the chorus of this new song when we move on to the next one — and then another.

After the opening set, one of the co-pastors comes up to also welcome us. She explains nametag Sunday, something new they're trying to help people connect with one another. Today we see no benefit from it, but for their first attempt, it's too soon to tell if it will work. I hope they continue this practice.

The pastor shares that two couples present this morning both suffered a death in their family this week. She briefly updates us on what happened, noting that the departed are now in a better place, where we will one day join them. She celebrates the support offered to these families by the staff and congregation. Then she asks those standing around the two couples to put a hand on their shoulders as she prays. My impulse is to extend my arm in their direction and when I see others do so, I join them.

After the "amen," several video announcements appear: professional productions that are engaging and command attention. Coming soon is their annual woman's conference. Candy expresses interest, and I encourage her to pursue it.[149]

The SUV on stage, as well as the bedroom suite on one side and dining room set on the other, are not props, but prizes for an Easter giveaway. Billed as "The Big Give," these extravagant gifts are to remind us of Jesus's biggest give of all: his life for us. They ask the congregation to pass out "invite tickets," encouraging visitors to come and join in their Easter celebration. They require advance nominations for the car giveaway, though presumably they'll distribute the other gifts at random.

I applaud the concept and appreciate the extent they will go to make their point, but I'm also uncomfortable. The cynic in me says they're bribing people to come to church. This, coupled with the concert atmosphere of the auditorium and highly produced feel of the service, strikes me as tapping too deep into the consumerism mentality of society. Yet, the progressive part of me celebrates their grand success in connecting with our culture in a way it can understand and accept, something most of the churches we've visited have completely failed at—and many don't even see the need to try.

The church is in the middle of a series on leadership, with the premise that God calls us all to be leaders in both our personal and professional lives. Today's message is an anomaly to their normal format. It's teaching some of John Maxwell's material on "The Law of Momentum," which the co-pastors re-

---

149 Though she's interested, she never signs up.

ceived training to present. Drawn from scripture, the instruction is most applicable to church leaders and easily adaptable to business leaders, but I have trouble understanding how it pertains to everyone else.

The other co-pastor of this husband-wife team presents the training. Intended for a conference, not a church service, it's too much information to condense into a sermon-length window. The teaching is good, and I retain the essential message, yet the presentation isn't representative of a typical Sunday message for this church and only hints at what might be the norm.

During the message, the video cuts out for several seconds. Since the speaker is live, this doesn't present a problem. Although when it occurred during the singing, we lost all the words to the song—and for a longer time. Such are the risks when depending on technology.

As the minister concludes his teaching, a slide appears on the screens, asking everyone to remain seated during the altar call. This confuses me. How can people come forward? I later realize the message is to keep people from leaving the service too soon, thereby distracting those who need to hear what the pastor says. He encourages people to rededicate their lives to Jesus. Several raise their hands, and the pastor prays for them as a group, while they remain at their seats. For those deciding to follow Jesus, he leads them in saying the sinner's prayer.

The keyboardist plays softly as the pastor prays, while the rest of the worship team reassembles onstage. He dismisses us, as the worship team launches into a reprise of an earlier song while everyone exits. I'd like to sing, but no one else does and without the words, I don't try. Still I linger to listen. Candy discovers the visitor card in the seatback in front of her, entering the information requested. Though I expect it to take several minutes to empty the auditorium, they only need about thirty seconds. By the time Candy completes the visitor card, only a handful of people remain in the sanctuary. The facility has an amazing traffic flow design. We get up and leave as well.

* * *

There's a bustle of activity in the rest of the facility. Candy wants to check out the coffee shop. As she does, I walk over to the information area near the main door. Two people give me their attention as I approach. I ask if I can give them our visitor card. They take it. "Would you like a tour?" I accept, just as Candy rejoins me. One of them guides us to the other end of the large lobby — to the visitor station — telling us about the church as we walk.

Two people at the visitor area welcome us, as our guide makes a smooth handoff, introducing us by name and relaying that we went to the first service and are interested in a tour. The visitor section is at the back of the facility. Had I turned on our four-way flashers when we arrived, we'd have been directed to the back. There we would have parked near this entrance and received VIP treatment, including a tour and preferred seating.

Our guide introduces herself and gets to know us. As she does, she occasionally struggles for words. After a while she reveals her predicament. "Let me turn this thing off. They keep distracting me." She points to an earpiece hidden by her hair and then turns off the radio at her waist. "Ah, that's much better. I can't listen to two things at once."

She gives us a visitor's packet, complete with information about the church and a CD of a message. We start our tour with the large Junior/Senior High section complete with staging area, pool tables, and staffed snack bar. Our kids are adults, but once she learns we have a grandchild on the way, she takes us through the nursery and children's section. Everything is highly organized, and the safety of the children is paramount. A methodical check-in and check-out procedure makes sure kids only leave with the right adult. I assume this is to guard against abduction by a stranger, but I'm sad to learn the primary reason is to keep the church from being an unwitting accomplice to a parent thwarting child-custody arrangements.

We pass the security center, staffed with volunteers who monitor the entire facility via closed-circuit TV. Next we go to the grade school area. A man standing at the door glances at our guide's name badge as we slide on in. It's an impressive place, offering games, prize counter, and a pair of two-story slides. In the back is a seating area, themed as a TV production stage. I'm sure the kids love it. As we exit, I grin at the man by the door. "Are you the bouncer?" All he's missing are the dark glasses.

With a tip of his head, he answers "Sort of." There's a glimmer of a smile. He could be an opposing presence if needed — and with his communication gear, more help is a call away.

As our guide shows us the facility and explains the church, she alternates between saying, "*when* you come back" and "*if* you come back." She's unsure which to use: the first could be presumptive, while the second could reveal a lack of confidence.

Then we go to the bookstore, where Candy spots a friend. As they talk, I'm able to ask our guide some questions. Concurrent to the service we were in, another one took place in the older building next door. Initially they used a video feed of the main service, but eventually they went to live music and a feed of just the message. This allows for a different format for the first half of their service, including more connection time and "music that is a little less rock and roll." Though it wasn't their intent, that gathering is a bit older. She suggests we might want to come back and check it out too. I don't bother to tell her I'd prefer a little bit *more* rock and roll, as well as a younger crowd.

Candy rejoins us, and we conclude our tour at the coffee shop. We thank our guide for her attention. She invites us to return, challenging us to come back for three months — so we can "see how our faith grows" — before deciding. "You can't evaluate a church on just one visit," she says, not knowing about our journey. We appreciate the tour and our connection with our guide. She's eager to serve and serves well.

In the information packet is a card for a free beverage at the coffee shop. Candy zeroes in on it. "I might as well use it to-day — because we won't be back." Though I agree with the first part of her statement, I disagree with the second. While waiting to place her order, we reconnect with a former neighbor we've not seen in years. Though we saw her son at Church #14 ("The Pentecostal Perspective"), her husband and daughter are here with her today.

Monitors are all around us, and I see the countdown for the next service. It hits zero and the beat of music emanates from the auditorium. I poke my head inside. There are more people than at this point during the first service, but not quite as many as when the first service ended. I suspect they'll end up with a full house. How will they ever manage to fit everyone in on Easter?

Candy's coffee concoction is a work of art, so much so that she snaps a picture of it before taking a sip. We head outside, hoping to find our vehicle in the many rows of cars. Between the two of us, we home in on it. Since we're leaving at an odd time, there are no traffic issues to deal with. We drive home with much to discuss.

* * *

This church is the largest one we've visited. They are the most progressive and presented the most professional service. They have much to offer and are a visible presence in the community. Abounding in excellence, they offer a notable example for churches to emulate should they desire to attract a bigger audience or reach a multigenerational crowd.

While connection was a concern last night at mass, forming meaningful friendships would be even harder here. But they do offer opportunities to meet people and form deeper relationships on Sunday nights and throughout the week.

If I were looking for a new church home, I'd give this one sincere consideration.

Takeaway for Everyone: The larger the church, the more important it is to do things well.

Church #52:

Playing it Safe

Our destination is not a church to visit but one to revisit, returning to the congregation we were part of a decade ago. Perhaps the second largest church in the area, they would be bigger, except they keep planting new churches and sending away their members to help. One of the churches they started was our home church, the one we'll return to next week.

The worship area seats twelve hundred, and they presently have two services: a blended one and a contemporary one. As is our practice for different services, we'll attend both.

The facility has expanded greatly over the years, with more additions than I can recall. The result is multiple driveways and countless doors to enter the facility. Inside is a sprawling array of corridors and rooms. We proceed as a visitor would, turning into the first drive and entering the closest entrance, even though I know a long trek awaits us to reach the sanctuary at the other end of the campus.

A greeter meets us at the entrance, opening the door for us. Just like last week, I quip that he needs a coat, and just like last week, he says, "I wasn't planning on doing this today." He grins. "But this is where they sent me." A most welcoming man, I expect him to direct us to the worship center. But he doesn't.

Insides are ample signs, pointing to every possible destination. Among the plethora of arrows, no doubt, is one pointing to the sanctuary, but without stopping to scrutinize our options, the signs offer little help. Since we know where to go, we amble toward our destination.

Along the way, I spot a few people who look familiar and most give me a confused glance, but no one comes up to talk. For the first time in fifty-two weeks, I've forgotten my Bible and journal. I hope to snag a bulletin to use for notes but see no one standing around to give me one. About to give up, I spot a rack of bulletins along a wall just inside the sanctuary. With my immediate concern addressed, we head in and sit down. That's when I spot an usher with bulletins.

Aside from last week, this worship space is the largest we've been in. A sloped floor gives way to a large stage in the opposite corner, serving as an impressive focal point. Padded pews, arrayed in four sections, sit at angles toward the front. Matching chairs, added in the front, in the back, and in every available nook suggest a capacity crowd. We've already seen hundreds of people, but aside from the greeter, no one has said a word to us. Once again, we witness a chief weakness of large churches.

People filter in, and the room is slightly more than half-full when the service begins. Though many are older, I see people of all ages.

Traditional organ music overwhelms the space. A rousing applause reveals the congregation's appreciation for the prelude. As for me, I'm glad it's over. On stage, an orchestra of about fifteen plays for the opening song set, with the organ taking the lead. The music director is our sole song leader, with his amplified vibrato filling the air. I think he does so brilliantly, though Candy disagrees. This isn't our first item of contention this morning. It probably won't be our last.

I question their description of a "blended" service, for it seems most traditional. In fact, we've been to traditional services that are more contemporary (such as the first service at Church #45: Another Doubleheader). Of course, we also attended one contemporary service that was more traditional (the second service at Church #17: A Doubleheader). I guess traditional, contemporary, and blended are matters of perspective.

Video announcements — professionally done and engaging — welcome visitors and update the congregation on key information. Today's theme is "True Sacrifice." They recognize and invite forward some members of the military, home on leave. The church celebrates their sacrifice for our country. While being far more than the sacrifice of most people, it's far less than the sacrifice of Jesus. We applaud their service. The minister gives a prayer of blessing for them and their families.

The minister asks everyone to complete an information card to put in the offering plate. Candy does so and drops it in, though most people don't. The card has space for prayer requests; the prayer team will pray over the requests during the service. Another video announcement plays during the offering.

There are cards at the end of each pew for members to pass out, inviting friends to their Good Friday event and Easter Sunday celebration. We learn that for their annual Easter egg hunt yesterday, 600 kids showed up. I'm not sure how I feel about this, but I'm ecstatic for such an effective community outreach, hopeful that some of the kids will come back with their parents on Easter and learn about the savior of the world instead of a bunny that lays eggs.

The church is wrapping up a yearlong teaching on the book of Mark. We stand for today's reading, first reciting 2 Timothy 3:16 as a preface, which appears on the screen: "All Scripture is God-breathed and is useful for teaching, rebuking, correcting and training in righteousness," (NIV). Then our leader reads the texts, Mark 14:32–36 and Mark 15:33–39. When he's finished, we recite in unison an affirmation that also appears on the screen: "This is God's word and we believe it is true."

Instead of a typical Palm Sunday message, the teaching focuses on Jesus's death, his sacrifice for us. Though normally reserved for the Good Friday service, this year they will not present a message on Friday. Instead they'll offer an interactive "Journey of the Cross" experience, starting with communion and proceeding on a path winding through the facility. I'd like to return for that, but we've already planned to begin our re-introduction to our home church that evening by attending their Good Friday service.

Their senior pastor stands on a smaller platform, in front of and slightly lower than the main stage. He acknowledges, without apology, that some arrived today anticipating a triumphant Palm Sunday message, not one about death, suffering, and sacrifice. "I'm not a Christian entertainer," he says. "I'm a minister of the gospel."

An outstanding communicator, he delivers his message about Christian martyrs and Jesus's death with excellence — oozing conviction. To portray the anguish of "the cup" Jesus was about to endure, we watch a clip of the Garden of Gethsemane scene from *The Passion of the Christ*. It ends dramatically with Jesus stomping on the serpent.

To wrap up the service, a different worship team comes out, a contemporary ensemble to lead us in the closing number, an updated version of a hymn, thereby fulfilling the "blended" element of the service. The pastor invites visitors to come to the front after the service to meet him. Though we're not the type of visitor he means, I consider making my way up to say hello if no one else does, but soon a dozen or more surround him, so I don't.

As we exit, a friend from long ago nods his acknowledgment of our presence, asking if he's going to be reading about their service on Facebook tomorrow. For some reason, I feel a need to be evasive, merely saying "could be." He recoils a bit, and I'm not sure if his grimace is in alarm or an attempt at comic relief. He moves on, and we pause, wondering if anyone else will approach us. When no one does, we meander out to the lobby.

It's thirty-five minutes until the next service, and we seek to fill the time. Candy is sure there's coffee in the fellowship area. Though I didn't hear any such announcement, searching for coffee seems a reasonable way to pass time. Nonetheless, we never make it as we see many friends along the way. A few say, "Welcome back" and are disappointed to learn we're only visiting. Some greetings occur in passing, while other friends linger for prolonged reunions. These are cherished interactions.

Never finding a beverage, I'm content for a quick stop at the drinking fountain as we make our way back for the second service. For an alternate perspective, we head to the other side of the sanctuary, finding more friends to talk to as we do.

* * *

In our thirty-minute absence, they removed the orchestra section and reset the stage. This gives more space for the contemporary worship team of eight, the same group that concluded the first service. There are three on guitar, a bass guitar, two on keys, a drummer, and a backup vocalist. The worship leader doubles as a keyboardist, while two of the guitarists have mics and sing backup. All the instrumentalists sing with joy, whether they have a mic or not.

Their song set offers three different tunes from the first service. Though they certainly have a contemporary sound, bordering on light rock, it lacks the edge that I hope to hear. "Safe" is the best description, far more reserved than what we enjoyed last week.

By now the room is almost full, I suspect surpassing eighty percent of capacity. Church growth experts claim that when a sanctuary is beyond eighty percent full, people begin to feel crowded, which stymies further growth. I can't imagine how they'll accommodate an even larger crowd next week on Easter Sunday. All age groups are present and more evenly represented than the first service, but I suspect there are still more Baby Boomers than Gen Xers and Millennials.

Most of the other elements of the service are the same, though this time, the pastor asks visitors to fill out an information card—a different one from the first service—and drop it off at the information center after the service. I urge Candy to complete it, but she refuses, reminding me that we aren't first-time visitors and that she filled out a card—albeit a different one—during the first service. This is the first time she's not complied with our plan to provide whatever information a church asks. Had we handed in a completed card, I'm sure we would have received a warm welcome, reminiscent of last week. Granted, I could do this myself, but I don't do it either. Perhaps the fatigue of our journey is showing.

A sermon outline is on the back of the bulletin. Like last week, there are blanks to fill in. I don't like this, as I fixate so much on filling in the next blank that I miss everything else. I didn't do this during the first service. This time I try, but for several blanks I end up copying from Candy. Though it took her both services, she did fill in every space.

The pastor ends by offering a time for rededication and then leads the congregation in saying a salvation prayer. Candy likes this, calling it a nice reminder of our decision to follow Jesus. I fear people could too easily misunderstand it, assuming they need to "get saved" every week. Alternately, it could become a meaningless ritual. I had this same angst last week, and after a week to cogitate it, my unresolved concerns bubble forth again.

The pastor invites people to come forward, afterward, for prayer with the prayer teams. I so appreciate serving people through prayer, but few churches do. Don't they see prayer as important?

The service concludes with the worship team leading us in the same song that ended the first service. Though I may imagine it, this time they play with more gusto.

Sitting with good friends who sometimes attend this church, we didn't have a chance to talk beforehand. Now we do. It's been a few months since we've seen them, so we catch up on family, life, and faith. They're also curious about our journey, and we share more.

The congregation disperses quickly, and we're among the last to leave, happy for the connections we enjoyed.

* * *

Today we had a delightful time of community after each service and heard an insightful message by a gifted communicator. We enjoyed worship led by talented musicians. Yet something didn't feel quite right. Candy sensed it too.

They have a "traditional soul." I offer this, despite them being one of the more progressive congregations we've visited.

Granted, this could be my issue. I could be cynical because of our weekly variations of worship styles, tired by the length of our sojourn, or simply anxious to return to our home church. The fault may be my past familiarity with them, or the ways I've changed since we've last been together, but something feels dated in their approach. I feel a tinge of disconnect between effort and effect.

I wonder if this may be the result of them trying to offer something for everyone, to keep all people happy, with the resulting arrangement leaving me unsettled. I suspect most people present would disagree. They attend because they like what this church offers. But what about everyone else, the greater community they long to reach?

Another issue, my common complaint at all large churches and a few not-so-large ones, is a lack of friendliness. Although having a greeting time during the service can be awkward or superficial, it does at least provide the potential for some connection, but they didn't offer that. Yes, I did have many meaningful conversations today, but they all were with people I knew. The folks I didn't know walked past me without a glance, or they looked through me as though I weren't there. If I had arrived as a true stranger, I would have left a stranger, feeling more alone when I left than when I arrived.

This is, of course, a dilemma that all large churches must grapple with and overcome.

Takeaway for Leaders: Having a safe service may keep folks from complaining, but Jesus never told us to play it safe.

Church #53:

❖

Home for Holy Week

O ur journey is over. I'm sad and excited at the same time. Our spiritual sojourn of fifty-two churches has ended. Reunion with our home church community looms large.

Today is Good Friday and our Easter celebration will be in two days, but I can't wait for Sunday. I desire a preview, a reminder of our home church. I want a sneak peak of what lies ahead. We head off for our church's Good Friday service.

This time, I leave my journal at home—on purpose. I'll not take notes tonight. Documenting my observations isn't the point: experience is, community is, and family is. Especially God. I assume a packed place, arriving early to find a good seat, but there's plenty of room when we get there. We sit and wait. I want to soak in the place. It's been too long. I need to remember.

I don't seek out others, but it's not long before a friend comes up to chat, and then another, and another. With a half hour before the service starts, the minutes pass quickly, as friends fill the time with smiles, hugs, and conversation. Some can't believe it's been a year, that our journey is over. But a few didn't know we were gone. This is the downside of a larger church. Absences can too easily go unnoticed. This isn't a lament, just an observation.

Including the balcony, the place seats 475, but the space seems small. And compared to the last two churches, it is. The worship team congregates on the stage. Our worship leader just had wrist surgery. He won't be playing guitar for a while, and tonight he's restricted in what he can do. There are two others on guitar (one acoustic and one electric), a bass guitar, a keyboard, a drummer, and two backup vocals. I recognize most of the musicians but not all.

They launch into song, with launch being the operative word. It's loud and energetic, worship at its passionate finest, full of joy and abounding in celebration. Though a few of the churches approached this, and Church #51 ("The Megachurch"), came close, these folks take worship to another level, being polished and spontaneous at the same time. People on stage jump and dance, with more movement in the congregation than I've seen in a long time. I don't need to wait to feel God's presence or seek him. Without question, he is here.

We sing for forty-five minutes and our pastor gives a brief teaching before we return to song. It's nice to be able to raise my hands and arms without worrying over committing a faux pas that might offend local conventions.

After ninety minutes, most with us singing, the service ends. I don't want it to. But our spent musicians have little left to give, especially our worship leader, whose sweat-drenched shirt confirms he gave his all to God.

I stand, looking for people I don't know so I can talk to them. My journey has made me more aware of seeking out visitors and those on the margins. Though I spot several to approach, others are already reaching out to them. That's what a church should do.

Now feeling free to move about, I seek out friends. It doesn't take long. Some conversations are brief, while others go deeper. We share prayers and give hugs. A few promise to email me and with another, I make plans to meet for coffee. After half an hour, the crowd begins to thin, but it takes several more minutes for Candy and me to meander to the door.

One friend says, "Have a Good Friday," and then questions her wording, given the sadness of Jesus's death.

"It's good for us!" I say. She nods in agreement.

"Besides, without Good Friday—"

"There'd be no Easter," we say in unison.

I tarry at the door for a final conversation as the sanctuary goes dark. We're the last to leave. After two and a half hours, I'm still not ready to go home.

But we'll be back in two days. Tonight is a foretaste of what is to come.

* * *

It's Easter and we're returning home to our church, the people we love and miss. This marks our first Sunday back since last Easter. I expect a joyful homecoming and a grand celebration: personally, corporately, and spiritually.

We arrive early to meet our kids. While our daughter and her husband attend this church, our son and his wife make an hour drive to spend Easter with us, beginning our day together at church.

My plan is to lay low today, but friends spot me as we enter the sanctuary. They're glad to see me and I, them. They're not sure if I'm back for good or just visiting. They seem relieved when I confirm our adventure wasn't a church shopping exercise and our plan all along was to return after a year.

Our reunion takes place in the aisle, and we're blocking people, so I excuse myself and look for my family. Even arriving early, there aren't many places left for six, but they did find a spot. Instead of roaming around to talk with others, I sit down and soak in the ambience.

There's nothing special about the building, except perhaps its age. Located in the central downtown district, the sanctuary is over 150 years old. Though not in disrepair, it's far from contemporary. Even with many enhancements, a dated feel pervades.

Our pastor welcomes everyone, telling visitors what the regulars already know: there's no plan for the service today, only a general intent. Its length is unknown, so it will end when it ends. He reiterates that we have freedom in worship: We may sit or stand or kneel. We may dance or move about — or not. As is our practice, the children remain with us during the service, worshiping along with the adults but often in their own way. There will also be adult baptism later in the service. A couple of announcements appear via video. With the place now packed, he asks the congregation to move toward the center and make room for those still needing seats.

The worship team is largely the same as Friday, but they changed out a couple of members and added a violin. They start the service with a prayer and then kick off the first song. The energy level is high, up a notch or two from Good Friday. Some of the songs are the same. Candy says most of them are repeats. She's probably right.

After thirty minutes or more of singing, we hear a brief message. The church is in a yearlong series — I've kept up by listening online. Today the lesson is about Abraham and Sarah, her scheme for her husband to produce a child through her servant, and his bone-headed acceptance of her suggestion. Our pastor ties this in with Easter: We all make mistakes, and we all need Jesus, who offers forgiveness and provides restoration.

Our pastor requests all elders to come forward to conduct the baptisms. The elder assigned for this service goes to the front of the church, and I join him — so much for keeping a low profile. Our fellow elders and staff assemble with us.

Our pastor shares the basics of baptism. The rite is the New Testament replacement for Old Testament circumcision, which he touched upon in the message. Baptism symbolizes the washing away of our sins,[150] a ceremonial cleansing, which publicly identifies us with Jesus.

People desiring baptism may come forward as the worship team leads the congregation in more songs. Even before hearing the full invitation, one person shows up and then another. A line forms.

For many churches, baptism is a somber affair, conducted with reserved formality. Not so for us. We treat it as a celebration with unabashed enthusiasm.

Our church leader prefers baptism by immersion, but the floor of this 150-year-old building lacks the structural integrity to support the weight of a baptismal pool. Instead, we use a traditional baptismal font, with the goal to get as much water on the recipient as possible.

---

150 Other creeds say baptism (by immersion) portrays the death, burial, and resurrection of Jesus. Can't we embrace both?

I talk with the second person in line, making sure she's there for the right reasons. With much joy, she anticipates taking this step as part of her spiritual journey. I pray for her as we wait our turn. The music is loud, and I'm not sure how many of my words she can hear, but God understands them all, and that's what counts.

After the other elder douses the first person, a raucous celebration erupts from the crowd, applauding and cheering her public step of faith. We're next. We step up to the font, and I cup water in my hands. "I baptize you in the name of the Father . . . " releasing the water over her head and then returning for more. "And the Son . . . " I get more water. "And the Holy Spirit. Amen." As the throng shows their approval in unequivocal terms, I hand her a towel to dry off.

There's not much room, so I try to usher her to the side and make room for the next baptism. But she won't budge. Her adult daughter is next. We gather around as another elder conducts that baptism. Afterward mother and daughter share a joyous hug, while friends hover nearby to share in the jubilation.

I return to the line of candidates, talking to the next person and baptizing her as well. We baptize a dozen or so this morning—and more will happen at the next service. What a glorious Easter and the perfect time to return home.

With the baptisms complete, I remain up front as the worship team continues. I sing along while I scan the crowd. Everyone is standing, and I don't see an empty spot anywhere, including the balcony. Even the back looks full. I wonder if some people stood the entire service, unable to find a place to sit.

After a couple more songs, the worship leader concludes the service and the crowd slowly disperses. I rejoin my family, wanting to focus on them instead of searching for visitors and friends. We eventually make our way out after ninety minutes. Some have already arrived for the next service, which starts in half an hour.

Today is an amazing reunion, a grand celebration, and a fitting conclusion to our yearlong pilgrimage.

Takeaway for Everyone: Is your church service a celebration?

—— ❖ ——

Part Four Perspective

To wrap up our adventure, we visited some of the churches (#45–52) on the western side of the area's largest city.[151] With many more churches on our list than the number of Sundays left, it was hard to pick which ones to include. Our decisions involved much discussion between Candy and myself, a bit of give and take, and a couple of last-minute changes.

We picked churches for this phase to provide the most varied experiences. Church #51 ("The Megachurch") is our area's largest, with #52 ("Playing it Safe") and #49 ("Large and Anonymous") being close behind. These comprised our extra-large church encounters, offering insight into the pros and cons of "big."

On the other end of the size spectrum was one small congregation, Church #48 ("Small, Simple, and Satisfying") and one medium-sized congregation, Church #47 ("Significant Interactions").

The rest of the churches were large congregations. Church #46 ("False Assumptions") had a huge facility—suggesting a once prosperous past—but it now has barely enough attend-

---

151 Our home church, which we returned to for Easter, is also in this city, located in the downtown area, but it falls outside of our ten-mile criteria at eleven miles away—and a twenty-one-minute drive.

291

ees to fit the large category. The other two sizable churches were Church #45 ("Another Doubleheader") and Church #50 ("Saturday Mass"). We included Saturday mass for multiple reasons: another Roman Catholic encounter, a church with a campus connection, and a Saturday night service. Plus, by doubling up this weekend and one other[152], we were able to complete our fifty-two-church journey in fifty weeks, allowing us to return to our home church for Easter.

On this, the final phase of our journey, my thoughts center on church size, with my overarching concern for community hovering in the background. I claim I want to attend a small church, one with a close-knit and spiritually-significant community. Yet, my actions belie that as our home church is a large one, bordering on extra-large. Also, and ironically, of the fifty-two churches we visited, Church #51 ("The Megachurch") appeals to me the most.

The reason I don't warm up to most smaller churches — the ones I claim I want to attend — is that they're frequently older congregations. They have traditional services, don't embrace newer methods, and are composed of aging parishioners. I've often criticized older congregations, but I'm not against older people. I'm concerned for people who coast toward the finish line, hoping to hang on to the status quo until they go to heaven.

Their focus is on maintaining what they have, not expanding their church or preparing it for the next generation. Yes, they

---

152 That weekend we went to a Seventh Day Adventist Church (Church #31, A Day of Contrasts) on Saturday, and an Episcopal Church (Church #32, Commitment Sunday) on Sunday. Although, it would have been possible to double up and visit two different churches on Sunday mornings, we opted not to do so as it taxed us to go to two Sunday services at the same church.

say they want their congregation to grow, but it's often little more than a hope. In vain, they expect that if they keep doing what they've always done, they will one day gain members. These congregations seldom do something different to attract new people. Even though using newer practices might help embrace visitors, that would make the people of the church uncomfortable. And comfort, as they drift toward life's end, is what they truly want. Though there are certainly exceptions, this is the attitude in most older congregations.

That brings me to Church #48 ("Small, Simple, and Satisfying"). By far the smallest church on the final leg of our journey, and one of the smallest overall, this church holds great appeal. They earn high marks for conducting their service without the help of paid clergy or a guest speaker, which they did with excellence. They tweaked many items from what most churches do. This includes the placement of the cross, how they communicate announcements, the congregation praying without first sharing their needs, many members being involved in the service, and the easy, informal fellowship time afterward. I assume these are all intentional tweaks made to maximize worship and strengthen community. They possessed a real sense of family, which all churches should have, but too many don't.

Though the service was more formal than I prefer, it's easy to overlook, given all the other pluses. But my one concern is their future. Candy and I were among the youngest present, so without an infusion of younger attendees, the church could be serving its final generation. Though many of these older members are young in their heart, this church offers little to attract a younger crowd who can sustain and perpetuate it.

This isn't their dilemma alone, but one shared by all the small churches we visited, as well as some medium-sized ones. If the solution to numeric decline was obvious, churches would pursue it, but the only small churches I've ever seen grow are new ones. The established ones keep getting smaller until they close. This isn't a lament as much as a reality.

The real problem is expectation. A congregation—or even denomination—shouldn't expect to continue forever. Instead, it's organic, following an expected life cycle: gestation, birth, growth, plateauing, slowing down, dying, and death. In fighting this natural progression, members turn their focus away from worship, community, and outreach to concentrate on survival, as if that's the goal. But it's not; God is.

Yes, leaders can take steps to lengthen the life of a local church or denomination, but to assume it can—or even should—live forever, misses reality. The only way to last indefinitely is to become an institution. With religious institutions, the primary focus switches from God to ensuring its survival. Paid staff eventually place their continued employment ahead of all else, losing passion for their primary mission. God isn't impressed with our religious institutions or the people who strive to sustain them. What he desires are followers who will make a difference, advancing his kingdom for his glory—not their own agenda.

* * *

Although outside our ten-mile requirement and fifty-two-week window, I shared about our home church. What happens there contrasts—often sharply—with many of our church visits. Although some aspects at a few of the churches were like our home church, none of them matched it.

Our home church remains the lens through which Candy and I evaluate other congregations. Our children did this, too, with their experiences at our home church forming their expectations when they moved and sought a new church.

I'm sad our adventure is over, and at the same time, I'm glad to reconnect with friends and once again establish a regular rhythm to our Sunday worship routine.

Takeaway for Leaders: Individual churches should be organic, with an eventual life cycle that will one day end. The only way to insure they last forever is to turn them into a religious institution.

Reflections

Our journey of visiting fifty-two churches is over, though the memories will last forever. With much to consider, this wrap-up pulls together key elements of our adventure. I hope this helps you and your church better interact with and respond to visitors, as well as find new ways to connect with and serve God.

Here are some of my thoughts.

A Lot Like Dating

Visiting churches seems a lot like dating: both parties are, in theory, on their best behavior and hopeful of a positive outcome. Dating is fun—for a while. There's variety and excitement for each outing, but eventually an emptiness emerges, and you yearn for more. You seek connection, you want commitment, and you desire permanence.

For me, dating churches was great fun for the first half of the year. After that, the allure of *new* started to wear thin, and I needed to work harder to have a successful date. This was even more challenging because we knew there would be no second dates, while the churches we visited usually hoped for more. Even after we told them we were visiting a *different* church *every* Sunday, most persisted in wanting that second date.

Even more so, visiting churches is often akin to going on blind dates. We had familiarity with five of the churches: for three, it was one visit, while for the two others our attendance was many years ago. However, for the other ninety percent of the churches, we arrived blind. We'd never been there before and knew little about them—except what we could find online.

I suppose church websites and Facebook pages correspond to a dating profile, with the best photos—sometimes out-of-date or misleading—and featuring positive traits while ignoring flaws. The effort of a few churches to put a positive spin on their online profile was more akin to lying. One church (#30, Mislead and Frustrated) gravely misled us. We couldn't recover from their deception and were still mad as we drove home. That date was an epic fail.

When visiting churches, just as with dates—especially blind dates—attitude is everything. Ideally you approach the outing with a positive outlook: seeking the good, striving to get along, and wanting to make things work. Either directly or indirectly, our pre-church prayer addressed this. Though I feel I went to each church with a positive attitude, twice Candy thought otherwise and offered correction.

Conversely, some people go on their blind dates with a negative attitude. They expect things won't work out, looking for the worst—and finding it.

Now take the dating analogy one step further. It's like going to your date's favorite restaurant, one you've never been to before. Your date knows the menu, addresses the staff by name, is friends with the manager, has a favorite booth, and orders "the usual." But you know no one, are overwhelmed by the food options, and find the ambiance off-putting. Strangers come up to your date, interrupting to have personal conversations as though you're not there and laughing over things you don't understand. You smile and try to make the best of it, but inside you squirm in agony. We often felt that way at the churches we visited.

If visiting a church is analogous to dating, joining a church might correspond to marriage. When you join a church you make a commitment, and you stop seeing other churches. There's a comfort in knowing what to expect, who you will see, and having community for the good times and the bad:

"for better, for worse, in sickness and in health."

Though our church journey was fun, educational, faith-expanding, and ecumenically insightful, I eventually grew tired of dating churches. I wanted to be in a church marriage, to have a church commitment and be in a faith family I could depend upon and support.

I think that's what most people want.

Greeting Well or Not at All

There are three opportunities for a church to interact with visitors: before, during, and after the service. Some churches failed at each occasion and only a few excelled at all three—though *every* church should.

First, greeting people before the service is critical, as it's the first impression a church makes on a visitor. Everyone *should* be a greeter. This is in addition to the official greeters stationed by the front door, the minister and staff, and the ushers—for those churches that still use them. Talking with friends before the service may be comfortable, but it's not greeting, and it certainly isn't welcoming to visitors.

Though a few churches treat their pre-service time with stoic reverence, you can always greet visitors *before* they enter the sanctuary. At the friendlier churches, people even approach visitors already seated. But at too many churches, we didn't interact with anyone before the service, leaving us isolated and alone. That's no way to form community.

Next, consider interaction during the service. When this occurs, it's an announced time of greeting. This can range from awkward to invigorating. It can last too long, be too short, or feel just right. There's an art to doing it well, but when done poorly, churches might be better off skipping it. Here are my suggestions for a successful mid-service greeting:

- Make eye contact.

- Smile.

- A handshake is acceptable, and not everyone appreciates a hug — and to "greet one another with a holy kiss" is just plain creepy.[153]

- Share your name and repeat theirs if they give it.

- Don't be in a rush to move to the next person.

- Focus on visitors first and friends only if time allows.

When the greeting time is a rote interaction performed with disingenuous intent, either overhaul it or omit it. Although there were exceptions, our general conclusion was that traditional churches struggled with greeting time, while charismatic churches excelled at it. Evangelical churches filled the continuum between.

One church redefined greeting time, making it more akin to an intermission, where people could roam around, get more coffee, or grab another donut, while having extended interactions. This church made it work well, but not every congregation could pull this off. And although we didn't see it on our journey, I've been to churches that provided time during the service for group discussion with those sitting near you.

Another way to extend hospitality during church is helping a visitor navigate the service — especially at liturgical services. Give them your hymnal when they grabbed the wrong one, share your bulletin to read the liturgy, or let them follow

---

153 This is biblical (see Romans 16:16, 1 Corinthians 16:20, 2 Corinthians 13:12, and 1 Thessalonians 5:26), but only greet the people you know this way, and don't subject visitors to this degree of intimacy.

along in your Bible. You can do this without saying a word.

As a final thought, if the official greeting time is the *first* time someone addresses a visitor, something's wrong.

When the first greeting occurs after the service, it seems too late to try, but it's better than not at all. Most churches did after-church hospitality reasonably well, but a few skipped this opportunity too. Sometimes there was a meal or snacks; food fosters connection. Other times it was just hanging out afterward, getting to know one another, making connections, and sharing our faith journeys.

All too often, one person made the difference between us feeling welcomed and ignored, singlehandedly forming our key perceptions of the church, with preaching and worship being secondary. While applauding the efforts of that one person, the lack of effort from the rest of the congregation is sobering. Granted, some people are naturally outgoing with a knack for hospitality, but everyone can smile and say "Hi."

Format and Size Matters

In our pilgrimage we found smaller churches (those under fifty people) generally offered more opportunity to make connections, with meaningful community apparent. But I grew weary of the ultra-small gatherings (those under twenty). Their miniscule size made Sunday worship a struggle, and there's little hope for their future. Without God's supernatural intervention, they'll plod along until their minister can no longer serve or until most of the remaining members die. Surely, they won't last the decade.

We also discovered that most liturgical churches — sometimes called high churches — weren't friendly. Though there were exceptions, the norm at these gatherings was no interaction with other attendees, not before, during, or after the service. And if anyone made contact it was often a rote effort with a disingenuous air.

This isn't to imply non-liturgical churches — sometimes called low churches, the opposite of high churches — were friendly. Though many were, some also kept visitors at a stoic distance.

Friendliness is a partner to community. At larger churches (those over a couple hundred), community presents a challenge, while anonymity unfolds with ease. Without concerted effort we would remain a part of the unnoticed masses at these larger gatherings. Though some people prefer to slip in and slip out of church unseen, interacting with no one, what's the point of going? The same outcome—perhaps a better one—could result by sitting at home in front of the TV.

At smaller churches, anonymity is impossible. Although experiencing community is much more likely, there's no guarantee, either. Arriving and leaving stealthily can't happen, but what's key is how they handle their visitors. Some churches do this gracefully, bordering on celebration, while others have an awkwardness that produces squirming and embarrassment. Granted, I'm an introvert—as is 51 to 74 percent of the population, depending who you ask—so my extroverted counterparts may think differently.

For medium-sized churches (fifty to two-hundred), some acted with large church anonymity, while others retained small church connection.

Candy's Take on 52 Churches

What do you do when God prompts your husband to take a one-year break from your home church to visit other congregations, a different one every week? You can't argue with God, so you go on a fifty-two-week adventure by your husband's side.

And what an adventure we had. We had the honor of worshipping with friends, old and new, that we never would have otherwise enjoyed. With many memories and thoughts that I take away from our journey, here are a few:

- With just seventeen people present, the pastor said, "If there are any visitors this morning, please raise your hand." I still giggle about this, as everyone knew we were visiting. What would have happened if we hadn't raised our hands?

- Seeing firsthand how a congregation can pull together, as a family, when dealing with heartbreak was truly inspiring.

- When a pastor is unavailable for a service, what a blessing when members step up and fill in.

- The many ways that others worship God are amazingly diverse.

- Worship in a group of five can be sweet, and a shofar is loud! This group met in a small office building. After the teaching, we went to a different room for worship: how breathtaking when they pulled the curtain aside for us to enter and we saw a replica of the Ark of the Covenant, cherubim and all. Awesome!

- Even with a language barrier at the Chinese church (#20), the joy of Christ came through.

- Just because you have guitars and drums doesn't make your service contemporary.

- Shared meals and conversation around a table are inviting and inclusive.

- After three experiences with Catholic Mass, I'm still unable to follow their services.

- It's so nice when someone, noticing you're a visitor, invites you to sit with them.

- Also appreciated is when others offer guidance throughout the worship service to help visitors follow along.

- I'm still uncomfortable when everyone shares the cup for communion. Just wiping the lip of the cup with a little white cloth is not going to remove the germs of everyone who drank before me. It's just not sanitary.

- There are some amazing husband-and-wife ministry teams who work together beautifully.

- It isn't necessary, but we appreciated it, when a pastor would make sure he or she reached out to personally welcome us. My favorite was the teaching pastor of one of the larger churches we visited. He welcomed us as we entered the building, simply introducing himself as "John." What a notable example he set for the congregation—if only they had followed his lead. He was the only one to welcome us that morning.

- Almost all churches had a cross somewhere in their facility, but the most meaningful was the one placed in the middle of the sanctuary, right in the center aisle.

- If you have a talented vocalist, no instrumentation is necessary. The beauty of a solitary voice, simply praising God in a room with good acoustics, is fabulous.

- A Belgian waffle breakfast for first-time visitors, with the pastor and his wife, is a great idea.

- I appreciate a pastor who will take a stand on hot topics and face them head on, sharing what the Bible has to say instead of ducking the issues.

- It was great to be included when most of the congregation headed to Arby's after church. Potlucks are delicious, but this was the next best thing.

- One church had a coffee bar. To help celebrate Lent, the barista topped my latte with a blue marshmallow Peep. What fun! Plus, their visitor packet had a coupon for a complimentary coffee, so it was free.

The most important thing I learned from this trek was how to—and how not to—make a visitor feel welcome. I need to take these lessons to heart as I reach out to visitors and those I don't recognize.

The church is the body of Christ, not a single congregation or just one denomination. We have a huge spiritual family, and it was so good to worship with them for the past twelve months.

After being gone a year, it was amazing to come back to our home church on Easter morning and celebrate Resurrection Day with all four of our kids by our side. God is good!

Generalizations

As already mentioned, we found liturgical churches less friendly and not as interested in fostering community, with charismatic congregations being the most embracing—even though their theology was often the most exclusive. Likewise, larger churches struggled to personally welcome us as visitors, whereas this was less of a problem at smaller churches.

Churches with a more traditional service tended to have older congregations, whereas churches with a contemporary service skewed younger, being either completely youthful or having a good cross-section of ages. At many churches we were among the youngest present, while at a few, we were among the oldest. When the entire congregation is over sixty-five, their future as a viable church seems bleak.

After only a few weeks of visiting, I developed a knack for predicting the type of service based solely on the appearance of the sanctuary: its condition and trappings. Likewise, the age of the congregation and how they dressed were also sufficient to gauge the type of service we would see. At only two churches did I judge incorrectly (#19 and #45).

One observation was particularly disconcerting: Churches with older congregations and traditional services tended to be friendlier than at contemporary services with younger people. This held true even within churches that offered both styles of service. What I'm not sure of is if the primary factor was the age of the congregation or the style of the service, because the two seem interconnected.

Last, based on a prior bad stint at an ultra-conservative Baptist church, I expected the Baptist churches we visited would be dogmatic, closed-minded, and exclusive. I'm pleased to say that, with one exception, this didn't prove true. Although I'm dismayed that we did witness dogmatic, closed-minded, exclusive attitudes at some of the charismatic churches we visited. This shocked me because I understood this was an old-school mindset, with the current charismatic perspective being more theologically inclusive and open-minded.

Tips for Improvement

We witnessed more than a few oversights, errors, and blunders that could turn off visitors. Sadly, many occurred more than once. Here are some pointers to consider to not scare away guests.

The Facility

Realtors stress curb appeal. So should churches. Make the outside of your building inviting for visitors and insure the inside continues the positive experience.

- Clearly mark the entrances. For big facilities, make the path to the sanctuary clear.

- Unlock the doors. And if there's a reason you want a particular entrance locked, make it apparent before people reach it.

- The facility needs to be clean, open, and well-lit—unless you're going for a subdued mood. At one church the pews were so dirty I didn't want to sit, even though I wore jeans.

- Address building problems and consider the décor. After a while, members overlook a building's flaws, but those are the first things visitors notice.

- Some buildings, especially older ones, have an odor. Eliminate them. And don't use one scent to cover up another one.

Online Presence

In today's culture, an online presence is critical to attract visitors. Short of a personal invitation, today's younger generation won't visit a church that lacks an inviting online presence.

- Keep websites and social media pages up-to-date. Though closed for two years, one church's website was still up and looked current. Avoid "coming soon" website pages, especially on sections relevant to visitors.

- Ensure a consistent message. We witnessed many glaring differences between churches' websites and Facebook pages (and bulletins).

- A visitor wants to know service times and location. Provide a street address, as many will use a GPS. Also provide both a map and a written description, as some will prefer one to the other.

- Let visitors know how to dress and what to expect.

- Have outsiders review websites. Two churches had sites that were off-putting and downright spooky. We thought one might be a cult. Seriously.

- Posting personal prayer requests online, in an unsecured section, is foolish and completely disregards privacy. Think through privacy laws carefully.

The Service (Ideas for Leaders)

People attend a church for the service. Make it easy for visitors to participate.

- If you don't provide Bibles, display the words overhead, as the Bible visitors bring—if they even bother—will not likely match yours. Visitors may also use a Bible reading app, but they'll need to know which version of the Bible you use.

- Make sure visitors know you don't expect them to participate in the offering. You don't, right?

- Clearly state communion expectations and traditions, since practices vary greatly.

- Don't continually address "visitors" as a special category. It's okay to welcome visitors and inform them they're exempt from certain expectations, but don't single them out or preach just to them—especially when it's obvious there's only one visitor.

- To attract new people, be accessible and user-friendly.

- Remove—or thoroughly explain—any practice or procedure that could confuse a visitor or keep them from engaging in the service and meeting God.

- Appoint friendly and outgoing people to seek out and engage visitors.

Have a Visitor-friendly Focus (Ideas for Laity)

To remain viable for the long term, a church needs to look outside themselves. This includes having a visitor-friendly focus. Here are some ideas:

- Invite a visitor to sit with you.

- Once you know a visitor's name, introduce them to others.

- Keep visitors informed. If you offer coffee and doughnuts, make sure they know where to find them.

- Ask if a visitor has any questions or concerns.

- Show, don't tell. If a visitor needs to find a certain room or asks about the restroom, don't point, gesture, or offer vague directions. Whenever possible, take them to their destination.

- Just because the church has appointed greeters, that doesn't relieve everyone else from also welcoming guests. Offer a smile and a friendly face to those you don't recognize. You may be the only one to greet them.

- Protect visitors from members who lack boundaries or don't comprehend social norms.

Conclusion

As we told people about our journey, everyone was intrigued. They wanted to hear more and expressed great interest in this book. A few were envious, wishing they could do the same, but most admitted they could never embark on such a bold quest and certainly not for a full year. When you see my wife, acknowledge her involvement. She was such a good sport and a great support the entire time.

The purpose of this book is to share our adventure. My prayer is that this narrative, especially the summary, will serve as a means for churches to improve what they do, be more visitor-friendly, and examine practices to make sure they do the right things for the right reasons. Unfortunately, we witnessed many practices needing overhaul.

More importantly, I hope readers will have a renewed sense of how diverse Christianity is. May we see other churches not as opposition or through heretical eyes but embrace them with acceptance. Jesus's church is vast, with many flavors and nuances. One version is not better than another, just different. Let's celebrate our variety and support one another on our faith journeys—regardless of which local branch we attend. We'll all celebrate together in heaven. Let's start practicing here on earth.

Appendix 1

Trivia

Interesting Notes

Here are some interesting notes about our journey—at least they're interesting to me:

- At only two churches did someone in the congregation know about our mission beforehand. Interestingly, this was near the beginning (#3) and at the end (#52).

- For three other churches (#22, 38, and 44), and possibly four (#24), the ministers knew why we were visiting.

- To my delight, we never showed up at the wrong time, though several times what we saw when we arrived made us question if we had the time right.

- We were never late, though we did cut things too close a few times.

- One church (#36) cancelled their service, leaving us with no place to go that Sunday.

- I drove right to most churches, but for a few I'd miss a turn or drive past, needing to make a second attempt. Only once did I have trouble finding a church and almost give up (#21).

- Fifty-one times we remembered to pray before arriving. Most days we did this prior to leaving home, but a couple of Sundays, we left late and prayed in the car. The only time we forgot to pray was when attending Saturday night mass (#50).

- Only once did I tell a church we would come back (#28). This wasn't a slip on my part but a sincere desire to return. (We did.)

- Candy or I knew the pastors at eight of the churches we visited (#2, 4, 7, 11, 22, 38, 44, 52).

- On three occasions (#25, 40, 48) someone asked us to sit with them—we knew all three couples. This is an ideal way for visitors to feel welcomed.

- Only two churches were minority congregations. Church #20 was Chinese and #26 was African[154]. This isn't surprising, as we live in a predominantly white area. See Appendix 3 for demographic information.

- We visited churches on two Saturdays. One also had Sunday services (#50), the other did not (#31). This allowed us to complete our journey in fifty weeks and return to our home church on Easter.

Things Change

We began our journey with fifty-seven churches on our list. We ended the year with ninety. Though this is pri-

---

154 It would be incorrect to label this church African-American, as the denomination originated in Africa and most of the attendees seemed to have been born there.

marily because we kept discovering more churches, a few moved, closed, or launched. Since we could only visit fifty-two, we had to eliminate thirty-eight of them, which was hard to do—but it would have been even harder to extend our journey for another nine or ten months to visit all ninety.

We also noted transitions in leadership.

Here are some of those changes:

- Five churches moved during the year. Three stayed within our ten-mile range (#7, 27, and 32), while two moved outside the area before we could visit.

- Two churches closed (#25 and one we didn't visit).

- One church started during the year (#26). We only learned of them through a friend who knew of our quest.

- Four churches were between ministers when we visited (#17, 23, 34, and 43).

- Four ministers—that we know of—left during the year. Number 9 and 12 occurred after our visit, while for #23 and 34 their departure happened before.

- The minister at one church arrived during the year, prior to our visit (#46).

- Two ministers serve two congregations (#5 and 6) In neither case did we visit their other congregation, as they were more than ten miles away.

Time and Location

For the past year, every Saturday night produced the same question: "What time is church tomorrow?" Although it seems insignificant, this tiny variable had far-reaching ramifications, including what time we needed to get up and how to adjust our pre-church activity. On a few Sundays, I misjudged the amount of time I had before church, needing to scale back my morning exercise routine or even curtail my time with God. This was not an ideal way to start my Sabbath.

It seems wrong to skip my personal intimacy with God just to make it to church on time, that my priorities must be askew. But it's hard to have a routine when church could start anywhere from 8:00 to 11:30 a.m.

Along with varying start times would also be different end times, with church lasting anywhere from one to two and a half hours—plus possible fellowship time afterward, be it planned or spontaneous. A few times we were gone for over three hours, a couple of Sundays we didn't return home until two in the afternoon, contrasting with as early as 9:30 in the morning. These variables greatly affected the remainder of our Sunday, dictating what could and couldn't happen the rest of the day.

This uncertainty in our Sunday schedule produced an unsettled aura hanging over the entire day. Disconcerted over not having a Sabbath rhythm, I felt spiritually out of sync for much of our journey. Some Sundays I honored God with how I spent my day—both before church and after—but too often I squandered many of my hours in disarray. Though we learned much about Jesus's church and the people we met at his various branches, I struggled in my Sunday intimacy with God for much of the year.

After confirming with each other the service times, our follow-up questions were "Do you know how to get there?" and "What time should we leave?" Though one of us knew how to get to most of the churches, a couple of mornings it was time to leave, but neither of us were sure where the church was located. Sometimes we'd scramble out the door with a hastily scribbled address and phone number, though my preferred resource was a printed Google map. Never once did my maps lead us astray—assuming I had one.

As our journey wore on, Saturdays sometimes found us still discussing which church to go to. Often the answer depended on which church had verified their service time and location with Candy.

We felt confirmation was important, no doubt fueled by our home church's former habit of changing service times and not fully informing everyone: the website might be wrong; the answering machine, incorrect; Facebook, out of date. Or they might only give one week's notice. Often people would show up at the wrong time, more than a bit peeved for the misinformation. Though our church eventually corrected these errors, they trained us to question a church's stated starting time.

Only once, however, did Candy uncover conflicting service times. A more common frustration was conflicting locations, with different addresses found online. One morning, we disagreed about their location. We scrambled at the last minute to figure out the right address.[155] In addition, three churches moved just before or just after our visit. One moved the week before.

---

155 Candy was right. I was wrong—enough said.

Appendix 2:

Facts and Figures

The purpose of *52 Churches* is to share our journey, for the narrative to serve as the means of understanding, not to present quantifiable facts. Even so, we did track a few items. Treat them as a numeric extension of our narrative, not as academic research.

Overview

- Churches that had Sunday school: 27 (52%)

- Churches with small groups: 10 (19%)

- Churches with an evening service: 16 (31%) — 12 (23%) were Sunday evening, while 4 (8%) were Saturday evening.

- Churches where we knew the pastor: 8 (15%)

- Churches where we knew someone at the service we visited: 31 (60%)

- Churches that moved during the year: 5 (10%)

- Churches that closed during the year: 2 (4%)

- Churches that started during the year: 1 (2%)

- Churches between ministers when we visited: 4 (8%)

Number of Services:

- One service: 41 (79%)

- Two services: 8 (15%)

- Three services: 2 (4%)

- Five services: 1 (2%)

The three churches with more than two services were Roman Catholic. Of the eight churches with two services, five of them offered distinctive styles — and for one, it was a different language. A ninth church had only one service when we visited in the summer, but in the winter they offer a contemporary service and a traditional service.

Starting times

The most common starting time was 10 a.m., followed closely by 11:00 a.m. All services that started at 9 a.m. or earlier were at churches with two morning services. The earliest starting time for a church with one morning service was 9:15 a.m.

On the other end of this range, the church (#31) with an 11:10 a.m. start time was for their Saturday service, while the church with the 11:30 a.m. (#36) starting time was for a unique situation. Few of their attendees lived nearby, so they would have church at 11:30, eat lunch together, and return for a second service at 2 p.m. Another church was also experimenting with having their "evening" service earlier in the day at 1:30 in the afternoon.

Here is the breakdown of service times. (For churches with multiple services, this is the time of their first service):

- 8:00 a.m.: 1 (2%)

- 8:30 a.m.: 2 (4%)

- 8:45 a.m.: 1 (2%)

- 9:00 a.m.: 4 (8%)

- 9:15 a.m.: 1 (2%)

- 9:30 a.m.: 5 (10%)

- 9:45 a.m.: 1 (2%)

- 10:00 a.m.: 15 (29%)

- 10:10 a.m.: 1 (2%)

- 10:15 a.m.: 2 (4%)

- 10:30 a.m.: 6 (12%)

- 11:00 a.m. 11 (21%)

- 11:10 a.m.: 1 (2%)

- 11:30 a.m.: 1 (2%)

Of the churches with a second Sunday morning service, their second service started at:

- 10:00 a.m.: 1

- 10:30 a.m.: 1

- 10:45 a.m.: 1

- 11:00 a.m.: 4

- 11:15 a.m.: 1

- 11:30 a.m.: 3

Size

The most subjective aspect of our numeric reporting is church size, which is based solely on the number of people attending the services we visited. Many times we could simply count, while other times we needed to estimate. Most of the time our projections were close to each other, but sometimes we had differing opinions. Once we disagreed by several hundred.

The average estimated size of the services we attended was 115 people, with a median of seventy. The median is the midpoint, with half the churches having less and half having more. The reason the average is so much higher is because of a few extra-large churches that shifted it.

Some churches had multiple services. If we attended both, we could count or estimate. If we weren't at all the services, out of necessity, I assumed the total at our service was typical of all their services and projected a total for the day.[156] This resulted in an average overall church attendance of 200. Again, the median was seventy. This makes sense because only large churches have multiple services, so the median would remain unchanged.

Musical Style

We heard all types of worship music on our travels, from traditional to progressive. We sang to bands, guitar, piano, and pipe organ. A few churches used accompaniment tracks and one sang to CDs. Another time we sang a cappella and once we didn't sing at all. And for one, we don't know because

---

156 From a statistical standpoint, this is sloppy, as the attendance at one service will seldom match others. But the intent of this extrapolation isn't to provide accurate numbers (because I can't) but to offer a general representation of size.

they canceled their service.

We sang hymns, choruses, contemporary tunes, secular songs, and everything in between.

In the most general perception, I categorized each service as being traditional, contemporary, or a bit of both—that is, blended. The results lean toward contemporary.

- Contemporary: 24 (48%)

- Traditional: 20 (40%)

- Blended: 6 (12%)

Hymnals

Most churches had hymnals. Although just because they had hymnals didn't mean they used them in the service we attended. Though we didn't keep track, I think that of the churches with hymnals, only about half used them. Some used hymnals for part of their singing, while a few used them exclusively. The common alternative to hymnals was displaying the words with a digital projector, with one that used an old-fashioned overhead projector and transparencies. Some printed the words in their bulletin or liturgy, while a couple passed out song sheets. One church had no singing because no one in the congregation could play the piano.

- No hymnals: 19 (37%)

- Had one or more versions of hymnals: 33 (63%)

- One hymnal: 21 (40%)

- Two hymnals: 9 (17%)

- Three hymnals: 3 (6%)

Bibles

Twenty-one (40%) of the churches had Bibles in their pews. Though in several cases, they didn't use that version in the service. Notably, two churches encouraged visitors to take a Bible home with them. The breakdown of available Bibles is (for the 21% that had them):

- NIV: 11

- KJV: 2

- NKJV: 2

- NRSV: 2

- ESV: 1

- NASB: 1

- The Message: 1

- Unknown: 1

All the churches read from the Bible during their services, though we weren't always able to determine which version they used. Of the forty-five times we could identify the version[157], the breakdown is:

- NIV: 16

- KJV: 12

- NKJV: 7

---

157 I use the corporate "we," as most of this was my wife's doing. She would write down a portion of scripture and later go online to find out which version it was. For my part, I couldn't write quickly enough to pull this off very often.

- NRSV: 5

- NASB: 2

- ESV: 1

- NLT: 1

- The Message: 1

Denominations

Overall, the churches didn't mention their denominations. For some, their affiliation was apparent from their name. We figured out their denomination for twenty-seven (52%) of the churches, either because they told us, by their online information, or through their name. Only four (8%) identified themselves as nondenominational. For those with a known affiliation:

- United Methodist Church*: 5

- Reformed Church in America*: 3

- Roman Catholic: 3

- Christian Reformed Church*: 2

- Presbyterian: 2

- Assembly of God: 1

- BMA - Baptist Missionary Association: 1

- Celtic Episcopal: 1

- Church of God: 1

- Disciples of Christ: 1

- Episcopal: 1

- Lutheran: 1

- Mennonite: 1

- New Apostolic Church: 1

- Redeemed Christian Church of God: 1

- Seventh Day Adventist: 1

- Wesleyan: 1

* We skipped one or more churches from these denominations to give us a greater variety.

Internet Savvy

If churches are to attract new people, especially younger generations, an online presence is critical, yet ten (19%) churches didn't have one. Of the rest, this is what we found:

- Website: 41 (79%)

- Facebook page: 27 (52%); one church had just Facebook but no website.

- No email address posted online: 10 (24%)

In too many cases, email wasn't an effective way to contact churches. Some messages bounced back, others received no reply—we found out one church had an obsolete email address they no longer checked, and a few replied weeks later—one attempted contact months later.

Though Candy's preference was to email churches, she did resort to calling a few. There the results weren't much better, with her often needing to leave a message and only sometimes receiving a return call. One number was disconnected, and another wasn't working. For a couple of churches, she couldn't find a phone number, either online or in the phone book. We did end up visiting these churches, but few others would have.

Follow-Up

Most churches requested our contact information. Often this was part of the service via a visitor card, though some churches still used a guest registry, and once or twice someone personally asked for our information. Except for the second service at Church #52, we complied with every request.

A few churches (I believe 12%) made no attempt to collect contact information. Of the forty-six (88%) who did, only a minority used it.

- Took no action: 30 (66%)

- Sent a follow-up letter: 14 (30%)

- Sent a follow-up email: 4 (9%)

- Added us to their email list: 2 (4%)

- Called us: 0 (0%)

The totals add up to more than 100 because four of the churches contacted us in multiple ways.

- Sent a follow-up letter and email: 3 (6% of the total)

- Sent a follow-up letter and added us to their email list: 1 (2% of the total)

Though we didn't keep track, a few churches followed up with us on Facebook because that was how we contacted them to confirm service time and location. There were also a couple of subsequent phone calls, but from our recollection they were all initiated on our part.

Appendix 3:

Census Data

The county we live in is predominantly white and every church we visited there was a white congregation. Often there were no minorities in attendance. This isn't to imply that non-white people in our area don't go to church. It's simply to say that we didn't see them at most of the churches we visited. Presumably they drive outside the area to attend another church, perhaps a minority congregation.

Some of the churches we visited were in the county to our east. There the population is a bit more diverse and more closely matches the average for our state. The two minority churches we visited are in this county. Although many minority congregations exist, the rest fell outside our ten-mile range.

Here are the 2017 estimates for our area, courtesy of the US Census Bureau. (These labels are what the US Census Bureau uses.)

<u>Our County</u>

White	91.5%
Hispanic/Latino	11.6%
Black	4.0%
American Indian	1.2%

Asian	0.7%
All other	2.5%

Adjacent County

White	81.5%
Hispanic/Latino	4.9%
Black	11.7%
American Indian	0.5%
Asian	2.8%
All other	3.5%

The totals exceed one hundred. A footnote on the US Census Bureau website explains this, stating, "Hispanics may be of any race, so also are included in applicable race categories."[158]

---

158 https://www.census.gov/quickfacts/fact/table/vanburencoun-tymichigan/PST045217 and https://www.census.gov/quickfacts/fact/table/kalamazoocountymichigan/PST045217

Glossary

Some terms in this book may not be familiar to all readers, such as those who don't go to church, those accustomed to one denomination, or those familiar with only one stream of Christianity. These definitions aren't comprehensive, as they provide only information relevant to this book. Also included are context and commentary when it might help.

Apostles' Creed: A formal statement of faith, concisely summarizing core Christian beliefs. Many churches recite this in unison during their church services. Widely accepted, it dates to the fourth century, possibly earlier. An alternative, and longer, creed is the Nicene Creed.

baptism: A religious ritual or spiritual ceremony involving water. It has various forms, ranging from applying, to sprinkling, to full body immersion ("dunking"). It also possesses various meanings, from a profession of belief, to preparation for a future faith, to a required ritual. Sadly, much disagreement, and even physical confrontation, has surrounded baptism and its various practices over the centuries.

baptistry: The place where baptisms occur. Depending on the method, the baptistry may be a font providing water to sprinkle on the recipient (especially infants) or a tub or pool for the immersion of a person into water.

Baptist: 1) Various Christian denominations include Baptist in their name and go by baptist. They fall into the evangelical stream of Christianity. 2) Generally, a baptist is one who practices baptism of adult believers as a sign of faith.

Bible: The central book of Christian faith. It is comprised of various genres, from many authors, written over a span of a couple millennia. It's often called God's Word or the Holy Bible, and believers regard it with reverence.

call: 1) A formal process by which a church congregation invites or hires a minister to work at or lead their church; they issue a call. 2) A supernatural sense of God's leading to direct Christians to take a specific action; they feel called by God.

charismatic: One of the three main streams of Protestantism. The other two are mainline and evangelical.

Chrislam: A comingling of Christianity and Islam.

Christian: A person who is like Christ or Jesus; someone who follows or aligns with Jesus.

Church/church: 1) The universal collective of people who follow Jesus. 2) A denomination or local congregation. 3) The physical building where Christians meet, often on Sunday.

clergy: Formally trained or ordained church leaders, often paid. Also known as ministers, priests, and pastors. Contrast to *laity*.

closed communion: Communion offered only to members or those formally approved to receive it. Contrast to *open communion*.

communion: An act initiated by Jesus of symbolically sharing bread (or crackers or wafers) and wine (or grape juice) to remind his followers of his sacrificial death. Christians have continued this practice in various forms. It's also called Holy Communion, the Lord's Supper, Mass, the Eucharist, or Holy Eucharist.

congregation: A group of Christians who regularly meet together as a formalized group.

consubstantial: (adjective) the persons of the Christian godhead, who are three persons in one. See *Trinity*.

contemporary service: A church meeting that follows present-day practices in their music, message, and format. Contrast to *traditional service* and compare to *seeker-sensitive*.

cross: The Romans—in collusion with Jewish religious leadership—executed, or crucified, Jesus on a cross. It became a symbol for his followers. It has taken on diverse meanings and significances over the centuries and across various Christian practices. Most church sanctuaries have one or more crosses. Many people expect to see crosses in churches. Crosses are common in Protestant faith practices, which celebrate Jesus as the risen savior. Compare to *crucifix*.

crucifix: A replica of Jesus on a cross, which celebrates him as the dying savior. Crucifixes are common in Roman Catholic faith practices. Compare to *cross*.

deacon: A person, often elected or appointed, to fill various service or leadership roles in a local church or denomination. Some churches have both elders and deacons, whereas others just have deacons. And not all churches have deacons.

denomination: An organization of like-minded churches sharing a common affinity, beliefs, or history. Some denominations exercise tight oversight of their local congregations, whereas others serve more as a resource or means for interchurch cooperation. Once important to most Christians, denominations now carry less significance, with increasing numbers of people seeking nondenominational or unaffiliated congregations.

Easter: A significant Christian holiday celebrating Jesus's resurrection, having nothing in common with the secular practice of Easter bunnies and eggs.

ecumenical: Generically, relating to worldwide Christianity or the universal church. There are also formal ecumenical organizations, which seek unity and the civil co-existence of diverse Christian expressions, beliefs, and practices. In a broader sense, but not used in this book, ecumenical can also embrace all religions and forms of spirituality.

elder: A person, often elected or appointed, to fill various service or leadership roles in a local church or denomination. Some churches have both elders and deacons, whereas others just have elders. And not all churches have elders.

elements: The two components of communion: bread (sometimes represented by crackers or wafers) and wine (or grape juice).

Enemy: Satan; the devil.

ESV: English Standard Version, a translation of the Bible.

Eucharist: See *communion*.

evangelical: One of the three main streams of Protestantism. The other two are mainline and charismatic.

expository preaching: A style of biblical instruction that can take many forms, but most of the time it's a minister or teacher explaining a passage of the Bible, verse by verse. An alternate style is topical preaching. Both have their advocates and detractors.

faith: 1) A set of religious beliefs. 2) Confidence in what is unknown or intangible.

faith community: 1) A local church. 2) Any gathering of like-minded people of faith.

fast/fasting: To give up something, usually food, for a time, often associated with Lent.

fundamental: See *evangelical*.

Gospel: 1) The good news or message of Jesus. 2) One of the four biographies of Jesus in the Bible: Matthew, Mark, Luke, and John.

high church: In a generic sense, a more formal church service that shuns modernism and uses liturgy. The Roman Catholic and Anglican churches exemplify this, as do many mainline ("name brand") churches. Contrast to *low church*.

Holy Bible: See *Bible*.

hymn: A religious song, typically older and traditional, usually formal and sung with organ accompaniment, and often in Old English. Some worship leaders update the words and use guitar accompaniment to make hymns more accessible to postmodern audiences.

hymnal: A book that contains the words and music for hundreds of hymns; some also include modern songs and choruses.

intinction: One method of taking Communion, by dipping the bread (or cracker) into the juice (or wine) and partaking of the two elements together.

Jesus: The central character in the New Testament and the basis for Christian faith. He is part of the Christian godhead, or Trinity, along with God the Father and God the Holy Spirit.

KJV: King James Version, a translation of the Bible, commissioned by King James of England in the early 1600s. Although formal, using Elizabethan English, it remains a popular version. It's the only English version of the Bible in the public domain and not subject to copyright restrictions. This is likely one reason for its ongoing use.

laity: The attendees of a local church; not a minister. Contrast to *clergy*.

layperson: A non-ordained (not a minister) participant in a local church. See *laity*.

Lent: The forty days before Easter, starting with Ash Wednesday and sometimes accompanied by fasting or penance in preparation for, or anticipation of, Easter.

Lectionary: A structured list of Bible passages designed to methodically cover the entire Bible over time, with three years being common. Some churches, often high churches, incorporate the lectionary into their weekly service and some ministers use it as the foundation for their teaching each Sunday.

liturgy: A formal, written portion of a church service, said in unison or responsively. Advocates of liturgy appreciate its standard wording, which has often withstood time. It offers a thorough, theologically inclusive faith practice. Detractors label it as rigid and not open to local expressions or the Holy Spirit's leading. See *high church*, which tends to be liturgical and *low church*, which tends to be non-liturgical.

Lord's Prayer: The prayer Jesus taught his disciples. Many congregations recite this prayer in unison as part of their service. The prayer is in Matthew 6:9–13. Some people call this prayer the "Our Father," based on its first two words. Some churches (often Protestant) include an addendum to the prayer, which isn't found in all Bibles. Other churches (such as Roman Catholic) omit this extra text.

Lord's Supper: See *communion*.

low church: A useful, but perhaps derogatory, term to describe the opposite of high church. Low churches are less traditional and more current than high churches. Their services typically avoid liturgy. Evangelical and charismatic churches are generally low churches. Contrast to *high church*.

kneeling rails: A piece of furniture found in some churches, often part of pews, to provide a more comfortable way for congregants to kneel, either before the service or as part of it.

mainline: One of the three main streams of Protestantism. The other two are evangelical and charismatic.

mass: Also known as the Eucharist, the main act of worship at a Roman Catholic Church. See *communion*.

May Crowning: A traditional Roman Catholic celebration that occurs each May to honor the Virgin Mary.

message: The sermon, teaching, or lecture portion of a church service.

minister: 1) (noun) A person, often formally trained and ordained, who heads up a local church. See *clergy*. 2) (verb) The act of serving or helping others.

Missal: A liturgical book of instructions and texts needed to celebrate mass in the Roman Catholic Church.

modern: In this book, used to reference the modern era, which is roughly the last five centuries. To minimize confusion, other applications warranting the word *modern* in this book use *contemporary* or *present-day* instead. Contrast to *postmodern* and *premodern*.

NAB: New American Bible, a translation of the Bible, often used by the Roman Catholic Church.

NASB: New American Standard Bible, a translation of the Bible, updating the American Standard Bible (ASB).

Nicene Creed: A formal statement of faith, concisely summarizing core Christian beliefs. Some churches recite this in unison during their church services. A more common alternative is the shorter Apostles' Creed. See *Apostles' Creed*.

NIV: New International Version, a translation of the Bible. It is one of the most popular and commonly used versions.

NKJV: New King James Version, a translation of the Bible that updates the Old English found in the KJV.

NLT: New Living Translation, a present-day paraphrase of the Bible

nondenominational: A church that is not part of a denomination. They are independent of outside influence, governance, or oversight. Contrast to *denomination*.

Non-liturgical: The opposite of liturgical. A non-liturgical church service doesn't use prescribed texts or scripts as part of its proceedings. Contrast to *liturgical*.

NRSV: New Revised Standard Version, a translation of the Bible that updates the older RSV (Revised Standard Version).

nursery: Many churches provide a nursery to care for children while their parents or caregivers attend the church service.

ordination: A formal approval process, often culminating in a reverent ceremony, whereby a church or denomination officially recognizes a person to serve as a minister.

open communion: Communion offered to both church members and nonmembers, albeit often with some limitations, such as affirming a basic set of beliefs or having been baptized. Some churches place no restrictions whatsoever on people partaking communion. Contrast to *closed communion*.

Our Father: See *Lord's Prayer*.

outreach: To go beyond oneself or church to serve, help, or tell others about Jesus.

pastor: See *minister* and compare to *priest* and *clergy*.

penance: An act often associated with Lent where people express sorrow over their wrongdoing. This can take the form of fasting, contrition, confession, the acceptance of punishment, and, in extreme cases, though not recommended, self-mortification.

pews: Wooden benches, sometimes with padding, used in many traditional church sanctuaries for attendees to sit on during services. Many contemporary churches opt for chairs instead of pews.

postmodern: That which follows the modern era; the present time. In general, younger people have a postmodern perspective, whereas older folks have a modern one. Contrast to *modern* and *premodern*.

praise: To exalt, extol, or worship God.

pray/prayer: Communication with God, sometimes formally and other times informally. Prayer can include praise, thanksgiving, confession, and requests for self or others.

premodern: The period of history just prior to the modern era and following the ancient era. Some of today's traditional church practices emanate from the premodern era. Although having pronounced differences, there are also similarities between the premodern and postmodern mindset. Contrast to *modern* and *postmodern*.

priest: The recognized authority in Roman Catholic Churches, and some high churches, who conducts worship services, administers the sacraments, and handles the daily functions of a local parish. Compare to *minister* and see *clergy*.

Protestant: One facet of Christianity. See *streams of Protestantism*.

pulpit supply: A formal or informal source of people—sometimes trained and ordained, but not always—who can conduct a church service and give a message when the regular minister is unavailable.

resurrection: To rise from the dead. Jesus was resurrected from the dead after his execution. Christians celebrate his resurrection on Easter.

ritual: 1) An established, prescribed order of a religious ceremony. 2) Part of an established religious routine or church practice, often subconscious. All churches have rituals, but not all realize it.

Robert's Rules of Order: An organized set of instructions used to conduct formal decision-making at meetings. Some churches conduct their meetings using Robert's Rules of Order, either directly or implicitly.

Roman Catholic: One branch of Christianity. See *streams of Christianity*.

sacrificial death: Christians see Jesus's execution on the cross as a sacrificial death, completely fulfilling the ritual sacrifices prescribed in the Old Testament of the Bible.

sacraments: a standard rite or religious ritual of spiritual significance. Protestants celebrate two sacraments: baptism and communion. Roman Catholics have seven sacraments, which include baptism and communion.

salvation: Brought into right standing with God. Within Christianity, there are varied understandings of what constitutes salvation.

sanctuary: The primary section of most church buildings where worship takes place.

seeker-sensitive: Making a church service as accessible as possible to visitors and those unfamiliar with church practices.

sermon: See *message*.

special music: A song performed at a church service. Many churches, especially contemporary ones, have moved away from this in favor of participatory forms of worship.

Stations of the Cross: A series of artistic representations of Jesus's final hours on earth, from his capture through to his resurrection from the dead. These are common in Roman Catholic Churches, as well as other high churches.

streams of Christianity: The three main segments of Christian faith: Roman Catholic, Eastern Orthodox, and Protestant. Compare to *streams of Protestantism.*

streams of Protestantism: The three main segments of Protestant faith: mainline (liberal), evangelical (conservative or fundamental), and charismatic (often Pentecostal). Compare to *streams of Christianity.*

supernatural: Relating to the spiritual, not corporeal.

tentmaker: A minister who doesn't receive compensation from the church they serve, but instead works a day job to be self-supporting. It is a reference to Paul in the Bible who sometimes worked his trade as a tentmaker to support himself in his ministry and not rely on donations.

tithe: Giving ten percent, or one tenth, of income to the church.

The Message: A present-day paraphrase of the Bible.

traditional service: A church service that follows older practices in their music, message, and format. Contrast to *contemporary service* and *seeker-sensitive.*

Trinity: The Christian godhead, or simply God, consisting of God the Father, God the Savior—Jesus, and God the Holy Spirit, but understood as being three entities in one.

Vacation Bible School: Also known as VBS, a short session of summer classes for children that focus on the Bible or biblical principles. It uses kid-friendly teaching, activities, and games. Usually lasting a week or two, Vacation Bible School sometimes culminates in a program for parents. Motivations for conducting VBS vary, from giving biblical instruction, to providing a break in the summer routine, to offering fun activities to kids, or as a community outreach.

Virgin Mary: The mother of Jesus, supernaturally impregnated by the Holy Spirit.

worship: 1) (verb) To show honor, reverence, and adoration to God in various forms, 2) (noun) A church service, as in a worship service.

Acknowledgments

I sincerely thank:

God, for giving me the desire to write about him and filling me with joy as I do.

The members of Kalamazoo Christian Writers for encouragement and support.

My valued assistant, Shara Anjaynith Cazon for doing some of my other work so I have more time to write.

James L. Rubart, my book marketing guru.

Joanna Penn's podcasts and books for helping me on my journey as a writer.

And I'm especially grateful for you, for going along on this amazing journey with me. May God inspire you to revisit your faith practices.

About Peter DeHaan

Peter DeHaan wants to change the world one word at a time. He writes and blogs about biblical spirituality, often from a postmodern perspective. His books and blog posts discuss God, the Bible, and church.

Peter DeHaan, PhD, urges Christians to push past the status quo and reexamine their practices. Many people feel church let them down, and Peter seeks to encourage them as they search for a place to belong. But he's not afraid to ask tough questions or make people squirm.

Peter earned a PhD degree from Trinity College of the Bible and Theological Seminary, awarded "with high distinction."

A lifelong student of the Bible, Peter wrote the 700-page website ABibleADay.com to encourage people to explore the Bible, the greatest book ever written. His popular blog addresses biblical spirituality, often with a postmodern twist.

In addition to his website, PeterDeHaan.com, connect with him on Goodreads, Twitter, Facebook, YouTube, Google+, Instagram, Pinterest, and LinkedIn.

His published books are:

Women of the Bible: The Victorious, the Victims, the Virtuous, and the Vicious

95 Tweets: Celebrating Martin Luther in the 21st Century

How Big is Your Tent? A Call for Christian Unity, Tolerance, and Love

Look for Peter's upcoming books, which include:

- *Dear Theophilus: A 40 Day Devotional Exploring the Life of Jesus through the Gospel of Luke*

- *Dear Theophilus, Acts: A 40 Day Devotional from the Book of Acts for Today's Christian*

- *Friends and Foes of Jesus: Explore How New Testament Characters React to God's Good News*

- *Woodpecker Wars: Discovering the Spirituality of Everyday Life*

- with more to follow

If you liked *52 Churches*, would you please leave a review on Amazon (and even Goodreads)? Your review will help other people discover this book and encourage them to read it too. It would be amazing.

Thank you.

To be the first to hear about Peter's new books and receive updates, go to www.PeterDeHaan.com/updates.